Ovid's Myth of Pygmalion on Screen

Also available from Bloomsbury

Now and Rome: Lucan and Vergil as Theorists of Politics and Space, Ika Willis

Ovid's Myth of Pygmalion on Screen
In Pursuit of the Perfect Woman

Paula James

Bloomsbury Studies in
Classical Reception

BLOOMSBURY
LONDON • NEW DELHI • NEW YORK • SYDNEY

Bloomsbury Academic
An imprint of Bloomsbury Publishing Plc

50 Bedford Square	175 Fifth Avenue
London	New York
WC1B 3DP	NY 10010
UK	USA

www.bloomsbury.com

First published by Continuum International Publishing Group 2011
Paperback edition first published 2013

© Paula James, 2011

All rights reserved. No part of this publication may be reproduced or transmitted in any form or by any means, electronic or mechanical, including photocopying, recording, or any information storage or retrieval system, without prior permission in writing from the publishers.

Paula James has asserted her right under the Copyright, Designs and Patents Act, 1988, to be identified as Author of this work.

No responsibility for loss caused to any individual or organization acting on or refraining from action as a result of the material in this publication can be accepted by Bloomsbury or the author.

British Library Cataloguing-in-Publication Data
A catalogue record for this book is available from the British Library.

ISBN: HB: 978-1-4411-8466-5
PB: 978-1-4725-0495-1

Library of Congress Cataloging-in-Publication Data
A catalog record for this book is available from the Library of Congress

Typeset by Newgen Imaging Systems Pvt Ltd, Chennai, India

For my wonderful daughters, Tanith Tinuviel and Jessica Luthien

Contents

Acknowledgements		ix
Introduction		1
Chapter 1	Ovid's Rich Text: Layers of Identity in the Pygmalion Myth	10
Chapter 2	Tragic Transformations: Making and Breaking the Statue on Screen	36
Chapter 3	Romancing the Stone: the Made-Over Woman as Comedy	65
Chapter 4	She Was Venus All Along: the Statue as Screen Goddess	91
Chapter 5	Pygmalion's Robots: the Horror and the Humour	115
Chapter 6	Bathos and Pathos: a *Simulacrum* among *Simulacra*	137
Chapter 7	Virtually Perfect: Hi and Lo Tech Gals of the Computer Age	150
Chapter 8	More Myth Making at the Movies	174
Appendix:	*Ovid's Pygmalion*	186
Notes		188
Coda to Paperback		207
Bibliography		211
Filmography		219
Index		222

Acknowledgements

I embarked upon a Latin degree at Southampton University in 1977. I was twenty-seven years old and had two young daughters. The experience transformed me, turning my life around personally, intellectually and professionally. I could never have contemplated going to college on credit – and if I had not been set on the path of lifelong learning, I would never have written this book! I would like to salute students of all ages (and their lecturers and teachers) struggling to stem the tide of reaction and to re-establish access to free higher education as a universal principle in the UK.

I would like to thank the Open University Arts Faculty (the research committee) for helping with the copyright costs so that the Burne-Jones paintings could be included in the book. The committee also contributed funds towards a ten-day contract for Dr Amanda Wrigley. Amanda has advised on images and also commented very helpfully on drafts of my early chapters. Regarding the choice of illustrations, I was constrained by the complexity of the permissions' process and the price of reproduction. However, the mainstream and more recent films discussed are all commercially available.

Dr Stacey Abbott (Reader in Film and Television Studies at the University of Roehampton) gave generously of her time and cast a critical eye over the chapters on the Make-Over Movie (tragic and comic). This benefited me as my knowledge of film is as a movie goer of many years and as a widely read student of the discipline not as a formal practitioner. Similarly, my husband John James (Open University Associate Lecturer) read drafts of the book from the perspective of a sociologist and suggested improvements in the form and the content. I am also deeply indebted to family, friends, colleagues and students who have added to my ideas (and disagreed with them!) during the years I have been working and reflecting upon Ovid's Pygmalion on screen. Special thanks to my brother Steve (Stephen) Deahl who viewed some very strange (and some really bad) films with me at the National Film Theatre, which were not always as germane to my research as I had hoped!

I very much appreciate the patience of my publishers and the support and encouragement of editor, Tom Crick, who put up with my redrafting chapters in the last stages of the book. Any errors or infelicities in the final product are entirely my responsibility.

Paula James (2011)

Introduction

Pygmalion and His Ivory Statue: the Myth According to Ovid

In Book Ten of his epic poem *Metamorphoses* (written in the first century CE, Common Era) Ovid relates the story of Pygmalion of Cyprus. In Ovid's version Pygmalion condemns the loose morals of the local women and carves a beautiful statue out of ivory to be his female companion. The wondrous work of art is so lifelike that the sculptor himself is fooled into thinking she is real. He embarks upon a daily routine of wooing his ivory girl with gifts and imagines that she responds. Finally, Pygmalion approaches the shrine of Venus, goddess of love (the Greek Aphrodite), at the island's festival in her honour. He hesitantly asks for a wife who would be like his ivory girl. When he returns home the statue responds to his caresses, and looks up at him with a maidenly blush. Venus presides over their union and nine months later a daughter named Paphos is born. Ovid never names the statue; she first became 'Galatea' in a French novel of 1841, see Joshua (2001, xv).

It Makes a Good Story

My relationship with Ovid's ivory statue goes back a long way. Reading selections from the *Metamorphoses* (in the original Latin) as a mature student at Southampton University in the late 1970s I became in turns entranced and irritated by this wonderfully inventive poet, Publius Ovidius Naso. Ovid inhabited a complex cultural world, living and writing in Rome, the capital of an extensive empire. Ovid's epic work on transformation, *Metamorphoses*, is a poem which moves through mythical and historical time from the stabilizing of the primordial elements into the ordered universe of Ovid's day when Augustus was securely established as the first emperor. The term 'flawed masterpiece', which so amused director and actor Orson Welles when applied to the films he made after his acclaimed *Citizen Kane* (1941), can be used to describe Ovid's magnum opus.

I became interested in the afterlife of Ovid's *Metamorphoses* through my friendship with Jane Miller (then Jane Keen) when we were students in the

University of Southampton Classics department. Jane was writing a doctoral dissertation on the legends of Perseus and Pygmalion in nineteenth-century art and literature. Ovid's influence was her starting point and she demonstrated that with Pygmalion Ovid had made a new myth out of a cultic practice, the ritual marriage between the king of Cyprus (Ovid cunningly suppresses Pygmalion's royal status during the narrative) and the statue of the goddess Aphrodite (Roman Venus). However, she discovered that many nineteenth-century texts (visual and written) reflected and refashioned Ovid's version of Pygmalion in a way that illuminated the ambiguous identity of the sculptor and his statue. Edward Coley Burne-Jones' series of paintings and George Bernard Shaw's play, *Pygmalion*, were part of her study. [1]

Jane's thesis reinforced my belief that placing classical and post-classical texts side by side is not just about tracing the influence of the ancient world on later cultures. The modern manifestation of myth can become an interpretative tool for probing the complexity of the original narrative. During my academic career, and in between publishing on a range of Latin authors, I have been enticed back to Ovid and published a number of articles on figures and motifs in his epic poem. I have always kept Jane's approach to the reception of Ovid in mind when tracing the before and after of his myths in the *Metamorphoses*.[2]

Over the last two decades I have taught Ovid in schools and universities, not continuously, but with plenty of gaps for reflection in between. I have very much benefited from a steady synergy between research (engaging with an ever-growing body of sensitive and scholarly interpretations of the *Metamorphoses*) and conversations in the classroom, the lecture hall and at seminars, to say nothing of feedback after conference presentations.

Initially my focus on Pygmalion was prompted by a teaching need rather than a research one. In 1998 a new Open University Level One course was presented. *Introduction to the Humanities* (1998–2008) included Classical Studies as a subject in its own right. In the unit on 'Myths and Conventions,' Open University students read the Greek tragedy *Medea* in translation and studied George Bernard Shaw's play *Pygmalion*. Cicely Palser Havely of the English Literature department wrote an excellent critique of Shaw, starting with a discussion of the myth and its function. Students were encouraged to explore the connections between the play and Ovid's narrative, so in my evening lecture at the residential school I suggested ways in which Shaw had reversed, refashioned and departed from the story of the statue.

To do this it was necessary to look at the before and after of the myth in Ovid's narrative sequence as these surrounding stories are intimately bound up with Pygmalion and the statue. I did a quick sketch of the women of Cyprus who were punished for impiety by the goddess Venus. She turned them into prostitutes and they seemed spontaneously to change into stone. The vices of these unfortunate creatures prompted Pygmalion to produce his own perfect woman. I also summarized the tragic fate of Myrrha (a descendant of Pygmalion and the statue), who fell passionately in love with her own father. Her story is told in the *Metamorphoses* immediately after that of the sculptor and his ivory creation.

I introduced students to the Burne-Jones' series of paintings depicting the myth of the sculptor and the creation of his perfect woman. I also distributed extracts from poems, plays and novels which had conjured with the Pygmalion theme before and after Shaw. Then there were the films, a modest and partly personal collection of screen texts that reworked the motif of the manufactured and the made-over woman with fascinating cultural and social implications. In those days visual aids consisted of the slide or overhead projector and the video machine. Technology in this kind of lecture has moved on, but sometimes the slick (PowerPoint) presentation allows no room for, or possibly inhibits, even a lively audience from intervening during the delivery. Of course, those who attended my Pygmalion 'performance' enthusiastically and imaginatively offered up other movies where the ivory maiden might have metamorphosed into a more modern but equally uncanny creature. The lectures invariably generated discussions about the unpalatable aspects of this tale, which on the surface celebrates the rewards of great artistry and piety.

Everyone Has a View on the Statue

The Pygmalion myth has proved to be all-pervasive. Whatever the place or time, starting a conversation about a myth that deals in the literal creation of a perfect partner or mate never fails to provoke a reaction. I was at the hairdressers in East Grinstead in August 2010 and mentioned I was writing a book about the pursuit of the perfect woman. Hair stylists know that good listening, diplomacy and acquiring some skills in therapy come with the territory. They frequently do far more than improve and 'make over' their clients' appearance. As it happens, hairdressers figure significantly in a number of re-workings of the Pygmalion story I discuss in this book.[3] Emma, the graduate stylist, and the assistant who was shampooing me and other clients listened with interest to my account of Ovid's myth. Emma is a twin and without prompting she raised the issue of Pygmalion's narcissism in carving something close to a second self and animating his own reflection. (She had produced a short film in college testing out viewer reactions to twins in profile closing in on a kiss.)

Other comments from her co-workers included the pornographic elements in controlling and forcing physical attentions on even an artificial body.[4] The conversation turned to the ethics of men forming and re-forming women and to perceptions of patriarchy. Strong feelings were expressed about the power of the fashion industry and the media in determining ideals of femininity. This nails one of the central issues about the legacy of Pygmalion, the cultural constructedness of beauty and desire.

Similar issues concerning concepts of perfection and the rights of manufactured beings came to the fore when my PhD student Amanda Potter set up a focus group of viewers who gave their reactions to an episode of *Buffy the Vampire Slayer* in which a perfect robot girlfriend named April is made and then discarded by her creator/manufacturer, Warren. The writer of the relevant episodes, Jane Espenson, was not consciously drawing upon or referencing Ovid's myth but our selected viewers pointed out parallels with films about ideal woman and the make-over movie in particular. We asked the group to read Ovid's Pygmalion myth and re-evaluate the *Buffy* episode.

The results were enlightening and I shall go over them in more detail in Chapter 6. Needless to say, the viewers of *Buffy* had some very definite ideas about the relationship between the screen robot April and Pygmalion's ivory girl, and I have incorporated a number of their responses into my interpretation. There was a consensus that robots and vivified statues have human rights and that Pygmalion's manipulation of his ivory girl and Warren's treatment of his technological triumph (April) had distinct similarities.

The *Buffy* case study was incorporated into the Open University Honours Level course *Myth and the Greek and Roman Worlds* to broaden out the discussion on Ovid's *Metamorphoses* and its modern reception. I am beholden to the Open University Arts faculty for allowing me to incorporate results from this case study into my book and for permitting me to reproduce, in this volume, aspects of my Ovid chapter written for that module. I am also grateful to the Open University for making me over into a creature of interdisciplinarity. As a lecturer in Classical Studies department since 1993, I have had the opportunity to work with Arts Faculty colleagues (English Literature, Art History, Religious Studies, History, Philosophy and Music) on courses that create subtle dialogues between disciplines, their content and methodologies, without in any way losing or silencing the voice of each subject.

So, my work on Pygmalion and his statue has developed out of all kinds of intellectual encounters and academic endeavours, as well as the occasional idiosyncratic, spontaneous and highly illuminating thoughts from 'innocent bystanders'. The beauty of this myth as metamorphosed by the mind of Ovid is its endless capacity for reinvention. A story simply (apparently) and briefly told by Orpheus, singer of songs, who takes the narrative reins from Ovid in Book Ten of the poem has become a slippery signifier for critical interpreters across the disciplines of arts, humanities, social sciences, and science and technology. It has reached out to novelists, dramatists, poets, painters and movie makers. The perfect woman of my title has become a trope or template for desiring the illusory ideal and the paradoxical disappointment of getting what you want.

The Singer and the Song

Although Ovid is the creator of the Pygmalion story in this (relatively) familiar form the internal narrator is the legendary Thracian bard, Orpheus. It is one of several stories sung by the singer to an entranced audience of wild beasts, birds and trees. It is appropriate that the bard who can move stones with his magical musicianship celebrates a divinely inspired sculptor whose ivory statue becomes a real girl. Possessing one's heart's desire has an added poignancy for the singer as Orpheus was bereft of his beloved. In the *Metamorphoses* at the beginning of Book Ten, Ovid introduces Orpheus as the tragic figure who has loved and lost, reprising the story told in the fourth book of Virgil's *Georgics*.

Virgil gives a moving account of the bard's journey to the realms of the dead to retrieve his wife Eurydice who had been killed by a snake bite. Orpheus charmed the king and queen of Hades (the Underworld) with his tuneful lament and they agreed to release Eurydice and let her accompany Orpheus up to the surface of the earth. However, in the final stage of the perilous journey, Orpheus broke the taboo the king of the dead had imposed not to look back at Eurydice. She vanished from view, reverting to a *simulacrum* (ghost) of no substance. The ruler of the Underworld proved pitiless in the face of Orpheus' pleas for a second chance. Ovid's decision to tell Orpheus' story and then make him the narrator of the Pygmalion myth is a deliberate one, as it seems as if the sculptor has succeeded where the singer failed. Pygmalion has in a sense brought a dead thing to life. Ovid may also be referencing the fifth-century play, *Alcestis* by Euripides. The king Admetus plans to have a statue fashioned as a substitute for his wife who willingly took his place in the underworld. The ghost of Eurydice and the story of Alcestis tend to lurk behind the cold inert statue in subsequent versions of the Pygmalion myth where the likeness of a dead woman is recreated by a bereaved lover or husband.

The Poet and His World

Publius Ovidius Naso (Roman citizens had three names) was born in Sulmo (Sulmona), Italy in 43 BCE. (Before Common Era). He was a prolific poet and we are lucky that most of his work has survived (with the exception of a tragic play, *Medea*, which, ironically, Ovid and ancient critics thought was the high point of his literary career). He was a wonderful wordsmith and enlivened every genre he turned his hand to. He started his first love poem in the collection called the *Amores* with an image of the love god Cupid propelling him away from serious epic tomes towards light-hearted 'songs for swinging lovers'. The *Amores* in which Ovid introduces Corinna (a pseudonym for his mistress but she could be as fictional as one of the many mythical figures he introduces into his poetic corpus) take the reader through the make-ups and break-ups of a furtive romance. Ovid just about exhausted the love elegy genre with his convoluted dramatic scenarios and his poetic gamesmanship. He worked to death the metaphor of the lover as a soldier undergoing all kinds of hardships and manoeuvres in the pursuit of sexual satisfaction.

However, he did eventually embark upon poems on the grand scale. His unfinished *Fasti* on the gods, cults and rituals associated with the Roman calendar is full of fascinating insights into ancient beliefs and practices with constant reference to the myths that are woven into the very fabric of the days dedicated to religious celebrations. In many ways, Ovid can be heralded as the supreme myth maker. He found a place for the matter of myth in all his works either in the form of sly allusions for the knowing reader or as an apparent diversion in the text, frequently introduced by a quirky bit of lateral thinking.

Ovid was popular and famous in Rome and beyond. Even if his sophisticated and self-conscious poetry targeted as its audience the educated and comfortably off, his literary works would have trickled down through the echelons of society and been recited relatively widely. He could be regarded as the poet laureate of his time. He seemed a natural heir to the poets of the late Republic (a period of great political turmoil and destructive civil strife) who survived into the reign of Augustus. Ovid's predecessors had been actively encouraged by this first emperor to put a positive spin on the new age of peace and prosperity he was promising the people of Rome and its empire. Ovid followed in the footsteps of Virgil and Horace in this respect, but he was a post-war baby and that made him a little more cavalier and relaxed in his style and in the subject matter he chose for his poetry.

It was around the time of composing the *Fasti* and putting finishing touches to the *Metamorphoses* that Ovid fell from grace, rather like a tragic hero. Up to this point, his decision to be a full time poet and to stay away from a career in public office had been vindicated. However, the approval of the emperor and of those through whom he exercised his power was easily lost. When Ovid was around fifty years old, he suffered banishment for an unrecorded crime (he may have witnessed or been implicated in a politically embarrassing incident involving the emperor's family). Ovid's considerable corpus of epistolary poems from Tomis (modern Constanza, Romania), a bleak outpost of the Empire and a cultural backwater, is a painful study in the psychology of an urbane and sophisticated middle-aged man who was destined to die far from home in spite of his constant pleas for a pardon. In his verse letters (*Tristia, Epistulae ex Ponto*) Ovid writes of a poem (*Ars Amatoria, Art of Love*) and a mistake that caused his downfall. At one point he hints at seeing something compromising and compares his unintentional error to the Actaeon myth, which he tells in *Metamorphoses* Book Three. Actaeon was a young Theban prince who accidentally stumbled upon the virgin goddess Diana while she was bathing with her nymphs. She turned him into a stag and his own dogs tore him apart.

Ovid's offending work, *The Art of Love (Ars Amatoria)*, had been in circulation for ten years before Ovid suffered his unhappy fate. Ovid's pastiche on the didactic genre in which the conduct of love affairs is taken as an appropriate topic for teaching and learning may have rankled with the emperor Augustus over the preceding decade. This manual of seduction was not exactly in tune with the imperial legislation designed by Augustus to promote family and family values, to encourage the continuation of the wealthier stratum and restore some dignity and status to the upper classes of Roman society. My thumbnail sketch of the emperor's motivation for a moral armament programme does not do justice to its economic and social ramifications. Ancient politics was as rife with contradictions, corruptions and dissembling as it is today, but obviously Ovid was out of tune with the ideological strategies of the regime. Ovid's elusive (for us) indiscretion may have brought the witty but unwise poem to the fore once again.

Although the following chapter deals with a myth in his weighty epic poem that Ovid may have completed in exile, his other literary ventures do have a bearing upon the *Metamorphoses* in general and Pygmalion in particular. Ovid was a man of many poetic parts and his exceptional artistry is very much tied up with the times he lived in. It is hard to say whether Ovid was simply a wild card or a conscious critic in the new era of Augustan *auctoritas*. The Latin word suggests authority legitimized by precedent and sanctioned by the gods. Of course, such authority was sustained by Augustus' control of the Roman legions and his ownership of the Imperial revenues. Ovid was writing under an autocratic regime and his treatment of the myths does seem to possess a subtext about the use and abuse of superior power by gods and mortals.[5] He also offers up for exploration complexities and intellectual conundrums that make his mythical narratives readily transferable to times and places far from the cultural world he himself inhabited and was to lose so tragically in the year 8 CE.

The Lasting Legacy of Ovid

In his lengthy (fifteen books' worth) epic, *Metamorphoses,* Ovid displayed his knowledge of myth in all its glory. His many stories of transformations still bear the hallmark of his distinctive approach to narratives that had already proved capable of moving audiences out of their comfort zone. The tragedians at Athens writing in the fifth century BCE had found myths and legends good to think about. Regarding themselves as teachers as well as creative writers competing for prizes, they recognized that the dramatic festivals celebrating the god Dionysus were a relatively safe space in which to explore the mortal condition and fearful 'what if' scenarios of social upheaval. They introduced contemporary resonances into legendary and traumatic tales of heroic suffering and the fragmentation of dynastic families, demonstrating the power of the gods and the precarious nature of human happiness.

So Ovid was by no means the first ancient poet to make myths multifunctional on an aesthetic and an ethical and ideological plane. However, Ovid has an almost modern approach to his mythic material in the way he synthesizes, theorizes and psychologizes his subject matter. He also has a keen sense of the dramatic nature of the myths and how these might be conveyed in a poetic narrative. The *Metamorphoses* conveys colour, tone and moving image so vividly in the re-enactment of mythical stories and the portrayal of heroic and divine figures that it has in turn inspired artists, authors and dramatists through the centuries to visualize, theorize and extemporize around Ovidian narratives. Picturing Ovid's mythical characters has helped me to expand my interpretations of his text in general and the myth of Pygmalion in particular.

Chapter 1

Ovid's Rich Text: Layers of Identity in the Pygmalion Myth

Pygmalion: the Full Story?

But the foul Propoetides[1] dared to deny that Venus was a goddess and they experienced the wrath and retaliation of the offended deity; for the consequence was (it is said) that they made their bodies and their reputations common property. As their sense of shame withdrew and the blood ceased to flow in their faces, it was but a small step for them to turn into unyielding granite. Because Pygmalion had witnessed these women leading reproachful lives and repulsed by the defects nature had bestowed in such abundance upon the female character, he took to living as a single man without a wife. For a long time he was deprived of a companion for his bedchamber. During this time he carved snow white ivory with propitiously wondrous artistry, giving it shape, a beauty with which no woman can be born. He conceived a love for his own work. Her appearance is that of a genuine girl, one you would believe to be alive and, if deference did not stand in the way, you would believe she was willing to make a movement. To such an extent, artifice takes cover under its art of artifice.

Pygmalion is in awe and stokes the fires of passion in his breast for the simulated body. Often he moves his hands over his work, testing whether it is flesh or ivory as before and he does not admit it to be ivory still. He plants kisses and thinks they are reciprocated. He speaks to the statue and holds it and believes that his fingers are sinking into the limbs he is touching. He even frets that bruising may appear where he has put pressure. One moment he employs flattery and the next he brings it gifts appreciated by girls; seashells, polished stones, little birds, flowers of myriad colours, lilies and painted balls and amber, the tears of the Heliades fallen from the trees. He adorns the limbs with clothes as well, puts jewels on the fingers, strings of necklaces around the throat, hangs delicate pearls from the ears and loops chaplets around the statue's bosom. All this becomes her and yet naked she seems no less beautiful. He lays her on coverlets dyed with Tyrian purple and addresses her as the partner of his couch and rests her neck on downy pillows as if she could feel them.

The festival day of Venus had arrived, most renowned in all Cyprus and heifers, their curved horns clothed in gold, had fallen under the blow to their snowy white necks. The altars were smoking with incense when Pygmalion performed his office (made a sacrifice) at the shrine, stood and falteringly prayed: 'If O Gods you can grant all things, I long for my wife to be (he did not dare to say "the ivory maiden") like the ivory one.' Golden Venus was present at her own festival and realized the import of his prayer. And as a sacred sign of the favouring deity three times, the altar flame blazed up and propelled its point through the air. When he returns, he makes for the image of his mistress and lying upon the couch, he kissed her. She seemed to grow warm. He closes upon her mouth again and with his hands he touches her breast. The ivory softens under his touch and with hardness set aside and letting his fingers sink in, it yields as Hymettian beeswax re-melts and made pliable by the thumb, it is moulded into many shapes, becoming usable by being used.

While he is in a state of awe and hesitantly rejoices and fears he is deluded, the lover persistently tests out his heart's desire. She was flesh: the veins throbbed under the pressure of his thumb. Then indeed does the Paphian hero produce fulsome words with which to thank Venus and at long last he presses with his own mouth a mouth that is not manufactured. The girl feels the kisses he proffers and blushes and lifts her hesitant gaze to the light. She sets her eyes upon her love and the sky simultaneously. The goddess is present at the union she has engineered and when the horns of the moon had nine times been curved into a full crescent the girl gave birth to Paphos from whom the island takes its name.[2]

Metamorphoses 10: 238–297
(translated by Paula James)

The Before and After of Pygmalion

The Pygmalion narrative has distinct echoes of other metamorphic moments in the poem, particularly the transformation of stone into flesh and the reverse process. The hero of Cyprus is himself a composite of characters who are less lucky in love and in artistic endeavours than himself, from Narcissus (in Book Three) who is fooled by his own likeness and falls hopelessly in love with his beautiful reflection in the pool to skilled craftsmen and women whose works are destroyed by envious gods (Arachne in Book Six for instance). Ovid's text is a landscape of intersecting myths and motifs, a literary canvas of metamorphic stories. The first ten books deal in narratives that might be happening simultaneously rather than sequentially and the poet appears quite consciously to allow his chronology to crumble at times. However, commentators have noted that the Orpheus stories mark a structural shift in the poem from a fluid mythological patterning to a focus on human history.[3] Pygmalion seems to sit at a crossroads in terms of Ovid's poetic structure, which gives this story of art and love particular significance. As Pygmalion and the statue have been remoulded over the centuries they have become ever more complex as signs and signifiers.

According to the narrator, Orpheus, before turning her attention to the Propoetides (usually translated as the women of Cyprus) Venus has already perpetrated a physical transformation on another family group in the Amathus region, the Cerastae, or horned ones. The Cerastae, a male household (Anderson, 1972, pp. 493–494), have indulged in human sacrifice at the very altar of Hospitality, so their crime is against Jupiter as protector of guests and a guarantor of the good treatment of strangers. The Cerastae's impiety, taking place on her own island, is an embarrassment to Venus; so much so the goddess considers leaving her shrines and the beautiful cities and meadows of Cyprus. Instead she devises an appropriate penalty for the Cerastae, turning them into fierce bullocks so interior savagery is now in tune with their external appearance. Venus is in vengeance mode but the Propoetides do not take heed of the warning implicit in the fate of the Cerastae.

We really are not sure who these women are nor their provenance other than they inhabit the Amathus region of Cyprus. The mythological plot thickens with the characterization of these women as *obscenae*, variously translated as foul, lewd and 'obscene' even before they are forced into prostitution when the adjective would be more appropriate. The derogatory description seems to prejudge the Propoetides and prefigure the punishment meted out by Venus in return for their denial of her. A challenge to the identity of a god is liable to result in a corresponding loss of identity for the mortal offender or offenders. Another way of translating *obscenae* is 'irredeemable', which would then refer to their impiety. Venus herself was associated with *obscaenitas* (obscenity) by an early Roman playwright and poet, Ennius. Commenting on the subject of temple prostitution in Cyprus he asks: 'Why should I speak of the lewdness of Venus prostituted to the lusts of all?'[4] Miller (1988, 205) briefly mentions the theory that the

Propoetides had pocketed the profits from their sacred trade instead of filling the coffers of the goddess. This would be a theft from and an insult to Venus but does not quite constitute a denial of her divinity.

Pygmalion is motivated to make himself a life partner because of his revulsion to real women with their innate vices. This is what we are told by the narrator, Orpheus, and yet the explanation does not quite gel with the punishment of those women who had denied that Venus was a goddess. The Propoetides[5] were forced by divine intervention to acquire those very vices Pygmalion abhorred. At least one scholar (Liveley, 1999, p. 202) has suggested that these women of Cyprus or Amathus may have chosen a life of celibacy and this is what Ovid means by their denying Venus. It is not altogether certain whether the Propoetides have questioned the existence of the goddess herself or are refusing to recognize her divine power in matters of passion, sex and procreation.

Whatever they have done, these women, the Propoetides, seem to teeter and then make the transition between pure and impure, celibate and meretricious. The verb *vulgo* indicating that they allowed their bodies and their reputations (their good name?) to be prostituted or made common property makes a pertinent contrast with the private nature of Pygmalion's passion and the secret and secluded existence he is to lead with his 'lover.' At first reading the Propoetides are negative role models for both sculptor and statue. Their metamorphosis into stone seems to be a natural not a supernatural corollary of their shamelessness; they can no longer blush once modesty has fled from their bodies. Pygmalion shuns these shameful women and the fate of the local girls motivates him to carve a creature with no earthly blemishes. We cannot know whether, before Venus' spiteful revenge, the Propoetides would have been potential partners for this young man looking for a pure and untouched wife.

Putting moral considerations aside, it is worth remembering that ossified creatures are hardly accessible ones, so Pygmalion has no marriageable material in his vicinity.[6] Otherwise it would be tempting to accuse Pygmalion of being like other haughty young men present in earlier books of the *Metamorphoses* who reject available partners. It is ironic that Pygmalion then makes a model which should be as impervious to feeling and as physically frustrating a bedfellow as those he has rejected.

The Propoetides certainly influence the production and the character of the ivory maiden in subsequent reincarnations. Painters, playwrights and film makers bring the ossified prostitutes to life, giving them a significant part to play in their narrative pictures and in unfolding dramas about the manufacture of an ideal. I plan to place the marginalized and immobilized beings much more centre stage in Ovid's version of the myth, for, with hindsight, they never really disappear from the story's frame.[7] For this reason I have gone into detail about the preamble to Pygmalion's story in Ovid, as it is important to my argument that from the outset they are seen as complementary and reflective of the statue rather than oppositional.

Commentators are quick to comment on the reverse process that occurs in Ovid's version of the myth with ivory or solid material becoming flesh and blood after living, breathing women have been turned into stone. I firmly believe that Ovid is not so much counter posing the Propoetides to the statue as suggesting they might be a mirror image (albeit distorted) of the initially inert carving. This point has been touched upon before but previous interpretations, even those of the art historians, do not focus upon the way the statue's tarnished 'sisters' tend to lurk in the background of the myth in visual as well as literary representations. Detecting a woman of Cyprus beneath the virginal statue's exterior will be a feature throughout my discussion of the screen texts.

The Ambiguous Identities of the Sculptor and the Statue

Given all these ambiguities about the stone prostitutes and the liminal ivory statue, it is clear to me that Ovid intended the Propoetides to be imagined as a sculptural group. Pygmalion is presumably aware of the ossified women and in the paintings of Burne-Jones they seem to be present in the artist's studio. In both series, marble statues stand in the background of the first painting in the series. In the earlier Sutton quartet of pictures they stare balefully out at the viewer, doubling for discarded attempts at carving perfection and for the women of Cyprus frozen in the pose adopted by the living girls on the left of the frame. Could these fallen women of Amathus serve as precursors of the pure and virginal future wife of the king? If they are part of Pygmalion's modelling process, then the ambiguity of the statue seems to reflect the problem of the Propoetides' provenance.

In her 1983 thesis (pp.130–145) Jane Keen (Miller) gives a detailed comparative analysis of these Burne-Jones quartets. She notes that both sets of paintings reflect the artist's longing for an elusive higher state. For Wildman (1995, p. 301) the series 'can be interpreted as a failure of the cerebral concept of beauty when faced with a physical reality which is impossible to resist.' Burne-Jones' model for the statue was his mistress, Maria Zambaco. Keen

Ovid's Rich Text – Layers of Identity in the Pygmalion Myth 15

The Heart Desires

The Hand Refrains

The Godhead Fires

The Soul Attains

FIGURE 1.1 Pygmalion and the Image Series 1868–1870, Burne-Jones, Sir Edward (1833–1898), Private Collection / By Courtesy of Julian Hartnoll / The Bridgeman Art Library.

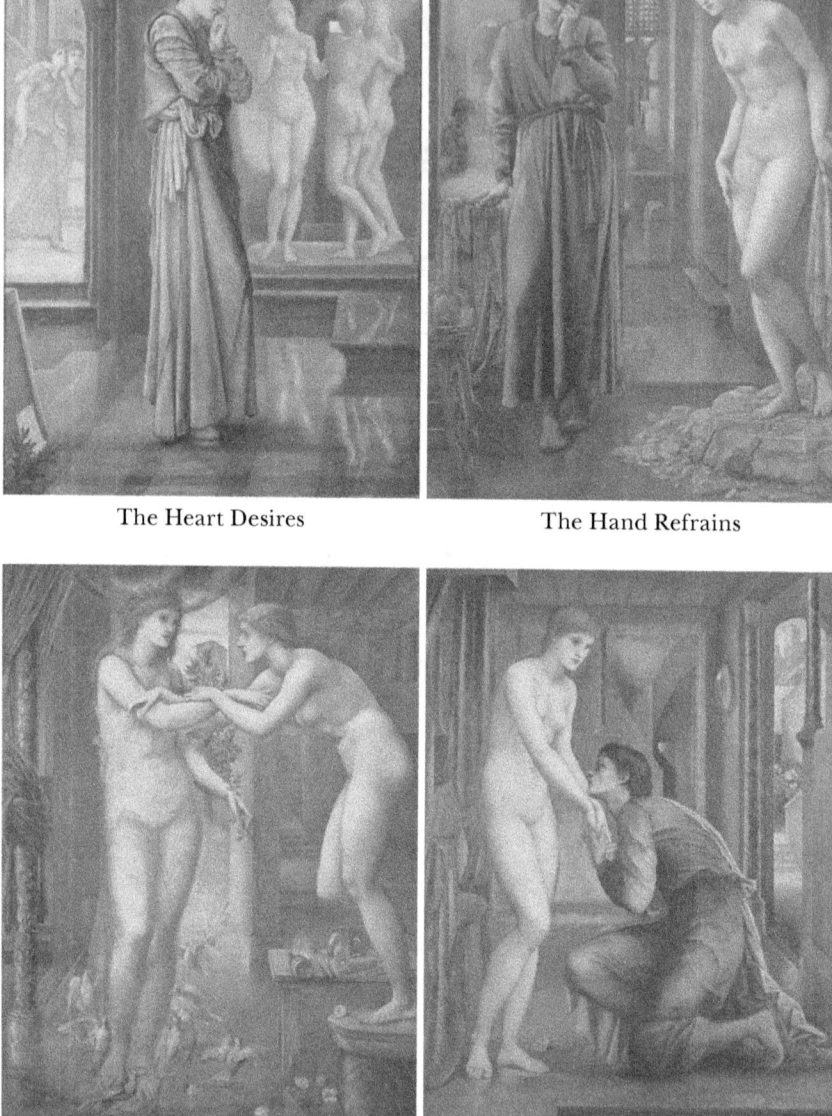

FIGURE 1.2 Pygmalion and the Image Series 1868–1878, Burne-Jones, Sir Edward, Birmingham Museums and Art Gallery.

observes that in the first painting in both series ('The heart desires') the artist uses 'architecture to create barriers that cannot be breached. His paintings are filled with steps, doors and arches, windows and distant buildings, all of which remind us of the worlds beyond.' (p. 131) This emphasizes Pygmalion's enclosed universe although Keen also notes the mirroring of poses that occurs with the real girls excluded by Pygmalion and the sculptural group at the back of his studio.

In the earlier Setton series, the sculpted women are in two groups and the floor is solid and without reflection. Although they would seem to be far better candidates for the petrified women of Cyprus with their immodest stares (like an audience according to Keen, p.132) the tasteful trio in the later series, which is modelled on Burne-Jones painting of The Three Graces, can also be associated with the trade of prostitution. (These three handmaidens of Venus were frequently used as a brothel sign throughout Renaissance Europe (Keen, p. 130).

The second painting, 'The Hand Refrains', is a distinct sanitization of Pygmalion's relationship with his (in this case) marble girl. The earlier painting emphasizes the sculptor's loneliness (Keen, p. 136) whereas the second series shows lively scenes outside the studio and Pygmalion is more obviously dressed in festive clothes. The statue however is less stiff and remote and seems, as Keen observes, to be in a kind of reverie. A major difference between the next two paintings, 'The Godhead Fires', is the figure of Pygmalion praying to Venus in the background of the picture from the earlier series. Keen suggests (p. 138) that this shows the sculptor's role in the miracle.

The final paintings 'The Soul Attains' correspond very closely in composition. Keen (p. 140) sees resignation and passive acquiescence in the statue's expression as though she is resigned to her fate and the prospect of death and decay. Keen concludes that Burne-Jones strived to capture the human beauty around him and immortalize it in art whereas Pygmalion achieved the antithesis by bringing the artefact to life. She detects a sense of unease in the last painting.

I continue to be intrigued by the statue's standing in the place vacated by the goddess. For a published and subtly different interpretation of the later series, see Arscott (2005, pp.109–118). Of particular note is her conclusion (pp. 117–118) that Burne-Jones is responsible for 'a very profound equivocation about the making of this sculpture.' Arscott sees the pots, the wrapping cloths and the clammy atmosphere as suggestive of the unwrapping of a corpse. She detects a subtext of clay to flesh and flesh to clay (or dust to dust) and also finds mirroring in all the main figures so that the substitution of the goddess for the sculptor and the sculpture can be readily envisaged as well as the interchangeability of Pygmalion and his statue.

Ovid's Mythic Materials

When Pygmalion starts upon his wondrous work he seems to be creating something quite new and without a model in mind. The sculpture has the face of a real girl but no-one sits for the artist and the statue appears to have sprung fully grown from his imagination. It would make Pygmalion very special, actually unique, if he had hit upon the perfect form of female loveliness rendering all other beauteous bodies mere copies.[8] Ovid who usually has an eye for detail and likes to add touches of naturalism to his descriptions is uncharacteristically silent about the making of the statue, but Pygmalion's skill must be outstanding if he is managing to manipulate ivory. Ivory lends itself to small-scale carving so the choice of material is possibly eccentric for a life-size doll (not that we are told the proportions of the statue).[9] The material figured along with gold in cult statues of the gods so presumably no expense was spared in the production of this snow white statue.

However, ivory is not naturally 'snow white' but, unlike cold grey marble, has a flesh-like tone. There is something deeply ambiguous about Pygmalion's statue in that she looks real but not fallible physically or morally. Snow white ivory symbolizes her perfection and simultaneously lends her naturalism. Ovid's ardent lover brightens up his statue by dressing her in finery and adorning her with jewellery but he becomes anxious that he might discolour or bruise the ivory sheen of his statue's skin with his passionate foreplay.[10] It is worth keeping in mind that Pygmalion has not painted any rosy glow on his ivory girl's cheeks. We are told that she blushes once she is vivified and has become conscious of her maker's embraces. Sharrock (1991, pp. 39–40) notes that the statue has not been made up in the cosmetic sense.[11] Statues on screen (including goddesses) do benefit from blusher and other commercial preparations. In the films under discussion in Chapter 3, the enlivened statues' submission to a superficial make-over marks the true transition into the contemporary world and their willingness to have natural and supernatural beauty enhanced by art.[12]

Whiteness denotes purity and also being one of the leisured classes in the ancient world; upper class women, like goddesses, did not become tanned or weather beaten by working outside. However, whiteness in a sculpture resembles the pallor of death, a quality and a state that subsequent versions of the Pygmalion statue story seem to attract. In literature and in painting artists and inventors modelled upon Pygmalion might, like Orpheus, be attempting to replace a lost and idealized woman and so they construct a copy which is paradoxically corpse-like in its inertness.[13] Ivory also represented illusion and liminality (being between two states) in classical times and this feature makes the nature of the statue and Pygmalion's self-deception all the more intriguing. The gates to the underworld are made of horn and ivory. Horn represents the portal for truthful dreams; ivory is the material for false visions. Ovid has introduced the horned Cerastae as part of the Cyprian cycle of stories (Ahl, 1985, pp. 250–254).[14]

The stone, the ivory and the horn all carry symbolic meaning and the simile of the Hymettan wax for the metamorphic moment (when the statue softens under Pygmalion's touch) adds another image. Bloom (2003) focuses upon the malleability and the multi-functionality of wax in her book, arguing that this material, a mere simile in Ovid's Pygmalion, has at least as varied and interesting a role in the myth's afterlife as the ivory itself. Wax may well have been used to cover up the joins of a sculpture made out of ivory parts and the simile of Hymettian bees wax for the 'melting' of the cold hard substance under the testing and moulding thumb of Pygmalion draws the reader into an increasingly complex visualization of the vivification process. Is the statue coming to life or in danger of falling apart? No one can quite equal Ovid for metaphorical mind games.

The Statue as 'Unique'

The narrator of the Pygmalion myth praises the artist for hiding artistry by artistry. After relating the story from ancient Greece about a veil so realistically painted that the viewer (another painter) believed the veil was cloaking a non-existent picture beneath, Gabriel (2004, p.17) writes:

> Perfect representation was an ideal for Greek art – and hence, perfect imitation or mimesis. According to this view, the perfect painting is the one that is so perfect one does not realise it is a painting. Note then that perfect representation, the perfect mimesis, is also a perfect deception, since it conceals its own standing as representation. Hence the closer we get to the truth, the more it deceives. This is the paradox of verisimilitude; the veil of deception.

Stoichita (2008, p. 2) outlines the art historical perspective upon an artificial construct that has no obvious original. In Stoichita's view, conjuring as he does with Plato's distinction between representation and imitation, art creates the perfect form of a virtual woman and Pygmalion is the medium by which the artistic ideal finds realization. Stoichita argues that Ovid's

Pygmalion myth confounds theories of Western mimesis in which the copy is the imitation of an original (2008, p.5). Stoichita refines his interpretation (2008, p.16) with the suggestion that the sculptor's *simulacrum* combines the original and the copy in one.[15] Cast (2009), in his review of Stoichita's book, points out that, in Platonic terms, the imitator is copying not the physical object but only its appearance.

If Pygmalion had stumbled upon a winning formula for accessing the ideal Platonic shape then any kind of model from the material world would be a poor imitation and an obstacle to retrieving and representing the original. In Plato's theory of perception, humans are only capable of experiencing shadows or poor copies (*simulacra*) of a perfect and essential form, all material objects being but inferior copies of their essence and appearance. However, the statue has the face of a real girl. What are we to make of the conundrum? Does Pygmalion have any model in mind?

The Statue as a Poetic Construct

Pygmalion's treatment of the ivory girl is simultaneously intimate and reverential. Although the nature of the frozen women was deeply flawed in the eyes of Pygmalion (a judgement voiced through Orpheus) the sculptor does desire a sexually compliant partner and, as noted by Miller (1983, p. 207) and significantly expanded by Sharrock (1991, pp. 39–46), he treats the statue as a mistress to be coaxed and seduced in the traditions of Latin love elegy. He brings the little gifts girls like and expect to receive from an attentive lover. This courtship suggests that Pygmalion has been reading the poetry of Tibullus, Propertius and Ovid himself who perfected the genre of elegy in which the writers document and dramatize their relationships with freeborn women.

Pygmalion also appears to be following the general advice about conducting love affairs given by Ovid in his work of three books, the *Ars Amatoria*, that mock manual of seduction (in verse form) which was instrumental in his banishment to Romania.

According to Sharrock, (1991, p. 49), the statue is a literary construction, an example of 'womanufacture' and a metaphor for the mistress who behaves submissively and obligingly, something the poetic *puellae* (girlfriends) were not always inclined to do.

> By foregrounding the lover as artist/artist as lover, the text consciously or unconsciously exposes the workings of gendered power relations in

erotic and specifically elegiac discourse. Love poetry creates its own object, calls her Woman, and falls in love with her – or rather, with the artist's own act of creating her. This is womanufacture.[16]

The socio-historical approach to the manufacturing of an ideal might be partially satisfied by Sharrock's 'womanufacture' interpretation, as this locks into the literary constructs of a specific time and place, Ovid's own world in fact. As the story of an ideal woman reappears through the centuries she is bound to metamorphose into a variety of cultural stereotypes. Perhaps we need look no further for an original for the statue than contemporary concepts of female perfection.

Whatever conflicting conclusions scholars might draw from Ovid's genre crossing (and this is not the first time he has brought an elegiac scenario into his epic poem) the comical courtship of the statue transforms Pygmalion into a Latin (poetic) lover. The sculptor sets about to win over an obdurate mistress as if he is expecting frustration before fulfilment and yet the statue is never shut away from his sight. The ivory girl is his exclusive property so Pygmalion achieves the elegiac lover's goal of ready access to his beloved. There are no other contenders for her favour. On the other hand, the lack of obstacles to and rivals for the ivory maiden take the excitement and erotic tensions out of the situation. The daily routine of courting, fondling, dressing and undressing this passive *puella* is potentially boring as well as blissful. The statue is a flinty and unresponsive creature not by choice but by nature. Pygmalion has and does not have what he wants.

In love elegy, the poets of Rome invite the reader into plausible situations even if the scenarios are fictitious and the women may or may not be 'mythical' or fictional rather than real and historical. In the *Metamorphoses* the narrator invites the reader to enter a world of myth and shape shifting and to share in the illusion that the statue might be real. The ivory girl is a mistress with a hard heart that nevertheless might be melted. We are told that 'you would believe that she wished to move or be moved if *reverentia* did not stand in the way'. The word *movere* can mean sexual arousal as well as simple movement. It also conveys the sense of self-propelled motion suggesting that the statue wished to move itself. For this reason classical scholars have struggled to convey the full register of meanings in their translation and to find an appropriate word for the noun *reverentia*, which seems to encompass reverence, modesty, and a sense of awe and respect.

Ahl (1985, pp. 247–260) teases out the wordplay within Ovid's narrative and does so with his characteristic comprehensiveness. For instance, noting a plethora of puns in the passage, he observes on page 248 that *reverentia* contains the Latin for truth (*re vera* means 'in truth' or 'indeed') and so *reverentia* reprises the previous description of the statue as *virginis verae facies*, a phrase suggesting the life-like appearance of the sculpture but also indicating Pygmalion's desire for a genuine and faithful maiden. If a sense of modesty or respect keeps the statue still then it is already acquiring some divine properties. Sharrock (1993, p. 174) points out that sculptures of the gods might be tethered down in case they went walkabout. This might happen if these were automata with mechanical movement; alternatively gods are assumed to inhabit their sculptural likenesses on occasion or have their *simulacra* hijacked by demons.

An aspect of *reverentia* which the modern reader might miss is its existence as a minor goddess, one of the many abstract concepts Romans liked to personify and appease. Such abstracts boasted modest temples and specific cults. It is tempting to visualize the deified Reverentia literally standing in the way of the newly carved statue and physically preventing it from moving. Reverentia in a physical, corporeal form would then be defending the virtue of the ivory girl just as immoveable door keepers and closed doors regularly excluded elegiac lovers from their mistresses and so scuppered their dishonourable intentions.

The Statue as Artistic Self-Delusion

There is an argument that we should look no further than Pygmalion's fevered brain and introverted personality for the genesis of the ivory girl. This is the psychological approach to the myth and it is fully and subtly expounded by Hardie (2002, pp. 143–152). There are distinct echoes of the Narcissus myth (told by Ovid in Book Three, lines 341–510) in the vocabulary and imagery of the Pygmalion story. The interplay between the two figures has been thoroughly explored but I suspect its implications have not yet been exhausted.[17] The lovelorn boy paralysed by the side of the pool which contains his heart's desire is compared with a statue, something of pristine loveliness and subtle hues. Like Narcissus who falls in love with his own reflection and embarks upon a hopeless courtship, Pygmalion also has to supply the responses of his statue and imagine his love and passion returned.

Ovid relentlessly exploits the paradox of Narcissus' situation as his self-love destroys him. His parents were warned by the seer Tiresias that their beautiful boy would be destroyed if he ever 'knew himself'. As the advice of the Delphic oracle, an ancient guide to rational living, was to 'know oneself' this utterance bemuses those who receive it. Hardie applies the theories of Jacques Lacan to the myth as Narcissus suffers from being locked into the mirror stage of childhood. Tiresias seems to be advising against the very encounter that will mark the moment when Narcissus should grow up and recognize his own reflection.

Narcissus' delusion is reprised in Pygmalion's concretization of an image, which should be nothing but a reflection or a phantom of the sculptor's mind but Pygmalion is rewarded by having his own idea of perfection come to life as a separate being.

For Narcissus who falls in love with his image before he realizes it is not some male nymph of the pool the recognition stage of his development breaks his heart. From the moment Pygmalion completes this miraculous and lifelike sculpture, which is so skilful that art is concealed by artistry, he loses his grip on reality in general.

The intertwining of themes (as well as bodies) across these stories is reinforced by the vocabulary and the imagery they share. Locating the parallels between Pygmalion and Narcissus does not necessarily resolve the issue of the statue's model but the former myth becomes a lens through which we can view the sculptor's love of a phantom. If Sharrock is right in her interpretation of Pygmalion's prayer (when he asks for his wife to be like the statue) Ovid has upped the subtlety stakes in the subsequent myth of Pygmalion: 'Although in the "reality" of our story there is no original for the *simulacrum* to be an image of, the text seduces the reader (and his own love seduces Pygmalion) into thinking, for a moment, that there is' (1991, p. 46).

Ovid has taken the motif or theme of realistic sculptures fooling even the most discerning eye to a whole new level with the artwork fooling the artist himself. This is a sea change to the story and pure invention on Ovid's part. Pygmalion was not the maker of the statue in the original story but one in a line of kings of Cyprus who ritually married a statue of Aphrodite (Roman Venus). Ovid is deliberately putting a particular psychological spin upon the myth so that Pygmalion temporarily joins other deluded and frustrated lovers pining after the unattainable. Then his statue comes to life and all is well. Or is it? The 'be careful what you wish for' caveat is applicable at this point.

The answer to Pygmalion's prayer is the destruction of a wondrous work of art: 'But the fact is when Pygmalion becomes a lover he sacrifices his identity as an artist' (Leach, 1974, p. 124). Pygmalion compensates for this loss of artistic immortality by immediately impregnating the vivified statue.[18] Pygmalion was never primarily an artist in that he showed no interest in celebrating his statue in public – it was always for private consumption. Nevertheless, Venus just may have subverted a prayer that was intended (if possible) to grant Pygmalion a facsimile of the facsimile so that the sculpture itself could be preserved for posterity.

The sculptor's equivocation about the statue itself becoming his wife could be prompted by discretion and circumspection but might be his attempt to have the best of both worlds. In at least one film, a latter-day screen Pygmalion is allowed this very thing in so far as a sculpted goddess returns to her pedestal while a mortal Doppelgänger appears to replace her. However, in this case the movie hero has not carved the statue he has vivified so no artistic capital has been invested in the process. Ovid's hero loses out as an artist at the moment he succeeds as a lover. According to Feldherr (2010, p. 261) who also questions the import of the sculptor's prayer 'Pygmalion is caught in the exquisite tension of wanting life to be like art and art to be alive'.

Leach (1974, pp. 127–135) contrasts Pygmalion with other artists in Ovid's epic poem who fail in various ways to preserve their skills and who invite the wrath of the gods by challenging divine artistic hegemony. Marsyas (in Book Six) suffers a terrible and tragic fate after losing the music contest with Apollo and Arachne (also in Book Six) is changed into a spider (the first of the species) even though her tapestry is described as equal if not better than Minerva's. Yet again, Envy with a capital E is deferred to – *Livor* could not find fault with her fluid pictures. When Minerva spitefully tears up her human rival's work, it is a self-defeating act in the sense that she is destroying an aspect of herself. Minerva embodies the craft of weaving in her divine persona and has warned Arachne that she must acknowledge the goddess for her remarkable skill.

Leach argues (p.107) that heroes fare better than artists in the *Metamorphoses* in holding their own against the power of the gods and nature. She does not remark upon the dubbing of Pygmalion as *heros* at the moment he prays for something like the statue to be his wife. Ultimately he has doomed his work to destruction and in this he joins company with the occasional divine *artifex* or a human artist with a divine gift as portrayed in Ovid's poem. The very first creation (the ordering of the cosmos by an unnamed god) is threatened with implosion and elemental chaos twice in rapid succession and other works of life and art are liable to be damaged or confounded throughout the *Metamorphoses*. It is almost as if Ovid brooks no rival and is the sole surviving artist upon whom we must rely for hearing about and picturing the creative achievements that have proved so fragile.

There is more than one scholarly trend in Pygmalion studies that identifies the statue as a 'literal' phantom, a ghost from beyond the grave. Orpheus the narrator has failed to bring his ideal woman (back) to life

(Viarre, 1968, pp. 236–237 and pp. 241–242). Ovid may also be refashioning a motif from Euripides tragedy *Alcestis* (written in Athens during the fifth century BCE). In Euripides' version of the myth, the king Admetus pictures himself with a full-sized sculpture of his wife Alcestis who has taken his place among the dead. In the play, Alcestis is rescued from Hades by the hero Herakles. The two bereaved husbands, Admetus and Orpheus, might be merging in the myth of Pygmalion and the ivory substance of the statue would take on added symbolic significance as a meeting point between the living and the dead.

It was Venus all along – the Goddess and the Statue

Miller (1988, p. 207) suggests that there could be a sub-text to Pygmalion's diplomacy and carefully worded wish for someone like the ivory maiden in that any sculpture of a beautiful naked female is likely to be a representation of Venus. In general terms the goddess of love is the model for all loveliness and in the specific context of Cyprus she is the cult statue with which the kings perform the *hieros gamos* or sacred marriage. For these reasons, Pygmalion, the artificer, does not presume to ask for Venus as a wife. Pygmalion is extremely hesitant (*timidus*) when he approaches the shrine of Venus, just as he has been with his ivory girl. If the reader did not know any better, the sculptor might be a mere humble artisan standing before the shrine. However, Pygmalion is revealed to be *heros* and, as Miller points out (1988, p. 208), the very fact that he is set apart in his worship at the festival suggests he has a special status. A private prayer to the goddess reflects the mixture of intimacy and awe Pygmalion demonstrates towards his statue at home.

As his descendants are the royal family of Cyprus we can only assume that Ovid decided not to reveal Pygmalion's kingly status until his identity as an artist and lover was firmly anchored in the reader's mind. Pygmalion's lack of daring demonstrates his deference to the goddess and is in sharp contrast to the women of Cyprus who had the audacity to deny Venus her divinity. Pygmalion's wish to marry a statue whose outstanding beauty makes her a generic match with Venus herself would be a dangerous presumption. And yet, the narrator (is this Ovid or Orpheus?) tells us that Venus understands what Pygmalion really wants. The statue becomes the consort of the king, a miraculous event recalling the ritual which inspired the poet's myth making in the first place. Kings of Cyprus did 'marry' a beautiful image, that of the goddess herself. The match or mismatch between myth and ritual deserves a little more probing. It all becomes very complicated if Ovid is in some way at this point in the story reverting to the historic cult aspect of Pygmalion because as king he could legitimately ask for the *statue* of Venus to be his wife.[19]

As Sharrock observes, the sculptor's adorning of the statue at home has elements of a ritualistic performance as if Pygmalion has been acting out the sacred marriage in the privacy of his own bedroom. The goddess of love is present at her own festival but we assume that Pygmalion kneels before her golden statue and that this is the form in which she attends the celebrations. Isolated from the festival throng Pygmalion now communicates with another *simulacrum*, which complements his own carving. If the reader becomes a viewer and imagines a combination of the ivory sculpture in Pygmalion's private apartments (or palace) and the golden one on public display, the two images merges into a chryselephantine replica of the goddess. And, indeed, the *simulacra* do meet as Pygmalion's bedroom is graced by the presence of Venus.

Pygmalion hurries home eager to be with his beloved ivory girl and finds her coming to life in response to his embraces. The word Ovid chooses for the statue's feeling his embraces is *sensit*. This is the very same Latin verb he employs in its other meaning of 'perceives' when describing Venus' response to Pygmalion. She perceives (*sensit*) or understands what Pygmalion desires. Liveley (1999, p. 205) mentions this wordplay and the interaction between Pygmalion and the two statues. Hardie (2002, p. 190) believes that it should raise the reader's suspicions when the narrator reveals that Venus is present at the wedding she has fashioned. I would add that the reader can visualize the statue, as Burne-Jones does, as a reflection of the living deity, as one beautiful and uncanny being staring another in the face.

There is an ambiguity about the form Venus takes at her festival and in Pygmalion's boudoir. She is both herself and her own *simulacrum*. Are we all dreaming the dream of Pygmalion about what is real and what is representational? Burne-Jones shows us the goddess Venus vivifying the statue. At least this seems a reasonable assumption but it is never stated in Ovid's text that she does so directly. In the second series of paintings, Venus steadies the statue which looks rather precipitate, lurching forward from the plinth.[20] What I find most interesting (and this does not feature in any analysis of the Burne-Jones paintings I have encountered to date) is the exchangeable positions of the sculptor, the statue and the goddess. In the last painting of both series, Pygmalion kneels before the statue, which now occupies the space vacated by Venus. Surely this suggests that for Burne-Jones there was an ambiguity about the identity of the lovely ivory girl and that it was only a small step for the statue to represent and supplant the goddess simultaneously.

The ivory maiden was carved with the face of a real girl not the appearance of a divine being. However, when Aphrodite visited Anchises of Troy on the hill side, this is just how she presented herself. She reassured him with a masquerade of virginity although he suspected this lovely girl was a goddess. Cyrino (2010, 89–92) dwells on this scene as described in *The Homeric Hymn to Aphrodite* and it seems to me that the preparations that Aphrodite makes before her seduction of the mortal shepherd encapsulate the mix we find in the ivory statue of simple girlishness and divine power and beauty. Salzmann-Mitchell (2005, p. 73) makes a comparison between Pygmalion and Anchises but only in a general way as a lover of Aphrodite. Films about statues of the goddess Venus coming to life tend to show us a female divinity who enjoys masquerading as a flirtatious girl with a mere mortal. The film *One Touch of Venus* (discussed in Chapter 4 along with other movies about supernatural beings) encouraged me to revisit Ovid with the Anchises factor in mind.

a Surfeit of Models!

There is one last candidate in this strange identity parade for a prototype ivory girl. Sharrock suggests there are distinct resonances in Pygmalion's adorning of his statue of the dressing and polishing of Pandora, who is introduced in the epic poem, *Works and Days* by the Greek author Hesiod (seventh century, BCE). According to Hesiod, Pandora was moulded out of clay by Hephaistus (the lame blacksmith god; his Roman name is Vulcan) to be launched upon an unsuspecting world. The materials used to make this first woman were the same as the earth and water, which Prometheus mixed to produce the human race. All the same, Pandora was a construct, a winning and fatal combination of heavenly features in a mortal shell. She was a synthesis of attributes bestowed by the gods, working together for once at the behest of Zeus. Steiner (2001, pp. 186–207) gives a subtle exposition of the Pandora figure as a craftwork embodying artificiality, inviting and frustrating desire and (p. 190) 'presentifying' a longed for and irretrievable absent model. She also notes (p. 91, n.25) that Ovid's ivory statue caps all previous versions and 'creates a being who, like the manufactured Pandora, corresponds to no mortal creature'.

Pandora was sent to be the bedfellow of a king, Epimetheus (his name means afterthought), and he foolishly accepted this baneful gift of the gods, which inflicted misery upon humankind. Pandora opened the jar full of evils and woes and henceforward became a byword for the curious and meddling woman. Prometheus (whose name denotes thinking ahead) had warned his brother against accepting any gifts from the gods, but Pandora was endowed with great beauty and charms including a persuasive and lilting voice. Epimetheus was destined to be wise after the event.

The presence of Pandora in Ovid's Pygmalion is more of a literary allusion than a mythical paradigm for the statue. The parallel could be stretched further if the vivification of the ivory girl to be a consort of the king constitutes a reinvention of the race of women. The women in Pygmalion's region of Cyprus are no longer flesh and blood and the female species may well need restoring. However, the myth of Pandora was not taken up by the poets of the Roman Empire. The poet Hesiod remains the principal source for this fascinating and misogynistic view, namely that the first woman was a burden and necessary evil to men. It is certainly the case, however, that in the afterlife of Pygmalion and the statue, artificial beings can become a bane to their creators and Pandora can be traced within the patterns of perfect women on screen.

Pygmalion inevitably invites comparisons with those scientists (real and fictional) who produce artificial life, from Frankenstein's monster to rogue robots parallels. The misfit monster has been realized with poignancy on film even though the horror genre is his or her natural habitat. Mary Shelley's early nineteenth century novel was subtitled *A Modern Prometheus*, referencing the descendant of the Titans (ancient elemental gods who gave way to the Olympian pantheon) and his role in moulding man from clay. Victor Frankenstein, the scientist, who creates the monster was intending to produce perfection from unpromising material but his story is readily conflated with Pygmalion in discussions about humans playing god and accidentally producing Pandoras.[21]

Pandora-like constructs access Western cultural models of flawed first women and the similarity between the statue, the first artificial construct of womanhood (sent to blight the life of man!) and the biblical Eve who is blamed for trouble in paradise has been noted by more than one classical and cinema studies' scholar. From the farcical rampaging robot at the end of the 1949 film *The Perfect Woman* to a positively murderous replica of an upright scientist in *Eve of Destruction*, and the cinematic prototype of destructive cyborgs, the other Maria in *Metropolis*, the submissive statue tends to turn into the stuff of the horror movie. The 'Pandora meets Pygmalion's sex toy' theme will feature in Chapters 5, 6 and 7.

The Desire for a Good Bad Woman

Beneath and beyond the dream come true of a made-to-order, compliant companion, Ovid implicitly raises questions and conundrums about the boundaries between bodies, divine, human and synthetic, as well as their porosity and permeability. This is hardly unexpected in a poem about transformations on the grand and the small scale. By bringing to life the beautiful ivory maiden which the sculptor has designed to be the first of her kind (like no woman born), the goddess Venus in Ovid's epic poem has sanctioned a new kind of gift giving – and favours bestowed by greater mortals upon lesser ones cannot always be taken at face (however fair a face) value.

Pygmalion's story has lent itself to positive and negative readings through the centuries. It can be Christianized, moralized and celebrated as the triumph of love and/or art but can also be retold or analysed as a lesson in the dangers of delusion, idolatry and human overreaching.

For a sociologist rather than a psychologist, the ideal in Pygmalion's mind will be a type or stereotype of beauty that is culturally determined. That should not deny his vision any individuality or particularity but it does suggest he is carving his perfect woman within the constraints of his classical context. Pygmalion may belong to a dynasty founded by the Phoenicians but Ovid is telling a story inherited from Greek sources and he overlays it with Roman social practices. The myth's protean possibilities and the ambiguity of its meaning have been set up by Ovid who places the episode between two narratives, the fate of the Propoetides, compelled to become prostitutes and then hardened into stone, and the story of Myrrha, descended from the statue and Pygmalion. As this great granddaughter commits incest with her father, gives birth to his child and then is immobilized into the myrrh tree, her metamorphosis is a disturbing counterpoint to the 'birth' of the ivory girl. Pygmalion is not really the father of his statue but she is a projection of his desires and has been carved out of his imagination, or so it would seem.[22]

But of course, the ivory girl is ultimately Ovid's creation. The statue has proved to be a cultural chameleon par excellence with persistent transformations in literature, art and cinema precisely because Ovid has kept her as *tabula rasa*, a blank canvas.[23] The poet could have taken the opportunity to produce an ecphrasis of the ivory maiden. Ecphrasis is the technical term for an elaborate description of an art work within a poem or prose piece. The ecphrasis was rarely just a literary tour de force but frequently took the reader beyond the boundaries of the text in a figurative and imaginative way. The author of such a detailed description might suggest that a static picture was full of movement or even of sound, thus celebrating the supremacy of written visualization over artistic representation.

Presumably Ovid would not have wanted to bring the ivory girl to life prematurely in this way. Paradoxically, he guaranteed her an afterlife by not describing her beyond her ivory surface and with the oblique information that she had the face of a real girl. The range of her reincarnations in film and on television displays the changing face of femininity and the celebration of as well as fears about female liberation and empowerment. The myth of Pygmalion and his ivory sculpture has also become a tool for interrogating the identity and integrity of the artist, the ethics and aesthetics of creating miraculous imitations of life, and the dangers and delusions of divine sparks in mere mortals.

The fate of the statue, a newly born and full grown girl, and the tragedy of Myrrha can become conflated in post-Ovidian stories about creating ideal partners. The myth also seems to have motivated storylines in which a vivified illusion is in turns passive, empowered, delightful and destructive. The statue on screen has taken the form of the made-over woman, the goddess of love, the robot girlfriend, the life size doll and computer programmes made flesh. The post-Ovidian metamorphoses of the Pygmalion myth invariably shed light (both diffuse and clear) upon the Latin poet's rich text. When a version of the ivory girl appears as a moving image on screen she can inspire us to re-visualize her in Ovid's text. Although this strategy runs the risk of superimposing a modern model upon an ancient narrative, it is surprisingly fruitful for confirming a range of complex identities for Pygmalion's statue in Ovid's own portrayal of the ivory girl.

a Sneak (Pre)View

My chapters on the comic and the tragic make-over deal in the disappointment and disillusionment felt by later Pygmalions towards the women they have re-created. They start out with the statue and end up with an all too fallible flesh and blood creature. Other controlling males make over an existing girl into something exceptional and realize they preferred the original model, however ordinary she was. The challenge of articulating without a shadow of a doubt what you really, really want survives in subsequent stories about men (and women) pursuing a perfect partner and then realizing they want the original flawed model after all.

Those forced to manufacture their own ideal in the absence of any ready-made model that fits the bill are not guaranteed satisfaction either. The ideal is no longer an exact fit and someone else with a flaw (in the judgement of Orpheus, the vices women are prone to) proves to be more attractive. Ultimately this is simple psychology and modern-day writers and movie directors would not need to read Ovid for inspiration. Several of the movies I have decided to discuss are about appreciating what it means to be human, warts and all, rejecting the illusion of perfection. For the heroes and in some case for the heroines playing latter-day Pygmalions these are films about growing up and, dare I use the pun, getting real!

There are so many movies that touch upon themes of make-over as well as television story lines, graphic and regular novels that it is tempting to parade Pygmalion at every turn, to see classical mythic moments where none exists. Films dealing in 'make-over' stories (discussed in Chapters 2 and 3) come with any number of cultural layers and Ovid's myth can be submerged under these nuances and accretions. In some cases it is, frankly, a stretch of Procrustean proportions to make meaningful comparisons between the modern and the ancient text. Is 'Pygmalion', maker of the ideal woman, just a short hand, a kind of cultural mnemonic or faint echo even when a direct citation is incorporated into screen narrative?

This brings me back to an earlier point about the myth's endless potential for unravelling and reweaving to suit each new cultural context and to maximize the medium's impact. The intriguing aspect of the make-over stories is that they fragment the statue's story in Ovid over a range of narrative lines and draw into the Pygmalion nexus other mythical figures, tropes and themes that appear in the *Metamorphoses*. The writers and directors of the films in question may not have accessed the episodes from Ovid by a direct route but he had certainly set his mark upon the myths for centuries to come. The connections implicit between Pygmalion and other tales of artistry, passion and playing god persevere into the creative consciousness – does it matter if Ovid's epic frame has not been uppermost in the minds of these relatively recent writers and creators of the statue's descendants?

In my 2003 article; 'She's All That: Ovid's Ivory Statue and the Legacy of Pygmalion on Film' I argued that a twentieth-century film (Alfred Hitchcock's *Vertigo* 1958) had enhanced my understanding of Ovid's text, particularly the function of the lead-in story about the Propoetides.[24] Stoichita's *The Pygmalion Effect* (translated from the French in 2008) traces the reverberation of the myth from its ancient erotic origins through sculpture, painting, photography and film, linking aesthetics, magic and technical skill. In Chapter 2, I have expanded my interpretation of *Vertigo* in the light of Stoichita's fascinating treatment of the film as a Pygmalion narrative with a focus upon the cinematic composition of key transformation, recognition and revelation scenes. Also published in 2008, Jane O'Sullivan's article took up the threads of the myth in *Vertigo* and analysed the re-emergence of its Pygmalion elements in the 1990 film *Pretty Woman*. I had reached similar conclusions about the correspondences between the two films but I have benefited from O'Sullivan's detailed insights.[25]

In fact, the twenty-first century has been rich in Ovidian reception. Joshua's 2001 *Pygmalion and Galatea* traces the cultural trajectory of the myth in the nineteenth century and the mixture of prurience and patriarchy each retelling or re-visioning reveals. Wood's 2002 *Living Dolls* explores the human quest for mechanical life with Pygmalion as her starting point. Enterline's analysis of Marston's 1598 poem *Metamorphosis of Pygmalion's Image* in her 2000 book *The Rhetoric of the Body from Ovid to Shakespeare* highlights Ovid's 'habit of moving between literal and figural levels of meaning' (p.130) and emphasizes the imagery of vocal animation at key moments of creation in the *Metamorphoses*.

Hersey's 2009 *Falling in Love with Statues* (posthumously published) looks at artificial humans from Pygmalion to the present with an impressive and sweeping survey of the nature of statues, human belief and rituals of worship. All these books demonstrate that Ovid's ivory maiden is a magnet for religious, historical, anthropological, aesthetic, scientific and sociological scholarship and speculation.

Pygmalion's Pervasive Presence on the Screen

However modern the location might be (cyberspace and all its technical wizardry spring to mind) the myth of Pygmalion always comes culturally layered (or sometimes filtered) through centuries of literature and the visual arts, presenting us with questions about the durability and changeability of mythological narratives and traditions. My method of putting a modern text in direct dialogue with an ancient one, using a film or piece of television to probe Ovid's influential refashioning of the cultic practices of Cypriot kings, does not (I trust) neglect the metamorphoses of the myth in between. I do however want to demonstrate that the visualization of Ovid's Pygmalion story on screen, as an act of performance, has the potential to reveal significant strands in Ovid's version.

Keeping Ovid in the picture is about picturing Ovid's myth as he tells it (or has Orpheus tell it). To borrow a term from cinematic techniques, 'storyboarding' the narrative is useful because it helps to visualize the proximity of the statue to the ossified Propoetides, to think of the ways the figure of Venus is being represented and her different relationships to the statue. This is my focus in Chapter 4. There are a number of subtle and highly theorized interpretations of the way we 'view' Pygmalion from classical scholars and experts in world literature, art history and film studies. These are complex and linguistically nuanced readings of Ovid. My approach to visualizing Pygmalion is in many ways more literal and my goal is to sustain a synergy so that both the ancient and the modern text stay in our sights.

According to Bloom, the cinema is, by its very nature, the privileged space of the Pygmalionesque as the

> very medium embodies the longstanding human desire for the animation of the inanimate. Even when the Pygmalion paradigm fails in film, the medium itself succeeds in creating the illusion of movement. (Bloom, 2000, p. 2)

She concentrates upon films that give life (or give the appearance of giving life) to corpses, body parts, automata, wax figures, statues, painted images and 'fake bodies' generally because the medium of cinema 'entails images of absent bodies (and objects)'. Gunning (2005) takes a similar view but asks (p. 262) what it is about the filmic image that specifically evokes the erotic and concludes (p. 263):

> the newly emerging institution of cinema accepted and standardised its erotic role, focusing the attention of its eroticised audience (already dwelling, Barthes claims, in a hypnotic state, immersed in the shadows) onto the incandescent illumination of the cinematic star as image of the perfect erotic body.

In her 2003 book *Waxworks: a Cultural Obsession*, on p. xviii of her introduction, Bloom champions the intermingling of high cultural and literary works with popular culture, literature and film, interrogating the viability of the distinctions between them in the process. I certainly share Bloom's inclusive approach to what constitutes an artistic remoulding of a myth from the classical past and her interest in keeping communication lines open between Ovid and the modern myth makers. If anything, my choice of screen texts, which do not overlap with Bloom's, cast the cultural net even wider, teasing out Ovidian strands from cult series to curios in the history of cinema.

For me, the intriguing aspect of all the movies I have selected is that they fragment the statue's story but also draw into the Pygmalion nexus other mythical figures, tropes and themes that appear in the *Metamorphoses*. This should invite classicists to revisit the source of the myth and its location within Ovid's poem with a fresh perspective. It will be an added bonus if films and television series of the distant past (some probably now less well-known than Ovid's *Metamorphoses*) are embraced and re-evaluated by those readers encountering them for the first time. I am sure Ovid would have approved of resurrecting recondite and 'legendary' films, which are still relished by a minority of cinema-goers today.

I indicated that there are a number of possible models for Ovid's ivory maiden. On the one hand she is non-specific in appearance, allowing future creators the freedom to alter her image physically and socially. On the other, Ovid has implied (or manipulated us to infer) that the statue just might be modelled upon a goddess or be a sanitized version of women of easy virtue. It should come as no surprise that the following chapters focus on films and a few key television series that give the various identities of the statue full rein. My choice is not exhaustive and never could be. I have selected screen texts that tease out the main motifs outlined in this introduction but there are bound to be other films, past, present and future with Pygmalion twists or timbres. I am sure anyone reading this book will gain great intellectual pleasure from applying 'the Pygmalion effect' to favourite and familiar films that are missing here.

My principal television text is *Buffy the Vampire Slayer* (1997–2003). In Chapter 6 I shall provide a whistle-stop tour through Whedon's well-crafted narrative arc before embarking on an interpretation of April, the robot girlfriend who appeared in Season Five of the show. Now more canonical than contemporary in television culture, *Buffy* might seem passé to some of the younger generation although it retains a lively fan base and has been reinvented in graphic novel sequels. Readers with classical backgrounds may or may not be *Buffy* fans (though I know a fair few who are). For anyone buying or borrowing my book and wondering about the prominent presence of a 'teen show' in Chapter 6, I recommend browsing Slayage online with its burgeoning bibliography of scholarly volumes and articles on Joss Whedon's ground-breaking series.

Buffy is full of fantastic elements but its vampires and monsters double for the inner demons of adolescence. Whedon's California setting (Sunnydale) was a realistic environment with a Gothic underbelly. Otherwise, I have sidelined some films set in a futuristic or fantasy world, so science fiction has received a raw deal in some respects. The reason for these omissions is my concern to keep intact the central core of the Pygmalion myth in Ovid. The statue stands out as something special and unexpected, a one-off albeit in a fantastic landscape of metamorphic events. It is too big a paradigmatic shift from the classical world and Ovid's myth to scrutinize robots when they appear as a species and as an everyday part of a fictional dystopian world.

Of course, robots en masse and as a genus in science fiction books and films can address and disturb the boundaries between being human and existing as a piece of technology (or being a human welded to or totally reliant on technological parts and aids). However, on balance, the advanced technological constructs being dreamed up in the modern world and the twenty-first century preoccupation with the dangers and delights of virtual reality are in general less useful issues for the dialogue I have set up with Ovid – and after all, Classicists do not want the wonderful Pygmalion narrative to vanish from the scene after the myth of the ivory statue has set such an intriguing cultural trajectory in motion.

The Tragedy of the Lost Texts!

This is a cause of frustration and sadness, but surprisingly does not apply to Ovid, at least as far as his epic poem is concerned. Nevertheless, classicists do face the challenge of missing or incomplete ancient written and visual sources which Ovid had sight of and we know of only second hand. For that reason, speculation has to reign supreme when it comes to the Greek and Roman traditions that fed into Ovid's refashioning of his mythic material.[26] Unfortunately, we have to say the same about the preservation of film and television series as this has a sorry history of loss and wilful destruction. My remarks upon the 1960s series *A for Andromeda*, the award winning *My Living Doll* (USA, same decade) and the film *Corridor of Mirrors* come with a caution about *lacunae*. (Mind the gaps!)

The fragility of early film (a highly inflammable nitrate base) rendered the cinematic world of representation as vulnerable to damage (from fire if not flood) as Ovid's cosmos in the *Metamorphoses*. Add to this the fate of films that were edited down before distribution for reasons of censorship or programming and marketing considerations. As Winkler has shown in an adroit discussion (2009, 32–3) Classicists working with diverse manuscripts traditions and reconstructing corrupt passages of Greek and Latin would no doubt empathize with the challenge and frustrations of these labours of love.

Chapter 2

Tragic Transformations: Making and Breaking the Statue on Screen

Introduction

This chapter focuses on Hitchcock's 1958 film *Vertigo* and provides a synthesis of views on this screen text as a re-working of the Pygmalion myth. However, I have prefaced this case study with an exploration of the director's development of an ideal celluloid woman whose enduring charisma relied upon her being apparently remote and unobtainable but simultaneously ready and willing to be sexually aroused. It would seem that Ovid's Pygmalion had hit upon a winning formula for mystique and allure well before the advent of Hitchcock's construction of the ice maiden image. However, Hitchcock's cinematic portrayals of the female predicament are closer to Ovid's poetic strategies for visualizing victims of assault and domination. Both ancient writer and twentieth-century director represent desire, delusion and disintegrating personalities with a mixture of empathy and comedy.

The reason that Hitchcock is more readily defined as a craftsman in the Pygmalion vein is because Ovid's sculptor has become a cliché for men making over women. The origin of this shorthand whereby the myth of Pygmalion means elevating the ordinary rather than normalizing the extraordinary will be addressed in more detail in Chapter 3. As a preamble to my discussion about Hitchcock's *Vertigo* and three other films (not by Hitchcock but with some similarities to his 1958 film) that deal in illusory women, namely *Corridor of Mirrors*, *Obsession* and *Stolen Face*, I shall contextualize the director's motivation in creating a distinctive kind of female persona for the screen.

Bloom's characterization (2000) of the cinema as a Pygmalionesque space where the inanimate may be animated works on more than one level. Hollywood studios have for many years encapsulated the film industry's manufacture and reduplication of culturally determined but also commercially driven images of perfection. Female stars continue to have less room to manoeuvre when it comes to ideals of beauty in the Western world. In the past, studio bosses but also directors (all invariably male) might mould actresses for private and public consumption simultaneously and they brought particular preferences to bear in the conscious crafting of their human material.

The world and the cinema have moved on but not necessarily as far forward or in the direction that we might have hoped. In discussing the American big-budget movie of recent decades and its success in appealing to 'both the stay at home mom and the high powered female executive, to the traditionalist and the feminist alike', Kord and Krimmer (2005, p. 4) conclude: When transferred from the real world to celluloid, neither type rules the screen; rather, both appear in curiously watered-down form. In answer to the question 'so what do we get from Hollywood?' they suggest (p. 9) that women's films

> aim to provide the answer to our identity crises, relieve us of our bad consciences, reconcile our differences with the world and provide comfort for our inadequacies.[1]

In fact, however weak, wicked or just plain fallible the women in these films might appear, however plain and normal they are tricked up to look, when played by the big stars, they invariably revert back to the screen goddess or the perfect woman.[2]

A Star Is Born: But It's a Painful Process

Ovid relates a number of myths in the early books of the epic which concern comely young women (frequently nymphs who tend to have an innate allure) and occasionally beautiful boys catching the eye of the Olympian gods. The unfortunate objects of desire are frequently elevated and reach the height of fame (Callisto whose story is told in Book Two becomes a constellation for instance) but only after suffering rape and then being subjected to a traumatic metamorphosis. Of course, these mythical victims do not seek out or invite the attention of those on high as an aspiring actor might but the manipulation of their identity interests Ovid on a psychological level. Their inner torment finds an echo in the testimony of actresses who had felt twisted into whole new shapes by the studio system.

George Cukor's 1954 cinematic tour de force, *A Star is Born* (still awaiting restoration to its full length), deals with the make-over of a promising actress into star material.[3] It is a self-conscious and often comical critique of the entertainment industry, which does not ignore the casualties of fame. Cukor's film demonstrated Judy Garland's dramatic range as well as the considerable emotional depth she could capture as a singer of showcase numbers. The heroine of the film (Garland playing Esther Blodgett) meets self-destructive alcoholic Norman Maine (James Mason) whose own career in acting is beginning to plummet. Entranced by her heartfelt rendition of the song, 'The man that got away', Maine becomes her promoter, manager and lover. However, he cannot cope with her success as his own star continues to fall. He returns to heavy drinking, in spite of all her patience, devotion and reassurance. Eventually Norman drowns himself, walking purposefully out of their beach house and into the ocean.

In a memorable final scene, Vicky (Esther) comes onto the stage after Norman's suicide and utters the immortal last line: 'This is Mrs Norman Maine'. Her tribute to her husband could be viewed as Vicky's willing sublimation of her own identity into that of the man who moulded her. She recognizes that his suicide has been partly precipitated by her success and growing autonomy. For a while the statue no longer needed Pygmalion but hers is a gesture for herself and the audience, a statement about her always being a part of Norman Maine. To a certain extent, this is a superficial link with the myth and underlines the pitfalls of seeing Pygmalion's shadow around every cinematic corner. It is possible that by mythologizing the moment that closes the film, I have marginalized the heartfelt loss that Esther/Vicky shares with her adoring public. After all, she is also asking to be applauded as a loving wife not as a celebrity construct. *A Star is Born* does, however, subject Hollywood and the movie industry to a satirical scrutiny while warmly approving of the individual who can rise above it.

Hitchcock's Crafting of a Complex Icon

Laura Mulvey's essay of 1975 'Visual Pleasure and Narrative Cinema' exposed the tendencies of mainstream movies to manufacture female images primarily for the male gaze. Mulvey's interpretation of the female icon gave rise to a raft of theoretical debates about the interplay between screen and spectator and took feminist film theory in a new direction. She argued from a Lacanian perspective that the man looks to and at the eroticized woman to fulfil his fantasies and fetishes about the ultimate object of desire. The cinema mimics the mirror stage of childhood and legitimizes, indeed encourages, the identification of the self with the other in a kind of narcissistic misrecognition, as the image on screen is a projection of the spectator's mind as much as of the camera. Hitchcock was a master of manipulation when it came to the gaze in this respect.

A number of Hitchcock's critics and several of his leading ladies have aligned him with Pygmalion in his manufacturing and manipulating of the female image. Brown (2005, p. 138) and Stoichita (2008, pp. 182–183) have drawn parallels between Hitchcock as a modern manipulator of artistic models (in particular female actors) and his mythical predecessor, Pygmalion. The director was surely aware of the myth and that the story of an inspired artist carving an ideal woman might be applied to him. Hitchcock was a cinematic sculptor but his inspiration came principally from canvas. He could deliberately evoke nineteenth-century paintings of fictional and mythical heroines when he wished to etherealize and idealize his leading ladies.[4] In Garrett (1999), actresses Janet Leigh, Tippi Hedren, Karen Black, Suzanne Pleshette and Eve Marie Saint did acknowledge in their panel discussion on Hitchcock that they took wing within the director's framework. His artistic vision was obviously inspiring even if his methods (frequently mischievous) left a lot to be desired.

The creator of Pygmalion was, of course, Ovid and in some ways the poet is a better fit with the auteur director as Hitchcock reproduced Pygmalion figures in more than one of his films. Both Ovid and Hitchcock portray men (and gods) who take control of women and manipulate them into new forms. However, there is a persuasive argument that Ovid and Hitchcock have produced texts which expose the fragility of male and female identities. The women are not always entirely disempowered.

Like Ovid, Hitchcock has been taken to task for focussing upon women as victims, as images to be manipulated and made over or metamorphosed by the male and, again like Ovid, he has his defenders or at least critical critics who think the texts of the director yield a complexity of attitudes towards female protagonists. Some interesting perspectives emerge from and through the screen beauties the film director parades before the spectator's gaze. Hitchcock's prime concern and preoccupation was with the aesthetics of his cinematic art and he was very much in love with his own talent. Fair enough – this was a criticism levelled at Ovid and the celebration of the great artist could be seen as a piece of narcissism on Ovid's part. Both Hitchcock and Ovid can cause discomfort with their probing into the pain of their characters, male and female, and neither is averse to importing comedy into the most tense and tragic situations.

Tania Modleski's introduction to her book on Hitchcock is worth quoting in conjunction with classicist Genevieve Liveley's observations on Ovid's apparently passive women. Modleski (1988, p. 3) states:

This book aims to account, often through psychoanalytical explanations, for the ambivalence in the work of Hitchcock. In the process, it continually demonstrates that despite the often considerable violence with which women are treated in Hitchcock's films, they remain resistant to patriarchal assimilation.

Liveley (1999, pp. 198–200) integrates various feminist perspectives on Ovid's poem and explores how a resisting reader (or viewer) chooses to open herself up to the plural discourse of the text while recognizing the limitations of male-centred critiques that legitimize and transmit only one reality (or reading):

> Ovid's *Metamorphoses* may encode perspectives that exclude the reader reading 'like a woman' and even give offence – particularly when these perspectives are presented or read in such a way as to dominate the discourse – but other perspectives are always available. Throughout the *Metamorphoses* characters and narrators continuously change: different views and different voices are seen and heard as perspectives and narratives change. (p. 200)

Liveley mentions the range of narrators in Ovid and suggests that this technique gives the reader a freedom of focalization. On more than one occasion in Ovid's *Metamorphoses* the reader bumps up against the issue of Ovid's narrative presence. When judgements are made by an internal storyteller this may be the poet's invitation to us to make judgements in turn upon (or form an opinion about) the fictional character who utters them. Ovid's voice is difficult to detect but there are literary devices that suggest actual authorial asides and evaluations – or are we supposed to think of Ovid entering his work of art, like Hitchcock,[5] simply to remind us about the fictional world and his genius as its creator. Both these image makers are not above artistic gamesmanship.

Here's Looking at You, Kid

Since her ground-breaking article of 1975, Mulvey has moved away in some measure from an exclusive focus on the male gaze. In 'Hitchcock's Blondes,' her introductory talk to a showing of *Marnie* at the National Film Theatre in London on 8 March 2010 (International Women's Day) she expanded upon her famous and influential interpretations of the portrayal of idealized and demonized femininity on screen. In this absorbing talk, Mulvey recognized and celebrated Hitchcock's distinctive contribution to the creation of beautiful and baneful women on film. While it is true that Hitchcock's unabashed intention was to heighten the voyeuristic enjoyment of his audiences by investing his heroines with erotic tensions under emotionally smooth exteriors, he developed a personal and distinctive vision of what kind of woman suited the cinematic medium.

Mulvey demonstrated that Hitchcock's heroines invite spectators, regardless of their sex and gender orientation, to idolize, fear, desire and pity them in various combinations. As examples, Mulvey traced the disintegration and reintegration of his leading ladies from Alicia (Ingrid Bergmann in *Notorious*) to Marnie (Tippi Hedren) and of course, Madeleine/Judy (Kim Novak) in *Vertigo*. Mulvey uses the myth of Pandora as a significant subtext to cinematic roles for women that involve their being deceptive and destructive, the sort of heroines who entice and entrap even when they seem at their most helpless.

Hitchcock excelled in constructing memorable images of women, some of whom move from distant, enigmatic, self-contained and self-controlled figures to bruised and broken creatures in need of protection and parenting. If Hitchcock's female characters are the modern equivalent of the ivory statue they mimic her qualities of solidity and resilience along with a suggestion of fragility and fragmentation. It would seem that the picturing of Hitchcock as Pygmalion is irresistible after all. In that case, his leading ladies should be reconsidered for their metaphorical relationship to the statue.

Hitchcock's Search for a Succession of Ivory Maidens

Hitchcock was privileged to be in a profession where artistry and creativity were rewarded and immortality more or less guaranteed. As a movie director, he could discard actresses who displeased, opposed or rejected him and replace them with more malleable models. In other words, Hitchcock was able to have the best of both worlds; Pygmalion had one shot at creating his notion of perfection and perhaps divinely inspired, in Ovid's narrative at least, we assume that he got it right first time. However, as noted in the introduction, painters through the centuries have presented Pygmalion as a sculptor by profession and depicted him in a fully equipped studio, with a human model or models and other statues in the workshop. These sculptures might represent work in progress, finished but imperfect attempts at the ideal, and even real women turned to stone (the Propoetides).

Perhaps Pygmalion prefigures the now equally legendary Hitchcock in these artistic interpretations of a man searching for and finding an ideal but then having to replace her or reduplicate her image several times over. Hitchcock had hoped to have Vera Miles playing Madeleine in *Vertigo* (Grace Kelly's departure from acting to marry the Prince Rainier of Monaco left him high and dry for a number of roles for which she would have been his preferred choice). Hitchock's ideal of the perfect screen woman has distinct similarities to Pygmalion's image of the ivory statue. Pygmalion's choice of ivory for the material of the statue produced the illusion of flesh-like tones, suggesting something warm and living beneath the hard surface. He too imagined a slow burn of passion beneath the cold exterior.

I have already explored some of the properties of ivory as substance and symbol in Chapter 1. Hitchcock's preference for fair-haired and alabaster leading ladies was bound up with a common cultural stereotype that set the dark and sultry look against the white European or Scandinavian female.[6] The director believed that such a Nordic look intensified the impression that seething (untapped) passions lurked beneath a frosty glaze and gaze. Hitchcock produced a number of films in which the hero is successful, as Pygmalion was, in bringing just such a beautiful creature to life.

The perfect woman for Hitchcock was 'blonde, subtle and Nordic'. His fantasy which he believed with some justification would be a winning formula with audiences was that 'deep down the ice queen was aroused and lubricious' (Wollen, 1997). Hitchcock possibly calculated that the Nordic or Scandinavian type of looks he favoured in his actresses evoked a cool and remote landscape in the mind of the viewer, which added to the idea of something remote and vaguely exotic, the ice or even snow queen of a fairy tale world. This transference technique (or the association game) makes the director a true artistic heir of Ovid who blurred boundaries between the physical environment and the personality of its denizens. Naiads and dryads could blend in with and become one with their surroundings (see the myth of Salmacis and Hermaphroditus summarized in Chapter 8).

Ingrid Bergman: the 'Statuesque?' Swede

The director had a fruitful working relationship with Swedish actress Ingrid Bergman and several of her roles combined the qualities of coolness and coquetry that heightened the sexual tensions in Hitchcock films. In *Spellbound* (1945), she plays the part of a professional psychologist (Dr Constance Peterson) working with patients who both rely upon and resent her attempts to stabilize them; she is a model of restraint and emotional coherence. The duality of woman, distant and desirable, impervious to seduction but waiting to be aroused, is clearly marked out in Constance's character. The storyline also involves masquerade, mistaken identities and a disturbed male hero with amnesia. John Ballantyne (played by Gregory Peck at the height of his male beauty) suffers from fragmented memories of a crime he may have committed. He is also under the delusion that he is Dr Edwards and arrives at the psychiatric institution, Green Manors, to replace the retiring head Dr Murchison.

Constance experiences an overwhelming attraction to the newly arrived 'Dr Edwards'. She struggles to understand this unscientific and inexplicable mutual feeling of love at first sight which the hero, JB, likens to a rare lightening strike. The image of electricity invokes an elemental awakening and reminds a viewer tuned into actual and metaphorical vivifications of both Frankenstein's monster and the miracle of Pygmalion's immoveable maiden opening her eyes and seeing her lover for the first time. It is expressed cinematically by the famous image of a succession of opening doors.[7]

Up to this point in the film, Constance has been impervious to male attentions and has established her superiority over a flirting colleague with a sunny smile and a verbal put down. She explains to him that he is deceiving himself if he thinks she is responding to his flattery, that he is sensing his own desires, none of which emanate from her, but which he has transferred to her nevertheless. This sums up the situation in Pygmalion very neatly, if we care to condemn the sculptor for indulging in delusions and deserving no more than Narcissus in wishing for the impossible. Conversely, Constance's name suggests the character's tenacity and fidelity which she exhibits towards the hero as her patient but also to older avuncular males. She seeks the help of and defers to the eccentric professor, Alex, who was her tutor and remains her mentor. Alex is played with comic genius by Michael Chekhov. Constance also shows great loyalty to Murchison (Leo G. Carroll), the retiring head of Green Manors. In the film's finale she gently reasons with the deranged Murchison who is holding her at gunpoint.

Spellbound rejoices in making a basic murder mystery an uncanny experience. The music for the film was composed by Miklos Rozsa. Rozsa incorporated the eerie sound of the theremin into his luscious score to reinforce the troubled and nightmarish world inhabited by the hero in waking as well as sleeping moments.[8] The atmospheric and surreal sets for John's disturbing dream sequences were designed by Salvador Dali. One of the discarded dream sequences featured Bergmann as a statue and this would have reinforced the two sides of Constance, encapsulating her wholesome beauty along with the breaking down of her brittle exterior. On reflection, this was judged as a crude symbolism and it may have been a wise choice to dispense with it.[9]

Nevertheless it intrigued the leading lady: 'It was beautiful', Ingrid Bergman recalled.

> We worked on it so much. That statue . . . my death mask was made and then this whole body of a statue. Then the body flew away, revealing the real woman underneath (Leff 1987, p. 165).

If retained, this image of Constance, the cool and rational psychiatrist, who frustrates JB by alternating in her treatment of him as patient or an object under study and lover, would have demonstrated his desire to see her protective exterior broken up. It would have complemented the appearance of a scantily dressed and accessible 'kissing bug', in the casino whom JB describes as looking a little like Constance in his casino nightmare, and cursorily dismissed by Chekhov's analyst as irrelevant, just 'plain wishful dreaming'.

In *Notorious* just a year later (1946), Bergman was paired with Cary Grant but the storyline required him to be cold and unforgiving, a man who manipulates her and then finds it difficult to declare his true feelings for her. Bergman plays Alicia, whose father has committed suicide in prison after being sentenced as a Nazi spy in an American court. Totally unsympathetic to his Fascist beliefs and estranged from her father, Alicia drowns her sorrows in drink and partying. Under a brittle exterior and a charade of loose living (i.e. like one of the Propoetides), she is courageous, principled and warm hearted. Alicia is persuaded by Devlin (Grant) to become an agent for the American government.[10] They embark upon a love affair but he rejects her when she agrees to marry a German industrialist (Claude Rains) and spy on the circle of top Nazi scientists meeting in his house. Devlin rescues her at the end of the film, carrying the heroine from the room where she is lying helpless and near to death from poisoning. Alicia is a less empowered role than that of Constance in *Spellbound* but it gave Bergman a chance to be sexually provocative on screen.[11]

American Beauties

Grace Kelly encapsulates the refined and remarkably lovely blonde in the Hitchock bevy of beauties. As Lisa Carol Freemont in *Rear Window* (1954), she was a dream casting as the immaculately turned out but refreshingly untroubled heroine. She enters each scene like an airbrushed photo stepping out of the fashion page. Judged by her fiancé (played by James Stewart) to be 'too perfect, too beautiful',[12] she is presented as calculating and superficial but the brittle and narcissistic exterior is tempered by Lisa's almost imperturbable acceptance of her identity, her self-knowledge. In a powerful critique of the film Tania Modleski (1988, pp. 73–85) argues that Lisa is an intelligent and resourceful female and much more complex than the part she plays as a spoiled privileged girl. However, Kelly was the muse that got away (to her fairytale marriage) and Hitchcock began to search for a *simulacrum* or copy of his ideal actress.

A one-off replacement was found in Eve Marie Saint (coincidentally three wonderfully and symbolically potent names) who played Eve Kendall in *North by Northwest* (1959). In the film, her character has been groomed (or rather trained as she is an FBI agent in the plot) to impersonate a calculating mantrap while preserving her masquerade and sustaining an aloofness and emotional distance in her demeanour. Eve turns out to be an heroic figure (from the American Cold War perspective) reprising to a certain extent Ingrid Bergmann's courageous spy dicing with danger in *Notorious*. These beautiful and successful agents of the American government (selling their bodies to advance the cause) are imperilled and need saving by the hero/lover, played by Cary Grant in both instances.

However, the character of Roger Thornhill in *North by Northwest* is more buffoon than buttress, being inferior to the leading lady in intelligence and resourcefulness. Roger's involvement with the daring do of espionage is accidental. He naively accepts the gift of a beautiful woman offering to help him as he runs from the police and the spy ring he has become embroiled in. Eve has to deceive Roger and send him to his death, but on learning the truth, he changes into the protective lover. Roger is a far cry from the emotionally closed down and embittered Devlin, the professional agent in *Notorious* who waits till Alicia is at death's door before he 'melts' and retrieves her from the mouth of Hades. However, both characters played by Grant need lessons in love and commitment and it is the plucky heroines who breathe life into them.

Tippi Hedren whom Hitchcock cast in *The Birds* (1963) and *Marnie* (1964) proved to be his most challenging choice on and off screen. In her second film, Hedren plays a frigid and compulsive thief who, on her own admission, cannot bear to be handled.[13] At the beginning of *Marnie*, Hedren is introduced to the viewer in fragmented form as a pair of legs walking away from a recently committed crime (stealing from the bank where she obtained a post without references). Her first act in removing her disguise is to restore her hair to its natural fair colour. The audience shares Marnie's view of her newly cleansed face in the mirror of a public cloakroom and presumably is supposed to react with the same delight and relief she shows as she shakes out her blonde locks.

Marnie then moves on to the Rutland bank and encounters the hero and her nemesis in the form of Mark Rutland who runs the family business. Sean Connery, cast as Mark Rutland, recalls her from a brief encounter at her last job (with the banker Strutt) and has already indulged in a bit of body part objectification, identifying her as 'the one with the legs'. [14] Connery, stylishly and very self-aware of his screen sex appeal, conveys amused and attracted as he plays Marnie's game and accepts her phony story and persona during the interview she attends for a secretarial position at Rutlands. Mark is fascinated erotically by Marnie's outward beauty and poise but this is spiced up by the hint of her pathological tendencies.

Mark waits for Marnie to steal from the bank, covers up the theft and then finds and 'captures' Marnie. He blackmails her into marriage but after a frustrating week of abstinence on their honeymoon, he forces himself upon her. There are aspects of the Pygmalion lover making love to an unresponsive statue in this and earlier scenes. Mark then becomes determined to solve the childhood trauma that has rendered Marnie so terrified of intimacy, so that he can sexually and emotionally 'bring her to life'.

Of course, Mark has not made Marnie the way she is but he professes an anthropological as well as a psychological interest in her condition. He also pursues her like a lustful god from the moment he sets eyes upon her. The scenario created by Hitchcock (and he makes a number of significant changes from the Winston Graham book set in Manchester, England) evokes the early books of Ovid's *Metamorphoses* when luckless women attempt to resist powerful deities. Not only do they become victims, they are liable to be punished for being victims as well. Mark does uncover the truth and the basis for Marnie's phobias and frigidity, so, in some ways, he fulfils the role of divine saviour and partially redeems his rape of the girl he earlier described as victim material ('such a fetching little thing').

Vertigo: When the Subtext Becomes the Text

Hitchcock's 1958 film, *Vertigo*, is a disturbing realization of the Pygmalion myth as it focuses on the transformation of a female figure in the most sinister of circumstances. Kim Novak who plays ethereal Madeleine and working girl Judy made a clear comparison between her role in the film and her experience of the studio 'make-over' of her body to fit the 1950s' stereotype of beauty. Novak commented upon her experience with the director whom she found intimidating in his insistence on a particular wardrobe designed to make her uncomfortable as Madeleine. Novak likened the make-over of Judy as a replay of the Hollywood studio's metamorphosis of herself:

> You know they want to make you over completely. They do your hair and your make-up and it was like I was always fighting to show some of my real self. So I related to the resentment of being made over and to the need for approval and the desire to be loved. I really identified with the story because to me it was saying, 'please see who I am. Fall in love with me, not a fantasy' (Auiler, 1998, p. 25).

The film has attracted an enormous amount of attention and critical acclaim as a cinematically ravishing and narratively disturbing achievement in the director's artistic corpus.[15] The text, context and subtext of *Vertigo* is as much mulled over as Ovid's Pygmalion myth and during the past decade more than one creative interplay has been suggested for these two tales of delusion set so far apart on the cultural spectrum. However, apart from my article in 2003 which I believe was the first to make a detailed study of *Vertigo* as a modern Pygmalion story,[16] its source text, the Boileau and Narcejac novel, *D'Entre Les Morts* (*From Among the Dead* but with an English title of *The Living and the Dead*) has been neglected or marginalized. Both titles of the novel (probably unconsciously) capture the symbolic associations of ivory explored in the introduction, its liminal qualities and its presence in the portals to the underworld where it denotes the doorway of deceptive dreams.[17] For Hitchcock, the fascination of the story was 'The man who wants to go to bed with a woman who's dead. He is indulging in a form of necrophilia' (Harris and Katz, 1996 Production Notes).

The psychological and figurative themes that come to distinguish this thriller-cum-murder mystery are accentuated once the book enters the medium of the moving image. Hitchcock introduces a distinctly ethereal ambience and an almost idealized landscape by transposing the action from France during World War II to a sunny San Francisco. He adds light and colour to a story, which in composition and plot has a much more *film noir* quality about it. However, glorious Technicolor notwithstanding, the film is full of real and metaphorical shadows. Brill (1988, pp. 207–208) writes of the vernal imagery of Persephone, queen of the dead, who brings spring on her annual visits to the earth, that accompanies Novak throughout the film. Brill identifies the flowers and foliage (real and representational) surrounding Madeleine and other Hitchcock heroines as a recurrent motif in the director's 'happier films'. 'Often lost themselves, they [the heroines] return to bring new life to the rescuers who must also be rescued and resurrected after their descent to figurative Hades'.[18]

Hitchcock sticks very closely to the novel for the basic thriller twist. In *The Living and the Dead* we learn from the protagonist Flavières he has left the Parisian police force and is now a practising lawyer. This emerges during a conversation with an old friend Gévigne who wishes to hire him to follow his wife. In any case the assignment does not appeal until Gévigne reassures him it is not to do with suspected infidelity. Flavières is initially unsure about physically demanding detective work as his reason for retiring from detective work was a traumatic incident. He now suffers from an acute fear of heights. The life-changing event that caused the hero's conditions made the perfect dramatic scene to open *Vertigo*. In the film James Stewart takes the part of the detective (Scottie) and we see him pursuing a criminal across the high roof-tops. This scene ends with the fall of a uniformed officer attempting to save Scottie. Scottie, like Flavières, is physically and psychologically damaged by this accident and his subsequent vertigo proves to be a tragic physical weakness.

Flavières is a shabby and unfit man isolated, lonely and ultimately cowardly, hardly heroic material. *Vertigo's* John Fergusson (nicknamed Scottie) behaves very differently from the protagonist of the novel at the crisis point in the narrative. Flavières has few redeeming features; James Stewart's Scottie is slim, handsome and elegantly dressed and scarcely distinguishable, at first sight, from other romantic leads he played in his more mature years. However, Modleski (1988, pp. 90–98) convincingly demonstrates that Scottie is a disempowered and to a certain extent feminized character, which is part of Hitchcock's mischievous manipulation of his leading man and our expectations of him.[19] In the film version, the detective's accident has put him in a temporary 'corset' and his long-term and close friend Midge (Barbara Bel Geddes) is cajoling and teasing him by turns during his recuperation.

She catches him as he faints on the step ladder only a foot from the ground, cradling him in her arms with the words 'mother's here'. She is clearly disappointed but resigned to the fact that he has never shown a romantic interest in her. Stewart still manages to bring his characteristic charm and humour to the part in these early scenes, and it is only with hindsight (*Vertigo* is a film that repays several viewings) that we realize just how much Scottie goes against the grain of Stewart's previous on- and off-screen persona. At the time of its release, the cinema audiences were likely to have accepted the illusion of James Stewart as a strong, sensitive and endearing hero who would ultimately prevail.

In the film, Scottie agrees to take on the assignment for his old college buddy, Gavin Elster (Tom Helmore). He is to tail Elster's wife Madeleine not to investigate an infidelity but to find out where she goes in a strange mesmerized state she has started to display. Madeleine (Kim Novak in a career defining role) cannot remember the places she visits in her daily drives but Elster is convinced she is unconsciously retracing the steps of a long dead ancestor, Carlotta. Employed as a private eye, Scottie becomes the prying eye upon Madeleine. At Elster's suggestion, he has observed her dining with her husband at their regular restaurant. It is obvious that Scottie is immediately intrigued and aroused by this beautifully turned out woman with a fey and distant look in her eyes.

The Deluded Lover

In the novel, Flavières sees Madeleine from the very first moment as an artwork, The Mona Lisa or *La Belle Ferronière*. The written text is peppered with images and allusions of this type, spelling out the unhealthy obsession of the hero with his human quarry and his immediate disgust at the thought of her body belonging to her husband, Gévigne, when he sees them dining together. Throughout *The Living and the Dead* Madeleine is continually viewed by Flavières as if she is the embodiment of enigmatic and lovely women portrayed in famous paintings. This finds skilful realization in Hitchcock's film version. Camera angles, filters, music, in other words, a whole host of compositional techniques are employed to suggest the start of Scottie's infatuation and the objectification of Elster's wife as a creature of hypnotic beauty, a vessel for heroic fantasy.

Scottie continues to look upon Madeleine from a distance, following her car on a labyrinthine route around San Francisco. The audience becomes the voyeur along with Scottie as we watch Madeleine from behind the wheel (of both car and camera). The cinematic Madeleine is placed in situations that intensify her appearance as an abstracted and other worldly creature. Scottie follows her to the art gallery and sees her sitting entranced in front of the portrait of Carlotta, her dead ancestor. Madeleine reflects this figure from the past with the bouquet she has just bought. It is a replica of Carlotta's posy and Madeleine has apparently taken on other physical attributes of her dead ancestor.[20] Madeleine also visits Carlotta's grave wearing a grey suit that integrates her among the marble monuments like a walking statue made out of memorial stone. This was the 'silly suit' Novak so hated (Auiler 1998, pp. 67–68) but which she admitted made her feel constricted and uncomfortable as Madeleine.

The audience continues to share the viewpoint of the increasingly intrigued and then obsessive Scottie as he tries to work out the mystery of Madeleine apparently haunted by her ancestor, the mad and sad Carlotta bereft of her lover and her child. Gavin Elster expresses his fears to Scottie that his wife is possessed by the spirit of Carlotta and unaware of her state and the cause of it she will nevertheless trace Carlotta's tragic footsteps and commit suicide. Scottie is enticed into what later proves to be a false narrative. Playing the hunter (following a lovely image of womanhood just as Ovidian gods might do) he pursues Madeleine with desire but also to fulfil the fantasy that he is her protector. As an assignment Madeleine is a temporary resurrection for Scottie as he is deceived into thinking he is in control, and will be able to save her. This self-deception is fed by his successful rescue of Madeleine when she throws herself in San Francisco Bay, apparently attempting to fulfil the worst fears of her husband. In the *Hitchock et L'Art* exhibition of 2001 the floating heroine was juxtaposed to Millais' drowning Ophelia. The correspondences between Madeleine and canonical works of art in Hitchcock's visual imagery mimic the direct comparisons with paintings (so direct they hover between simile and metaphor) Flavières makes in the novel.

The censors were extremely unhappy with the subsequent scene in the film. Scottie has clearly undressed Madeleine as her clothes have been hung up to dry in his apartment and she emerges in his dressing gown. This very erotically charged (but not explicitly sexual) situation was difficult to film to Hitchcock's satisfaction. The end result is nothing like the equivalent episode in *The Living and the Dead* which is anti-climactic once Flavières has fished Madeleine inelegantly and with a great deal of physical effort out of a murky river Seine. Instead of Madeleine leaving abruptly (as in the novel), Hitchcock's heroine is subjected to Scottie's scrutiny and his tenderness as he has his first chance of intimacy with her. Scottie utters a proverb about a life saved belonging to the saviour as he talks to Madeleine in the cosy setting of his lounge. Stoichita (2008, p. 183) notes that the colours of the red and white robe she has borrowed are symbolic of resurrection and animation.

Film critics have recognized that Madeleine has a rebirth in this scene and that it represents a turning point in the film, although she does not quite wake to her lover as the statue did to the sculptor: 'By pulling her up from the water of San Francisco Bay, Scottie has given birth to her; when he puts her to bed in his apartment, she is naked as a baby – At this point, Scottie is the benign creator, the artist who gives life' (Kehr, 1984, p. 2). To bring additional Pygmalion effects into the equation, the total submersion of the heroine in the water recalls the washing of a sacred statue and just might reinforce her status as a goddess to be worshipped by Scottie. Venus was born from the sea and Madeleine seems to embody divine perfection and also the allure of the ivory statue Pygmalion was accustomed to place so reverently upon his bed within his private quarters. This is what Scottie does to the unconscious Madeleine.

It is only much later in the film that we realize, as viewers or as voyeurs, the extent of the fantasy played out before our eyes in the secluded environment of Scottie's apartment. The cosseting of the illusory Madeleine (as she turns out to be) is akin to the care lavished by Pygmalion upon his statue. She seems so real to Scottie and to the spectator. Her tantalizing remoteness and dignity suggest that she, like the shy statue in Ovid's version, wants and waits to be aroused. It is a mixture of feigned modesty on her part and Scottie's genuine reverence that delays their love making.[21] He does persuade her to accept him as a companion the next day when he follows her back to his apartment. She says she intended to leave a thank you note and vanish from his life, but this is part of the elaborate manipulation devised for Scottie by Elster.

Scottie and Madeleine are to enjoy a first passionate kiss during one of their days 'wandering' together and the embrace occurs against the background of a surging sea. This is a deliberate cinematic cliché, which could be the director's clue or double bluff to the audience that Scottie is unknowingly enacting a romantic moment that has been orchestrated and scripted within the film. However, it is not that simple as we are to find out much later that by this time Madeleine is really falling for Scottie, an event not predicted by herself or Elster. The added value for the classicist, the image of the breaking waves invokes the sea as birthplace of the sea as the birthplace of Aphrodite / Venus whose presence would be appropriate in this scene of heightened sexual passion. For, the moment of mutual love and desire is genuinely felt even if it has been artificially engineered.

On the surface, Scottie and Madeleine are two characters concealing their true identities and deceiving each other about their motivation. Scottie has subordinated all sense of professionalism (the detective with an assignment) to the unfamiliar feelings of passion his friend's 'wife' has inspired. Midge, Scottie's increasingly distanced friend, stands by helplessly while Scottie's obsession takes hold. She tries to make fun of the belief that

Carlotta could be controlling Madeleine but this badly misfires. When she realizes that Scottie is seriously involved with this apparently unstable and enigmatic woman, Midge asks herself with a wry smile 'Was she a ghost?' perhaps realizing that Madeleine is in some sense as illusory as the spectre of Carlotta.

Scottie has all along been set up for a fall. His function is to witness Madeleine's suicide and this he does after a few halcyon days with Elster's 'wife' in which she continues to play the haunted creature subject to reveries, 'the beautiful phony trances' (as the bitter and disillusioned detective later dubs them) that make her so mysterious and alluring to the hero. Scottie is taking Madeleine on a tour of the places she allegedly dreams about as Carlotta and he has identified the old Spanish mission from her description. Madeleine tears herself from their embrace, runs up the steps to the bell tower and throws herself off. Scottie falters in his pursuit, held back by his debilitating dizziness, and can only look on in horror. He suffers a complete mental breakdown and no amount of music therapy (not even Mozart) provided by Midge during his convalescence can pull him out of his catatonic trance. It would seem as if Scottie has become the inert statue of the myth. Brill (1988, p. 208) casts Midge in the role of a failed Persephone and a failed Orpheus but of course she was never the vernal heroine of the film.

Scottie goes on to 'haunt' the places associated with Madeleine when he finally leaves the hospital and Midge is now out of the picture. He imagines he sees his lost love if a woman dressed or coiffured in a similar style passes by him. For Scottie, San Francisco is full of ghosts, of *simulacra*. Then one day, in the street he notices Judy, an office worker, laughing and bantering in a group of girls. Under the make-up she is remarkably like Madeleine. Judy seems at this point to have a clear and distinct identity. When Scottie follows her to the small and shabby apartment she rents, she admits to being picked up before, with more than a hint of a slightly murky past. Singer (2008, 75–79) makes interesting comments on the physical and moral flaws and falls of Judy/Madeleine as a failed Eliza.

The audience is soon to find out that a very specific person had 'picked up' Judy, namely Gavin Elster. Once she served her purpose, she was paid off and returned to her pedestrian existence as a working girl. Restored to her former persona, Judy has none of Madeleine's refinements or ethereal qualities and from Scottie's perspective will need some radical remoulding to become Madeleine. The brash and tarnished Judy allows herself to be separated from her group and to be sculpted for a second time into the ethereal and mystical Madeleine.

The Self-Deluded Lover

> Yet Love at length forc'd him to know his fate
> And love the shade, whose substance he did hate.
>
> Marston's *Metamorphosis of Pigmalion's Image*, stanza one[22]

In refashioning and making Judy over as Madeleine, Scottie is surely accepting second best, wilfully creating something like his ivory maiden for personal possession. The successful (if temporarily so) transformation of *Vertigo*'s flawed Judy into the idealized Madeleine was what first motivated me back in 2003 to reassess the relationship between Pygmalion's statue and the implied statue group formed by her tarnished Cypriot 'sisters', the Propoetides. The view we are first given of Judy is among workmates. Her separation from the group by Scottie who sees the image of Madeleine beneath Judy's brighter make-up and colourful outfits culminates in Scottie putting the finishing touches to the transformation (or creation) of his beloved in the privacy of her room. Hitchcock has framed the separation sequence in a way that invites comparison with the Burne Jones' paintings. The women of Cyprus pass by Pygmalion's studio while he stands bereft of inspiration.

Could a modern Propoetis provide the model for the ideal woman preserved in Scottie's memory? Judy encapsulates the polarity and similarity between the perfect *simulacrum* of the statue and the flawed females with the vice or weakness of not just having but acting upon sexual urges. Barr (2002, p.7), in discussing the theory that most of the film is Scottie's dream or fantasy, regards the whole scenario as an expression of the classic Madonna/whore dichotomy, the opposition between the romantic female image (Madeleine) and the more earthly available one (Judy). In *The Living and the Dead* this is spelt out in Part Two, chapter Two when Flavières scrutinizes Renée (Judy) in profile at the bar:

> the way the other Madeleine did her hair to match Madeleine's colour lacked style, her mouth had lost its line, despite the efforts of lipstick. Not that it mattered; she was almost better as she was, because less intimidating. He could approach her more easily now, feeling her to be made of the same clay as he was. He had been afraid of embracing a shadow. He found her a woman, and he reproached himself for desiring her already, as though he was profaning something very profound and very pure.[23]

Readers of Ovid's Pygmalion have their vision of the statue tunnelled through Orpheus' portrayal of the sculptor. Scottie as sculptor of Judy reprises Scottie as viewer and lover of Madeleine. His confusion of what is real and illusory is what guides or misguides the spectator through much of the film. Once Judy comes into the picture, the character of Scottie seems to be partly Pygmalion but partly Orpheus, striving to bring his beloved back from the dead. He fails on both counts. Scottie had taken the directorial role with Madeleine, as the eye of the camera that followed her around San Francisco.

With Judy he performs another function of the film maker, becoming an incongruous costumer and insisting on a grey suit identical to Madeleine's for the protesting girl. She squirms at the insensitivity with which Scottie pursues his artwork upon her. Begging her to dye her hair, he says 'It can't matter to you'. Judy is the lump of ivory to be remoulded, just as she provided the physical material for Elster as he fashioned a likeness of his wife. In spite of his protestations, Scottie, unlike his counterpart in the novel, does not want Judy for herself. As Joshua observes in relation to Ovid's narrative (2001, 148) 'Pygmalion is unable to experience the real without wishing it to be the ideal'.

However, this Propoetis, Judy, has played the part of Madeleine before (the grey suit hangs in her wardrobe, another souvenir, along with the fateful necklace, of a crime). Scottie will discover the deception but only after the cinema audience hears Judy's internal monologue when Scottie leaves. Hitchcock made the controversial decision to uncover the twist before the end and allow the audience into the irony that Scottie is about to transform Judy back into Madeleine. (Hence the following paragraphs carry a spoiler warning for readers unfamiliar with the film.)

Hitchcock had considered having his heroine discussing her fate with her original 'Pygmalion', Elster, who was creating a Doppelgänger of the wife he had murdered and whose suicide he and Judy had faked. In this discarded scene, Judy was to express her fears at being abandoned by Elster and would ask him 'What will become of me?' (Auiler,1998, pp. 53–54).[24] Instead Judy has a brief monologue starting with 'So, Scottie, you found me'. She confesses to us that she had played the part of Elster's wife and hidden in the tower while he threw the body down. They had relied upon Scottie not reaching the top of the mission to witness the crime.

In bringing Madeleine back to life, Scottie is unknowingly destroying his dream. Through love of Scottie, Judy takes an unimaginable risk in resuming their relationship and allowing Scottie to resurrect the Madeleine persona. She sacrifices her true identity in order to win his love all over again.

The newly clothed and transformed Judy is as sexually significant as the naked Madeleine had been after the San Francisco Bay episode. Visually the scene in Judy's apartment when she emerges as Madeleine from the bathroom evokes the last kiss between Scottie and Madeleine before her flight to the tower. The finishing touches to the transformation are provided by the cinematic techniques at Hitchcock's disposal, filming Judy through the soft focus filter used for Madeleine. Stoichita gives a detailed exegesis of Hitchcock's techniques for representing Judy and reprising Madeleine during the painful scenes of the make-over of one to the other. He also does a superb analysis of the moment she becomes Madeleine for Scottie, which is climactic not least because of Bernard Herrmann's Wagnerian score. Auiler (1998, p. 141) is eloquent on the subject of its impact:

> Swirling harps and blaring brass provide an aural equivalent toe the vertigo effect Hitchcock committed to screen. And a steadily ascending and descending scale drives forward the anticipation and eroticism of the final transformation on Judy into Madeleine.

However, to complicate the mood and resonances, it also replays and counter poses the apartment scene as Hitchcock, dubbing Scottie's clothing of Judy as an inverted striptease, cynically remarked:

> Cinematically, all of Stewart's efforts to recreate the dead woman are shown in such a way that he seems to be trying to undress her, instead of the other way around. What I like best is when the girl comes back after having her hair dyed blonde. James Stewart is disappointed because she hasn't put her hair up in a bun. What Stewart is really waiting for is for the woman to emerge totally naked this time and ready for love.

The director also stated that it was a striptease in reverse with the woman being forced to make up not take off, (Katz and Harris, DVD production notes, 1996). Judy's request that Scottie 'muss her up a little' is a cry to be made less perfect and less impenetrable.

In the recognition scene which follows (a revelation in more than one sense for the utterly deluded detective), Scottie is restored to near orgasmic happiness by the vision he has created and surrenders himself to the illusion, which is only a recreation on the surface of Madeleine, as far as he knows at that point in the film. It seems to satisfy Scottie that he has superficially reincarnated the woman he so adored from the rough and raw material of Judy. The delusion demonstrates just how psychologically sick the hero still is. Like any tragic figure, his knowledge is fatally limited. It is significant that he is satisfied with the appearance not the essence of Madeleine, although Durgnat in a charitable reading of Scottie's state of mind argues (1974, p. 283) that 'a sound instinct has spotted the real, the unique person, all but emancipated from the hazards of the superficial lifestyle. He is reincarnating Madeleine-Judy in a profound and a true way, not in a superstitious one'. Durgnat also suggests (p. 283) that 'one has also to allow that Madeleine, sane, is Judy's creation, and an aspect at least of herself'.

The sight of Carlotta's necklace breaks the illusion for Scottie and the suspense of knowing is at last over for the viewers of the film. Scottie recognizes the souvenir of the crime, which Judy, wanting to be discovered perhaps, decides to wear to complete her ensemble for their dinner date. Scottie rapidly pieces the puzzle together. The most traumatic realization for him is that Elster had created Madeleine out of Judy before him. Scottie is an imitation of Pygmalion just as Judy is a mimicry of the manufactured Madeleine. As Sharrock (1991, p. 46) observes about Ovid's Pygmalion, 'there is no original for the *simulacrum* to be the image of, although the text seduces the reader into thinking, for a moment, that there is'.

When Scottie realizes that he copied Elster step for step in metamorphosing the roughly hewn Judy into the polished sculpture that is Madeleine, he bitterly accuses her of being a very apt pupil. Scottie is the third man (following Hitchcock and Elster) to make-over Judy / Kim, to remove her naturalness, to airbrush out her flaws, to reverse the Pygmalion process in one sense and confirm it in others. Stoichita (p. 183) pinpoints the proliferation of Pygmalions in the tale *Vertigo* tells:

> Both Elster and Scottie (each in his own manner, with his own motivations) are in a certain way lodging a challenge with respect to the profession of the film director who retains an exclusive power of creating simulacra.

This reconnects Hitchcock with Ovid as both have an ambiguous attitude to the creative characters in their texts. Ovid visualizes and celebrates artists who reflect and rival him in telling and showing wondrous transformations. In Chapter 1, I made the point that artists and their works, even that of the demiurge who orders the elements of the universe, are subject to sudden destruction within the *Metamorphoses*. On the other hand, I cannot help wondering if Hitchcock's decision to have Elster succeed in getting away with murder and go scot free was partly to allow a triumph to this Pygmalion, the original maker (in the film) of Madeleine. If Elster is closer to Hitchcock as the orchestrator of the plot, he cannot be punished for producing the ultimate in a persuasive screen image, the double delectation of Kim Novak playing Judy playing Madeleine.[25]

An Alternative Vision of *Vertigo*: Love's Labour's Lost

We have already seen that Ovid's Orpheus, narrator of the Pygmalion myth, intrudes upon *Vertigo* and distils the tragedy of the hero of a man who has loved and lost not once but twice. Judy's accidental fall from the tower which Scottie forces her to climb as an action replay of the false death is the shocking finale to the film.[26] Gunning (2005, p. 262) makes the observation that: 'Cinema does not simply carry the old myths and stories as inert freight but gives them a new twist, imbuing them, as it were, with aspects of the nature of film itself'. He does not address its Pygmalionesque qualities; instead he sees the unfulfilled yearning in Scottie's desire for Madeleine as 'a revelation of both the pathology and the emotional depth of Love as pursued in the Western tradition'. Gunning focuses on *Vertigo* as 'perhaps cinema's most beautiful and bitter image of this erotic quest for the object of desire' (p. 266).

Gunning cites a long line of writers, critics and directors who have emphasized the erotic experience of the cinema (pp. 263–264) where an audience plunged into darkness is aroused by the filmic image that by its nature evokes the erotic. His classical connection is Aristophanes' satirical fable told in Plato's *Symposium*, which explains, in a farcical picture of double sexed spherical bodies split in two by Zeus, why love is both wholeness and lack in the Western tradition. The separated selves are always seeking physical reunion. Ovid's two lovers made into one motif is a mischievous distortion of the fable, for bodily melding in the *Metamorphoses* might be a guarantee of thwarted passion instead of a restoration of primal bliss and reintegration. Gunning views *Vertigo* as a tragic gloss on Plato/Aristophanes' satiric yarn:

> We experience the seeming impossibility of recovery of a lost wholeness, not simply because the two parts never seem to cohere but because the original time, the primordial epoch of union before division, remains unattainable. Not only the body but time is out of joint. (p. 273)

This approach leads Gunning to interpret the scene set among the Sequoias, when Scottie and Madeleine stand against the huge redwood tree, as follows:

'One of the most beautiful and disturbing sequences of the film presents cycles as an image of deep time' (p. 266). In spite of the falseness of the whole scenario and the cue for another phony trance from Madeleine, Gunning argues that the evergreen and ever living tree (*Sequoia sempervirens*) is a symbol of the unattainable past and of the uncanny nature of the creature (a voice from the grave) that Scottie so painfully desires. Brill would no doubt cite the Sequoia as a vernal portal to Hades, prefiguring both the feigned and actual death of the heroine.

The meaningful Redwood also evokes the fate of Myrrha, descendant of Pygmalion (wanting to be between the living and the dead and being transformed into the myrrh tree) and the audience to Orpheus' song, the sentient forest. Like Stoichita (2008, p. 200), Gunning (p.269) believes that the green filter around Judy retransformed into Madeleine renders her phantom-like. The green also reminds us of the Sequoia, of mortality and of the relentless nature of time which cannot be turned back for the reunited lovers. I particularly liked Gunning's question (p. 271) about Elster as truly the demiurge of Scottie's world of desire. It is precisely the hero's reinvention of Elster's narrative that guarantees its illusory and destructible nature. There are most definitely shades of Ovid's transient and metamorphic world here.

The Myth Refracts: Before and after Vertigo

Although there are many astute and critical responses to Hitchcock's remarkable film, it remains a challenging text, which continues to function as a seemingly inexhaustible source of new definitions and interpretations in the world of film criticism. Hitchcock bestowed his legacy upon subsequent movies with similar themes of deception, illusion and thwarted desires. Does Pygmalion have any presence in the cultural continuum of related cinematic narratives? In the next chapter, I shall engage with O'Sullivan's 2008 reading of *Pretty Woman* as a film accessing both Hitchcock's and Ovid's mise en scènes. To conclude the chapter I shall briefly focus on three other movies that share narrative and visual features with *Vertigo* and Ovid's Pygmalion.

Corridor of Mirrors went on general release in 1948.[27] This British film directed by Terence Young has been judged as a showcase (or more cruelly a vanity vehicle) for Edana Romney. This striking looking actress was a combination of Deborah Kerr and Valerie Hobson in appearance but she did not enjoy similar success as a screen star. Romney plays Mifanwy who

FIGURE 2.1 Corridor of mirrors poster (author's collection)

falls under the spell of Paul Mangin, a role taken by Eric Portman giving the edgy sort of performance at which he excelled. Portman could convey something simmering under a brusque and brittle exterior and the part of Paul required this sort of understated charisma. Paul is a haunted hero searching for his perfect woman as without her his life has no meaning. The Albert Lewin film of 1950, *Pandora and the Flying Dutchman*, deals with a similar theme but is far less successful in spite of stunning colour photography and Ava Gardner at her most breathtakingly beautiful. *Corridor of Mirrors* is a highly accomplished film in terms of cinematography and musical score but it also struggles to make sense and find its generic niche.

The story of Paul's obsession with Mifanwy and of his attempt to transform her into an ideal from the past is told in flashback by the heroine.

In the opening scene, Mifanwy has settled down to normal family life with Owen (Hugh Sinclair), an uncomplicated man whom she has known from childhood. She introduces herself as a perfect wife and mother with a dark secret. She then reveals that her respectability is superficial and that she very nearly became embroiled in a bizarre enactment of a Gothic horror novel. The architect of this strange dream like interlude was Paul Mangin. Paul is long dead, hanged for murder, but she has received letters from him, summoning her to London for a last meeting. We see Mifanwy speaking to her husband and reflected in the mirror (obviously mirrors, reflections and doubling are major motifs in the film, so it connects with Hitchcock's cinematic corpus where such tropes are recurrent). Mifanwy informs Owen that she must go to London. We know that this is to resolve the mystery, to face the ghost of Paul and her past.

The film then retraces her relationship with Paul and her attraction to this enigmatic recluse. Behind a corridor of mirrors in his mansion, Paul shows the heroine a gallery of dummies in period costume. The designer of the costumes, Edgar Orsen (played by Alan Wheatley), has a wife, Caroline (Joan Maude), who loves Paul passionately but Paul is obsessed with a painting of a Renaissance Italian beauty, Venetia. Yet Paul has no illusions about his ideal; he sketches her character as morally sick and corrupt just like the age in which she lived. Mifanwy closely resembles this tantalizing and faithless femme fatale (who was strangled with her own hair) and not just in appearance. She exhibits mercurial behaviour in both resisting and submitting to Paul's infatuation with her. We are informed at one point that Mifanwy means 'devil woman', suggesting that Paul knows she will not stay with him but will break his heart.

After some months of dalliance, Mifanwy agrees to attend an elaborate masked ball Paul has organized in her honour. There is even an open air carnival to recreate the sumptuousness and decadence of Venetia's environment. However, Mifany chooses this night to leave Paul, saying that she will no longer be part of his doll collection, she has already described herself as turning into a wax figure, all head and shoulders. She refuses his ring, extracts herself from a dizzying dance in the corridor of mirrors and departs. Mifanwy returns to Owen, the childhood sweetheart she has been seeing in between the strange interludes with Paul.

The morning after the ball Caroline is found strangled in Paul's bed and the portrait of Venetia has been slashed to ribbons. Paul, bereft of his illusion (both the living girl and her artistic representation), nobly allows himself to be tried, convicted and hanged for the murder of Caroline although all we have seen is his rejection of her in his bedroom. It will emerge that

Caroline has actually been strangled by his pathologically jealous housekeeper, Veronica (Barbara Mullen). The film moves back into the present day with Mifanwy's arrival at Madame Tussauds where Paul's waxwork stands in the gallery of famous murderers. Veronica has sent the letters to Mifanwy to entice her to London but she does not succeed in killing the real rival this time (she had strangled a poor imitation before). Escaping the mad and murderous Veronica, Mifanwy returns to the land of the living, her husband and children.

Corridor of Mirrors suffers from a *satura* (mixed dish) of ingredients drawn from Gothic horror, fable and fairytale, with a generous dose of romantic fiction. Paul's mansion with its many rooms and labyrinthine corridors recalls Bluebeard's castle and has elements of Robert Browning's poem, *My Last Duchess*. Shot in a Paris studio, it also has visual and thematic echoes of Jean Cocteau's 1946 film, *La Belle et La Bête*. The audience is possibly supposed to find the hero sinister, or in some way uncanny and monstrous, and to expect the worst or the best for Mifanwy. However, she teases and tantalizes Paul and relishes behaving coarsely when he is perfecting her make-over with wonderful gowns and jewellery. Their relationship is one of mutual manipulation and deception.

Oddly enough the film moves more into Pygmalion territory with the fate of the hero not the heroine as Paul is unjustly executed and then immortalized as a wax figure at Madame Tussauds. Pygmalion takes the place of the statue and the material used to mould his image brings a trail of associations in its wake. In her detailed study of 2003, Bloom focuses on films in which a wax figure substitutes for the illusory beloved and relates its porosity and pliability back to the simile in Ovid. As Pygmalion tests out his statue hoping that Venus has answered his prayer, he feels his fingers sinking into the ivory and the sensation is likened to working with wax. Solid wax figures replace ivory ones in key literary texts of the nineteenth century in which Pygmalion fails to vivify his creation or does not actually want a live partner.

It seems fitting in the symbolic order of things that Mifanwy bids farewell to Paul in the gallery of wax models. He has regained heroic status in her and the viewer's eyes. In his Shadowplay film blog (27 May 2009), David Cairns points out that Mifanwy comes across as too mature and worldly ('we don't feel for her') whereas Portman conveys a character of mystery and ethereality. Thus Paul appropriates another aspect of the ideal female represented by the statue. Different though this film and its resolution is to *Vertigo* there are elements in its portrayal of obsession with an illusion that may have inspired Hitchcock to give his duped detective a more complex, tormented and sympathetic personality than the hero on offer in Boileau and Narcejac's novel. Cairns suggests that *D'Entre Les Morts* may have been inspired by *Corridor of Mirrors*. Mifanwy, the heroine in *Corridor of Mirrors*, see-saws between wanting a routine and conventional existence very much in the present and being seduced by the glamour of being Venetia living her luxurious and decadent existence as reinvented by Paul. Mifanwy, like the false Madeleine, is haunted by a figure from the past.

There are also visual motifs of reflection and a focus upon thresholds that link the two films,[28] as well as a vertiginous spinning (actual movement or camera contrived) symbolizing the irresolution of desire for both sets of lovers. As with *Vertigo* aspects of the Pygmalion myth and other Ovidian narratives from the *Metamorphoses* appear in *Corridor of Mirrors*. The quest in this film for a *simulacrum* or *umbra* and the tragic consequences of attempting to transform an all-too-real and fallible woman into this ideal demonstrates the dangers of replaying and especially reversing the story of the statue.

Stolen Face: Scenes That Inspired Hitchcock?

This British film directed by Terence Fisher in 1952 and starring the Hollywood stars Paul Henreid and Lizabeth Scott is regarded as a curio and sometimes acknowledged as a forerunner to *Vertigo*. It has been unfairly dismissed as it boasts excellent performances from Henreid and Scott. As plastic surgeon Philip Ritter, Paul Henreid manages to be charming with a hint of compulsion first about his work and then in his adoration of concert pianist Alice (Scott) whom he meets while on holiday in the countryside. He treats this beautiful woman (a fellow guest in the quaint B & B) for a cold recommending whisky and aspirin and tenderly tucking her into bed. So the love affair begins with the elegant, warm and accomplished Alice returning his love; but she cannot bring herself to leave her fiancé and manager/mentor. She departs for home to resume her concert tour and will not take his calls.

The 'bereaved' and lovelorn Philip returns to his practice and decides to remould the face of a disfigured girl into the likeness of Alice. Unfortunately the embittered criminal Lily who receives the make-over does not reform but after promising to be whatever Phil wants reverts to her vulgar and grasping personality. This plot turn undercuts the liberal and humane message of an earlier scene where the prison governor extols Philip's work on physically damaged prisoners. The sceptical governor has been impressed with their rehabilitation once they are physically repaired, improved and able to face the world.

Just after Philip has married Lily (Lizabeth Scott is nicely nasty and does a convincing impression of an irredeemable cockney) Alice arrives to declare her love. Her gentlemanly fiancé has released her from the engagement. Lily is already driving Phil to distraction and to murderous thoughts but the horror of the situation is resolved with her falling out of a train. Alice and Phil can live happily ever after – a very different denouement from *Vertigo* as the *simulacrum* dies but the original is saved for the hero.

However from the opening shot of the marble bust of Alice (full face with a superimposed profile) this film does seem to prefigure *Vertigo* cinematically. When Lily has been transformed into the likeness of Alice, she and Philip are seen sitting with a hairdresser. Philip suggests that blonde would be a nice colour (Alice is very fair) and then starts to choose an appropriate dress for his new wife, selecting the kind of demure outfit that Alice would wear. (The costume designer for the film was Edith Head who went on to do the designs for *Vertigo*.) Lily is happily compliant at first but the marriage becomes a series of taunts as Lily exploits Philip's desire and destroys his delusion. She really does seem to be a *simulacrum* that has no intention of being further moulded or polished by her creator. This is no pathetic and compliant Judy.

She flaunts her drinking and her infidelity at Philip and continues to steal compulsively. Lily hones in on Philip's hypocrisy accusing him of being a thief, a stealer of faces. There is a significant and Pygmalionesque moment in an earlier sequence when Philip reassures and distracts Lily before the operation by telling her which part of her hip bone and other areas of her body will be used to sculpt her new face. Learning the truth about his obsession, she furiously objects, sometime after the event, to being metamorphosed into the image of another woman but tells Philip 'you wanted this face; you're going to live with it'. The underlying concept of this film (partially reprised in director Fisher's *Four Sided Triangle* discussed in Chapter 5) or more precisely its realization on screen seems to have dovetailed with Hitchcock's vision for *Vertigo*. The pitfalls of playing Pygmalion provide the common denominator of both films.

Obsession: A Homage to Hitchcock and A Hint of Pygmalion

This 1976 film directed by Brian de Palma and starring Cliff Robertson and Genevieve Bujold also boasted a Bernard Herrmann score. Its referencing of *Vertigo* was quite deliberate both in plotline and cinematic techniques. No sooner has the idyllic marriage between a rich and successful Robertson and lovely and elegant Bujold been established than the wife and small daughter are kidnapped and held to ransom. A rescue attempt goes awry and Robertson witnesses his wife's death and believes his daughter has been murdered as well. He blames himself for not bringing the ransom money in the suitcase and spends the next years in guilt and grief. While on a trip to Italy Robertson meets a girl who is the image of his lost wife. He pursues and courts her although he is considerable older and she is an independent and feisty young woman completing an education in the arts.

She is not averse to his attentions and allows him to suggest refinements to her which will enhance her resemblance to his dead wife. They marry and he is blissfully happy but his young wife is almost immediately snatched away in a second kidnap and ransom. Robertson moves from devastation at the second loss of his ideal to determination to pay the money this time and save his beloved. However a revelation is in store because his faithful friend (and partner) has engineered the second kidnap just as he planned the first. The girl is a willing accomplice as she is the daughter spirited away by 'uncle Bob' and for her this is a test for her father. She needs to know if he will value and love her enough to pay the ransom for her life. So a cruel deception as well as a crime has been played upon the hero who finally learns the truth. Amy, the daughter, is guilt ridden by her action and slashes her wrists on the plane but she and her father are reconciled at the airport. They circle around in each other's arms, reprising the waltz between Robertson and his wife at the beginning of the film – she sobs and calls him daddy – a happy ending?

The elements of crime, deception, illusion, make over, repetition of loss and the blurring between the living and the dead make this a film in the mould of *Vertigo*. It also imports a rather uncomfortable conundrum. Father and daughter certainly kiss as lovers and it would seem they have committed incest with Amy at least perfectly aware of the aberration. *Obsession* wanders into Ovidian territory but it is the aftermath of Pygmalion that is being reprised. Myrrha's passion for her father and her subterfuge in sleeping with him provides the mythical narrative in this case. Robertson's/Pygmalion's child is reborn for him but his ideal woman has proved mortal and will not return to life. Amy's seduction of her own father telescopes the stories of the sculptor and his royal descendant in the *Metamorphoses* demonstrating once again that Pygmalion and the statue rarely appears in any medium without bringing a trail of associated mythical material in their wake.

Chapter 3

Romancing the Stone: the Made-Over Woman as Comedy

As it happens, the very first erotic myth Ovid relates in his epic poem about a god being smitten by a beautiful girl has a quirky 'make-over' moment in the narrative. Apollo is literally love struck by Cupid's arrow and pursues the nymph Daphne, daughter of a river god. Daphne is an outdoor girl who models herself on the huntress goddess, Diana. She has no interest in men and is careless about her appearance. Apollo manages during the chase to picture her in a more relaxed pose and looking less dishevelled. Unsurprisingly the encounter does not end well. The myth is worth reprising at this point because it is both a tragic and a humorous story and forms an appropriate transition between this and the last chapter. The portrayal of Apollo as a less than accomplished seducer is Ovid in comic mode. The fate of Daphne prefigures fictional heroines and screen stars who become decorative and marketable symbols. The made-over women find it difficult to retrieve their real identities after the Pygmalion treatment.

Apollo and Daphne: *Metamorphoses* Book One, Lines 452–567

Ovid is sensitive to the terrifying predicament of female victims pursued by lustful gods but fully capable of striking the odd humorous note in the most traumatic and tragic situations. If he is critiquing the abuse of power, he is simultaneously intrigued by the paradoxes of the Olympian gods in the thrall of passion. Daphne's plea to her father Peneus not to marry her off and her rejection of available suitors is reprised in the maidenly modesty of Myrrha, descendant of Pygmalion, except that Myrrha is concealing a strong sexual passion for Cinyras. Daphne is desperate to enjoy a life like Diana whose father Jupiter, ruler of the gods on Olympus, granted her the gift of perpetual virginity. (However, Daphne has been shot by a lead tipped arrow, which Cupid uses as an antidote to love, so her desire for celibacy is contrived by a god and not a free choice.)

Her unwanted divine lover finds no fault in Daphne other than, interestingly, a little lack of polish. As he chases her through bush and briar, he becomes worried that she will scratch those shapely legs in her strenuous efforts to get away from him.[1] He promises he will chase her more slowly if she runs at a more sedate pace. The god also thinks Daphne's streaming locks would become her better if they were properly styled. This is the god playing hairdresser and wanting to make over a child of nature. The pursuit is an altogether burlesque scene with Apollo pointlessly praising all his own attributes and accomplishments in order to win over the unresponsive nymph.

The comedy does not alter the horror of the predatory race. Daphne utters a desperate prayer to her father to destroy the beauty that has attracted the god. The escape strategy provided is her transformation into a laurel tree. She is rooted to the spot, and has become the very antithesis of her energy, mobility and swiftness as a huntress nymph. Apollo wanted to tame her tresses, wayward in the wind, and he finally embraces her paralysed into a tree, the leaves of which tremble in repulsion at his touch. For an outdoor girl with minimum concern for her looks and no interest in luxurious adornments, there is a further irony to Daphne's metamorphosis into the laurel, which as a leafy crown will become Apollo's identifying attribute.[2] The laurel was adopted as a symbol of victory and Ovid's allusion to laurel wreaths signifying the imperial triumphs of Augustus at Rome means that Daphne has metamorphosed into a cultural commodity and an ideological statement. This was not Apollo's goal but paradoxically his pursuit of a perfect woman ends in her becoming an abstract, a representation and joining the ranks of female figures that embody a virtue (in this case, victory in endeavour or battle, generally associated with the male sphere). Such female figures are no longer individuals but the ultimate in alienation and objectification.[3]

The Metamorphosis of a Myth: Shaw's Pygmalion

I wish to boast that Pygmalion has been an extremely successful play, both on stage and screen, all over Europe and North America as well as at home. It is so intensely and deliberately didactic, and its subject is esteemed so dry, that I delight in throwing it at the heads of the

wiseacres who repeat the parrot cry that art should never be didactic. It goes to prove my contention that great art can never be anything else.
– 'Shaw's Preface to *Pygmalion*', Penguin Books, 1957 edition, p. 9.

George Bernard Shaw's play *Pygmalion* had its first production in April 1914 and has become an almost unavoidable reference point for subsequent screen dramas about 'improving' and remoulding unpromising and perhaps initially unyielding material. Its heroine Eliza Doolittle is a cockney flower girl, a far cry from a statue waiting to be awoken. Professor Henry Higgins makes a bet with Colonel Pickering that he can refashion this rough young woman into a refined lady and pass her off in public as a duchess. When Eliza arrives at the professor's door willing to pay for elocution lessons, Higgins finds the challenge irresistible. Shaw's comedy about a lower class girl being transformed into a refined young lady (at least on the surface) is what most people think of as the Pygmalion story. Shaw's reworking ensured the myth a pivotal place in mass culture, but this is not Pygmalion as Ovid would know it. Shaw is largely responsible for the myth accruing a special meaning for subsequent stories about social elevation and dislocation. The lightest of romantic comedy (Rom Com) movies with a make-over theme retains traces of Shaw's satire upon the superficiality of appearances and usually a modicum of moralizing about the faults of contemporary society, its hypocrisies and hierarchies.[4]

Shaw heralds his play as a celebration of phoneticians. More broadly it is a critique of education, self-improvement, social mobility and the problems of patriarchy, notwithstanding certain patronizing attitudes to women within its pages.[5] The further modernization of the myth and updating of Shaw's play for a contemporary cinema audience has produced as many post-feminist and retrogressive messages as enlightened and progressive statements about the objectification of women. Garry Marshall, director of *Pretty Woman* (1990), did not deceive *Sight and Sound* (February 2002 Review, p. 58) with his later film *The Princess Diaries*. On the contrary he invited further opprobrium because he tried to amend his philosophy and throw a bone at feminism, by telling his young female target audience: 'You don't need a man', only to crush them under a heavier oppression: 'You need a makeover!'

Pygmalion, the play, is nowadays most familiar to audiences through its cinematic incarnations and particularly through the popularity of the musical version. *My Fair Lady* was a hit on stage with Rex Harrison and Julie Andrews and transferred successfully to screen where Andrews was replaced by Audrey Hepburn, an established star.[6] As O'Sullivan (2008, p. 136) points out:

> In this film, however, there is also a much greater emphasis placed upon the technicoloured (sic, it should be Technicolored) spectacle of Eliza as she is transformed by hairstyles, make-up, and a range of fashionable garments from the capacious wardrobes of Twentieth Century Fox.

Pygmalion in Pedagogy

Carole Newlands (2009, p. 2) in an article about teaching Ovid's *Metamorphoses* pinpointed the original Pygmalion narrative as a 'the most troubling text where misogyny and aesthetics are closely linked'. My previous chapter focused upon the tragic consequences of men transforming women, usually in an obsessive way. However, Ovid's myth lends itself equally effortlessly to lighter touch dramatizations on the same subject. Humour is a long established tool for teaching and the comic make-over movie is fruitful ground for exploring the parallels between Shaw (the Ur or source text for these films) and Ovid's statue story (the Ur text for those working with or interested in classical myth).

Shaw would have been gratified to know that the ideological aspects of the make-over movies have inspired a distinct pedagogical programme. At the university of Ghent, Ive Verdoodt and Kris Rutten have designed a teacher training course called 'Film Choices for Screening Literacy: the "Pygmalion template" in teacher education.' Recognizing that 'movies in particular can be described in contemporary everyday life as important tools of representation and influential meaning makers', Verdoodt and Rutten (2010, p. 519) encourage the exploration of the learning journey, which is part and parcel of movies about making over a central figure. The two acclaimed films of Shaw's play *Pygmalion* are an obvious reference point or inspiration for such films: 'Typically these movies present a mentor–mentee relationship in which mentor (creator) introduces a "pupil" (creation) into new literacies, an act which causes a radical transformation or metamorphosis, often resulting in a (temporary) crisis of identity of both protagonists.' (p. 525)

The authors discuss different discourses in today's heterogeneous societies and the way in which film has helped teachers to cross cultural divides as classes of students discover the pleasure of close and critical analysis of familiar visual media. In the conclusion to this book I shall engage more closely with this thought-provoking article which poses the questions:

'What do popular movies teach us?' and 'How can we use popular movies to teach?' The Ghent experiment elicited a range of responses from students, and these have informed my interpretations of *Educating Rita*, *Pretty Woman* and *Miss Congeniality*.7

Verdoodt and Rutten also place Woody Allen's 1995 comedy *Mighty Aphrodite* among the make-over film as the hero (Allen) attempts to refine actress-cum-hooker Linda (Mira Sorvino) whose baby he and his wife (Helena Bonham Carter) have adopted. They might have included Allen's earlier 1987 nostalgia fest, *Radio Days*, in which there is an ongoing narrative about waitress and aspiring actress, Sally (Mia Farrow). Sally takes herself in hand and improves her prospects by paying for elocution lessons (thus physically and linguistically moving from Brooklyn to the big time in New York).

One of the questions in a critical evaluation of the make-over movie is to what extent the metamorphosis benefits the woman concerned. At first sight such films are culturally remote from Pygmalion's ivory statue, which has no voice or choice in her making and her transformation. Anderson, in his commentary on Ovid's *Metamorphoses* (1972, p. 496), makes the pertinent point that 'it was not until the late Renaissance that dramatists and poets began to speculate about her [the statue's] personality: how does it feel to be brought into the world a fully grown beauty without any experience at all?' This is Eliza's Doolittle's dilemma once she enters high society. In her altered state, Shaw's heroine looks like a real (upper class) girl but struggles to fit into her environment.[8]

Reversing and Reflecting the Myth?

Shaw's play and his playfulness with the myth of Pygmalion, the fact that he is turning it around, is touched upon by Anderson (*ibid*) and discussed by Joshua (2001, 97–102.) Jane Miller's 1983 doctoral dissertation, an engrossing interpretation of Ovid's Pygmalion myth in nineteenth century literature and art, gives an in-depth discussion of the reflections and refractions of Ovid's text set in motion by Shaw. Miller distilled her interpretation of the Pygmalion play in her contribution to *Ovid Renewed* (1988) and my discussion of Shaw is very much indebted to her insights (both in her published chapter and the unpublished thesis). Shaw's play has helped launch the myth in all its metaformations across the media so it is important to trace where Ovid's figures and motifs surface in Shaw's *Pygmalion* and continue to feature in films that reference a play written a century ago.[9]

In Ovid, Pygmalion is a man manipulating inert material and bringing it to life to play a conventional and gendered role in society. Shaw's play deals in the tensions, conundrums and comedy of transforming an all-too-human and fallible creature into something unreal and constructed who then has to reinvent herself to survive. Eliza is an apt pupil and plays part of a socialite so well that eventually everyone is fooled, even entranced by her. There are those willing to worship her and put her on a pedestal but she is not a comfortable 'fit' anywhere in her new body. Unlike the statue, which was programmed from vivification to be a royal repository of future kings, Eliza is in peril of losing her place in the lower classes. Instead of integration she faces alienation and objectification, a loss of identity equivalent to other metamorphic victims in Ovid's poem of transformations.

The direction in which Shaw took the myth of Pygmalion and the distinct thematic overlays in his play can be readily explained. Shaw was locking into the Cinderella story, which, as Joshua (2001, p. 97) points out, was a very popular 'rags to riches' romance from the eighteenth century onwards. *Pygmalion* reprises aspects and motifs from the fairytale with a typically Shavian and ironic deconstruction of the sanitized and sentimental elements that retellings of the Cinderella story acquired. There is an equivalent to the palace ball in the play, the Ambassador's reception, where Eliza exudes elegance and mystique and does not put a foot wrong. Much to Higgins' amusement she is 'unveiled' by Nepommuck (Higgins' former apprentice; he is called Karpathy in the films) as a Hungarian princess.

Gabriel Pascal's 1938 screen production of Shaw's play (directed by Anthony Asquith) and George Cukor's film of the musical, *My Fair Lady*, made the most of Eliza's public debuts.[10] These become spectacular visual feasts, as O'Sullivan points out, and the addition of the sumptuous set piece (the Ascot races number) is now a famous movie moment for superb cinematography.[11] Later make-over movies invariably boast a big scene where the newly polished and refined girl is displayed to the public in all her glory, completing her metamorphosis into the beautiful butterfly. The privacy Pygmalion preserved for his statue in Ovid's narrative is subverted and invaded by the Cinderella filter and Shaw is largely responsible. As Holroyd (1989, p. 327) observes: 'Shaw is at the same time conducting an experiment with the Pygmalion legend by making Higgins create a petrified social statue of Eliza'.

Joshua puts Shaw's play firmly in the cultural context of other Pygmalion plays of the nineteenth century. Both Joshua and Miller also give very valuable historical and social background to the myth's refashioning in the Victorian and Edwardian eras. However, they do not mention that, as well as drawing upon the Cinderella story, Shaw reworks and expands a comic interlude in Tobias Smollett's eighteenth-century novel, *Peregrine Pickle*, in which the eponymous hero passes off a guttersnipe as a duchess for a bet.[12] The girl in question reverts to vulgar swearing during a game of cribbage, sweeping out and inviting the other players to kiss her arse, revealing that she is 'deliciously low' to borrow a phrase from Shaw's play. The scene in Smollett's novel has an equivalent in Eliza's nicely modulated but totally inappropriate small talk in the play (when at tea in polite society). Her reply 'walk, not bloody likely' when upper class Freddie offers to escort her across the park caused a storm of shock and mirth when *Pygmalion* was first performed at theatres.[13] This is reinforced by a memorable moment in the musical with Eliza at the races and bellowing out to the horse to 'move its blooming arse'.

Nevertheless, Shaw's *Pygmalion* is rich in resonances of the Ovidian myth. In the play's epilogue, Shaw imagines his Eliza wanting to pull Higgins down off his pedestal and see him making love like any ordinary man, which turns around Pygmalion's imaginary scenario with his ivory girl. This artful reference to the statue motif reminds those familiar with the Ovidian narrative that Pygmalion probably needs bringing to life as much as the ivory sculpture. Miller (1988, p. 210) also notes the tendency for the sculptor to replace the statue on the pedestal and quotes the epilogue to the play in which Shaw observes that Higgins has much too godlike a power over Eliza for the relationship to be anything but disagreeable.

Shaw's comments on Higgins' character and behaviour remind the classical reader that in Ovid's story Pygmalion will completely control the statue once she is vivified, however subservient, love-stricken and deferential he was to his ivory girl in her inert state. Pygmalion possesses the statue only after praying to Venus for something like his ivory girl and doing so with reverence and diplomacy. The ivory sculpture's natural place is on a pedestal but Ovid's Pygmalion subordinated art to desire and pulled her (however reverently) down from her lofty plinth (and had done so before she was vivified). She never was an artwork but the *puella* (girlfriend) of the sculptor.

Pygmalion has exhibited a divine skill in his artistry and then acts like a god in moulding, manipulating and finally sexually possessing and penetrating his ideal of perfection. As superior and patriarchal figures abound in the afterlife of the myth, it should come as no surprise that in its most well-known refashioning, Shaw raises the issue of control in the relationship between creature and creator. Higgins reveals himself throughout the play as a bombastic bully and he continually threatens Eliza with physical violence (although much of this is comic hyperbole and a steady stream of exuberant language forms the drive and momentum of his very being). His treatment of the new-found protégée is the very opposite of his mythical predecessor and he is actually closer to Mary Shelley's Frankenstein in his ruthless re-fashioning of human material into a new hybrid being.[14] Eliza is tortured by technology once Higgins ties her to the phonograph and this is brought out forcefully by Anthony Asquith's 1938 film of *Pygmalion* starring Leslie Howard and Wendy Hiller. Shaw's set instructions for Act Two emphasized that Higgins has a laboratory (rather than a study) with state-of-the-art equipment. This is the workshop of the modern speech sculptor. However Martin argues (2001, p. 41) that Howard is a more charming and civilized hero than Rex Harrison in the 1964 musical, *My Fair Lady*.

Before Eliza embarks upon her daily elocution lessons, she has to be dressed appropriately and look the part she is being groomed to play. It is worth remembering she has offered Higgins a generous payment to better herself and learn to talk 'proper'. Both screen versions of the play could show a bath scene in which Eliza is stripped and scrubbed within an inch of her life. Moving this moment from an offstage to centre stage scene throws the transformation and physical manipulation of the girl into sharp relief. Some critics still find this an uncomfortable moment. Higgins is *in loco parentis* for a vulnerable young woman who has put her trust in him but his attitude to her fear of washing hardly elevates him above her uncaring father. (Alfred Doolittle later encourages Higgins to whip Eliza into shape if she is recalcitrant or rebellious.) The professor responds to Colonel Pickering's question about the girl's discomfort with the careless remark that he does not believe that Eliza would have any feelings worth bothering about. This gives Eliza a further affinity with the statue and the Propoetides in Ovid's narrative.

The burning of Eliza's clothes along with the cleansing of her body lends a strange sort of ritualistic timbre to the proceedings (the washing of a divine statue perhaps). There is also a sense in which Eliza is beginning to be reborn. In removing the surface dirt from this modern-day ivory maiden (who scrubs up well as her father observes, so much so, he fails at first to recognize his own daughter) the servants of the Higgins household are simply revealing the true and good-looking shape under the detritus. The ancient belief that a marble slab had the form of the statue within it and needed only the talent and chisel of the artist to carve it out is remarkably residual, as wannabe Pygmalions after Shaw like to claim that they are simply bringing out the beauty within (not playing god but simply releasing an innate and natural quality of the material). Ritual cleansing and total immersion in water reveal and enhance the perfect woman hiding within a grimy and crusted encasement.

In her astute analysis of this and other key scenes in both Pascal's *Pygmalion* and Cukor's *My Fair Lady*, Martin (2001, p.43) observes that Eliza looks at herself in the huge mirror opposite the bathtub once she has been symbolically cleansed of her working-class identity. In a previous scene she had scrutinized her features in a small looking glass in her cheap lodgings. Martin also points out *(ibid)* that her speaking part at the later embassy ball is largely suppressed in favour of a focus on her as a manifestation of loveliness:

> Her greatly improved looks, and the fact that her words are hardly heard at all, suggest that the extraordinary new physical appearance, which both discovers her natural beauty and covers it with a mantle of artifice, is at the core of her metamorphosis, not just phonetics.

Eliza, the Statue and the Women of Cyprus

Commentators and critics who have written about the connections between play and myth have never really done more than mention Eliza's relationship to the women of Cyprus, the Propoetides. Eliza protests on more than one occasion that she is not of dubious character in spite of appearances: 'I'm a good girl, I am', which could be interpreted as an unconscious attempt to distance herself from those forced to sell their bodies by the goddess Venus in the Ovid original. Eliza struggles to be the statue and yet shuns the polarized position of the Propoetides, the fallen women of Cyprus. In Shaw's day, numerous lower class women would have teetered upon the brink of prostitution. It is also significant that Eliza is in danger of having her reputation compromised by being a kept woman in Higgins' household.

The position and exploitation of women is a recurrent motif in the play. As noted earlier, the play is intentionally didactic. Shaw highlights the pitfalls of individual betterment, especially for females: 'Ambitious flower girls who read this play must not imagine that they can pass themselves off as ladies by untutored imitation' ('Preface to Pygmalion', p. 9). Eliza's fear of being thought a woman of easy virtue was well founded and it would have been much better understood by the contemporary audience. It is not uppermost in our minds because of the comedy of the encounters and our own cultural distance from Victorian/Edwardian mores. Higgins' housekeeper and Higgins' mother question the morality and the practicality of making Eliza, a human being, into a living doll to be played with. 'What's to become of her' is a worry expressed by the sensible and practical women of the play. They realize that Eliza is in danger of belonging nowhere once the experiment is successfully completed. As Martin (2001, p. 44) argues, Henry has lost his bet because 'far from succeeding in raising Eliza socially he turns her into an outsider in her own country'.

Henry's mother, Mrs Higgins, has the wisdom and ability to see the broader picture (a godlike overview?) and an awareness of the unfortunate if not exactly tragic predicament Eliza's grooming could set in motion. Higgins is oblivious to the problem of giving Eliza aspirations above her station with only a minimum of training and that mostly in social superficialities. Similarly, Pygmalion's statue comes to life but will be totally reliant upon her lover in a new and strange environment. Did she undergo a rapid training programme in regal rituals and behaviour? We can only imagine her being kept in protective custody, the seclusion which characterized the life of women in the Greek world. In narrative terms, Ovid leaves us with a vivified statue, as submissive and passive as she was as the ivory model tucked away from sight in Pygmalion's quarters.

Eliza may be bullied but she does fight back, a feature that increasingly characterizes descendants of the statue in Western culture. She puts her own stamp on the remoulding of her character by Higgins and Pickering whereas the Ovidian ivory girl has a limited repertoire of passive resistance.[15] The 'battle of the sexes' element in Shaw's play sharpened up during the later twentieth century and by the 1960s the nature of Eliza's social subordination had significantly altered.

In *My Fair Lady* Eliza articulates the mix of fear and loathing she feels for Higgins in the song 'Just you wait, Henry Higgins, just you wait!' and in a later refrain, 'Without You' she starts to exorcise the Svengali-like influence of Higgins, declaring that he no longer seems like the earth and sky to her. I doubt if the composers Lerner and Loewe had read Ovid before penning the lyrics, but there is an interesting coincidental echo here of the ivory maiden waking to sky and lover simultaneously at *Met.* 10:294. The record cover shows Eliza as a smiling puppet but she still sings out her exasperation with gusto in the musical. The image possibly implies that she is a marionette with a mind of her own. Shaw had always wanted his heroine to cut the umbilical cord (chord!?) between herself and Higgins.

FIGURE 3.1 My Fair Lady record cover (author's collection)

The Fate of the Sculptor, the Statue and Supporting Cast

As Miller observes (1988, p. 210), Doolittle, Eliza's father, is forced to undergo a metamorphosis engineered by the meddling professor who recommends him to learned societies as a peripatetic lecturer in original thinking. Ultimately embracing middle-class morality, Doolittle experiences a similar process to his daughter's education and elevation. His original philosophy, acute self-awareness and the ability to communicate in a lilting rhythmic rhetoric are seized upon by Higgins at their first encounter. Higgins explains this attribute as an inheritance from the Welsh side of his family and laughs at its persuasive effects. Eliza and Doolittle just need the veneer of vulgarity to be stripped away to reveal their considerable potential. Father and daughter end up speaking a new language and fulfilling what the Ghent training programme has identified as the literacy goal common to this sort of transformation and elevation story.

In spite of the refining and polishing, Eliza retains features of her lower-class background (impudence, brashness and forwardness) under a lovely, elegant and demure exterior. This combination of raw and refined is what attracts the aristocratic Freddy Eynsford-Hill. The duality of Eliza (embodying the best and worst of two social worlds) provides a clearer correspondence with Ovid's statue in fulfilling the conflicting desires of men. Another popular tune reinforces Freddy Eynsford-Hill's romantic attachment to and elevation of Eliza. In the film Jeremy Brett (actually dubbed by Bill Shirley) sings 'On the street where you live' as he looks longingly up at her abode like an excluded elegiac lover in Roman poetic traditions. Higgins' apparent exasperation with the pupil who has disrupted his bachelor routine, voiced through the half-sung, half-spoken 'Let a Woman in Your Life', recognizes the qualities of the newly formed creature who has 'got under the skin' of two very different males with competing romantic and scientific / intellectual desires and curiosities.[16]

Higgins is so indifferent to others' feelings he seems as self-obsessed as his mythical namesake. Although it is the women of Cyprus who are turned to stone, Shaw's male creation could be accused of detachment and a lack of human kindness, which equal emotional ossification. Pygmalion's statue has the ability to bring her creator to life and this is what Eliza strives to do to Higgins in the play (and harbours a desire to do physically and sexually in the Epilogue). She succeeds in exasperating and frustrating him but eventually he confesses to companionable feelings towards her. Ovid's Cyprian hero has shunned women and, if we read against the grain of the text (or put more simply between its poetic lines) it is possible to speculate upon his lonely and obsessive life in the company of an inert block of ivory. Shaw shows us a Pygmalion brought to life by Project Eliza.

In Act Four, Pickering and Higgins totally ignore Eliza after she has won their bet for them. Angry and hurt, she wails 'what's to become of me?' and Higgins responds with the offer of finding her a husband suited to the liminal social status she has acquired. She immediately picks up on the dubious morality of such human trafficking. She retorts that they were above such things on the corner of Tottenham Court Road: 'I sold flowers; I didn't sell myself!' In Act Five, the finale, Henry's mother is the means of their reconciliation (bringing them together, a little like the goddess Venus presiding over the encounter between Pygmalion and the statue).

In this final confrontation, both Higgins and Eliza are trying to convince themselves that they can do without each other and yet their interdependence as well as their independence is unmasked.

Higgins is goaded into claiming he can do without anybody, including Eliza: 'I have my own soul; my own spark of divine fire'. The imagery here resonates with the ambiguous relationship Ovid has set up between Pygmalion and the vivified statue. The spark of divine fire evokes the favourable sign from Venus in the Latin narrative and echoes the subtitles Burne-Jones uses for the transformation of the ivory girl to flesh and blood, 'The Godhead fires', 'The Soul attains.' Were there not so many turning points in this closing scene, I would suggest that this remark about divine fire is a sign for Eliza truly to come to life and come into her own.

It marks the moment when Higgins has to admit he shall miss his pupil if she moves out and moves on. One thinks of the ancients tethering their statues down. Eliza suggests that the gramophone and the photographs can keep him company but Higgins protests that hearing her voice and seeing her face (in other words, *simulacra* not the real thing) are no substitute for having her feelings in his presence and being able to turn on her soul. Eliza retorts: 'Oh you are a devil. You can twist the heart out of a girl as easy as some could twist her arms to hurt her'. This is a Pygmalion with the skill to 'sculpt' his subject's vital organs and he will not let go of that.

In the course of the exchange and stung by her accusations of coolness and cruelty, Higgins utters a stinging speech about his protégé's option of submitting to a brutish husband who has a thick pair of lips to kiss with and a thick pair of boots to kick with. He dares Eliza to turn her back on betterment, and exchange a comfortable existence for the gritty life of the gutter where emotions are raw and without restraint. He accepts that this sort of relationship has its warmth as well as violence, that you can feel it through the thickest skin. Far from the idea that loose morals and unrestrained passions lead to hardening into stone through shamelessness (the original Pygmalion motif) he suggests that cheap sentiment (snivelling love) and cruelty, worship and wife beating are all features of the uneducated who wallow in an excess of emotion.

When Eliza protests that she has could no longer live with a low common man and threatens to marry Freddy, Higgins blusters back that he has made her a fit consort for a king (which must remind us surely of the destiny of the ivory statue). However Higgins rejoices when she stands up to him and makes an eloquent speech about existing and succeeding apart from her creator. He celebrates 'making a woman of her'. He said he would do it and by god (which god, Venus perhaps?) he has. Higgins is not Eliza's king as Pygmalion was to his statue, although as Martin concludes (2001, p. 41) she would make the perfect wife if not the royal consort.

In the epilogue, Shaw explains that Eliza will indeed marry Freddy, but Higgins is never entirely out of the picture. The 1938 film firmly embedded the image of Higgins and Eliza as 'an item', something Shaw never intended. He despaired of an audience that from the early days wanted 'his Miltonic bachelor to be transformed into the beautiful lady's lover' (Holroyd, 1989, p. 331). Miller (1988, p. 209) notes Shaw's fury when in the early theatrical production Beerbohm Tree (Higgins) threw a bouquet of flowers to Mrs Patrick Campbell (Eliza) as the curtain fell. Martin (2001, *passim*.) teases out the variety of factors that worked for and against the realism of a romantic relationship between Henry and Eliza in the screen versions. Shaw had disapproved of a boyish and attractive Leslie Howard in the lead (Pascal's 1938 film) while the much older Rex Harrison in *My Fair Lady* was less convincing as a partner for the youthful looking Audrey Hepburn as Eliza (with handsome Jeremy Brett waiting in the wings as Freddy). [17]

The relationship between Henry and his mother is sidelined in the screen versions, which are very much in favour of the fairy tale ending. In the epilogue to the play Shaw says of Eliza (p. 134 in the Penguin edition) that: 'It would be sorely strained if there was another woman likely to supplant her with him' but also observes that: 'When Higgins excused his indifference to young women on the ground they had an irresistible rival in his mother, he gave the clue to his inveterate old-bachelordom'. Higgins, like Pygmalion, has no time for flawed females (and that includes those of his own social stratum) as none of them equals his mother, his perfect woman.

Shaw spells out Higgins' idealization of his mother in the main body of the play and reiterates it in the Epilogue. She alone can scold Henry for his thoughtless behaviour when he will not give up his experiment. As Miller notes (1998, pp. 209–210), Higgins worships at the shrine of his mother and rejects available partners. He is not the marrying kind. Shaw's own relationship with his mother had been truncated and he idolized her as a consequence so some personal issues may just have intruded upon the play, as did Shaw's attachment to the leading lady in the early productions of the play. This could account for an epilogue that slightly fudges the identity of Higgins' ideal woman.[18]

Miller sees Mrs Higgins as a Venus figure, the measure for all womanhood and Eliza is endowed by Higgins with some of the external grace and poise of his mother. I have stretched a point by making Mrs Higgins stand in for Venus towards the end of the play. My defence is that in allowing Henry's mother to be both model for the sculpted Eliza and the means by which Pygmalion and the statue recognize and reflect each other's feelings I am reinforcing the duality of Venus in Ovid's text. I am disinclined to take Miller's sensitive treatment of Higgins' (and Shaw's) adoration of his mother into the realms of the Myrrha story, tempting though it is to detect a hint of incestuous love implicit in Ovid's Pygmalion. Higgins is not in love with his mother but he does recognize her as a superior being. In the original version of the play it is Higgins and his mother who exchange a kiss at the final curtain.

Pygmalion and the Statue Get the Common Touch

So powerful is the paradox of a living creator who needs to be humanized and transformed by the very person he is eager to improve or refine (the motivations are varied and culturally determined – they can be scientific, aesthetic, narcissistic and downright mischievous), that it has become a leitmotif and one that has been realized in a variety of unexpected ways. In her 1989 book, *Hard Core; Power, Pleasure and the Frenzy of the Visible*, Linda Williams analyses a satirical spin upon *My Fair Lady*, which has an amoral Eliza and replaces or replays the set songs of a musical with choreographed and explicit sex scenes. This is the 1975 film, *The Opening of Misty Beethoven* directed by Radley Metzger.

The heroine of the film, Misty, is an unequivocal Propoetis, selling her body in public. She starts out as a small-time whore who makes her living pleasuring old men (giving hand jobs to be precise) in the pornographic theatre in Pigalle and working in the adjacent brothel in between times. Dr Seymour Love, a sophisticated sexologist, comes into her life and thinks she is suitable material for an upgrade. Additional refinements to her art are developed during her training to be a high-class hooker once she has been discovered by this wealthy pimp and recruited into the big league. He actually degrades her into a desired sexual performer amongst the international jet set. To quote Williams (1989, p.142):

> Seymour's apparent goal is to transform Misty from an honest whore who gets direct payment for her services into a pleasure giving automaton whose indirect payment is access to a higher social class. In the process, however, he forces Misty to rely increasingly on complex technological aids, which in turn become a necessary fetish for the pleasure.

Misty becomes a symbolically synthetic creature, a sex machine and in the process she struggles to retain spontaneity in her work. Misty turns the tables on Seymour by the end of the film and, rather like Georges Méliès' teasing statue[19] she arouses him to an erotic frenzy, so much so, he acknowledges himself as her biddable pupil appearing in dog collar and chain. This 'made-over' woman has managed to pull her male manipulator off his pedestal and shake him out of his physical detachment. Misty fulfils Eliza's fantasy by finding her Higgins' emotional soft core. *The Opening of Misty Beethoven* (later made into a musical) manages to complicate the play of Pygmalion and the myth of the passive and virginal statue by modernizing the ivory girl into a warm and volatile whore who loses a different kind of innocence or simplicity in being 'improved' by an insensitive male.

Pretty Woman (the 1990 film directed by Garry Marshall), and starring Julia Roberts and Richard Gere, starts with a similar scenario to *Misty Beethoven* but goes in a very different direction. The Shavian subtext was noted by more than one reviewer at the time. A prostitute is passed off as a Beverley Hills beauty but, like Eliza, decides she wants more from her Pygmalion than money. *Pretty Woman* also incorporates elements from the nineteenth-century play *Pygmalion and Galatea* by W.S. Gilbert of Gilbert and Sullivan fame. Joshua and Miller (1988, pp. 210–211) identify this work as one of the 'feeders' into Shaw's *Pygmalion*, inspiring him to see the potential of the myth for satirizing society. In Gilbert's play the Victorian art world is parodied with its corruption and double standards although the setting is ancient Greece. A world of buyers and sellers is shamed by the statue's innocence and capacity for unselfish love.

The Gilbertian Galatea is embarrassingly honest and genuinely bemused at the cruelty and (paradoxically) the artificiality of the wealthy and successful world of her creator. Cynisca, the wife of Pygmalion and the model for the sculpture, is taught true feelings by the statue before this incongruous creature retreats to her original marble state: 'It is the statue who possesses the qualities of warmth, kindness and pity, while the woman is cold, pitiless and hard' (Miller 1988, p. 211).

Pretty Woman produces a heroine who is equally bemused by large-scale corruption in the business world of 1990s America. Julia Roberts plays Vivian Ward, a hooker picked up by the wealthy Edward Lewis (Richard Gere). The emotionally ossified Edward definitely needs to 'melt', lose his frigidity and be brought to life. Julia Roberts in her first starring role, and aided by a now trademark wide open and dazzling smile, gives a pitch perfect performance as a modern Cinderella with a twist. The storyline was an ideal vehicle for exploiting Roberts' skill in portraying a wide-eyed and luminous Lulu figure. [20] Unlike the tragic heroine in the silent film Roberts' character triumphs in a cynical world of manipulative men when she could easily have fallen victim to its seamy and psychotic side. The suggestion is that her character's Propoetidean qualities were only ever skin deep. It is hinted in the film that she is relatively new to the profession so she is only slightly sullied.

The 'make-over' theme in the film takes a little time to kick in. In what seems subsequently an uncharacteristically spontaneous act, Edward picks up the prostitute Vivian after asking her for directions to the hotel. Kord and Krimmer (2005, p. 20) see a latent impotency in Gere's character from the outset. It is Vivian who is good with (gear) sticks, denoting a technological but also a physical and phallic attribute. They also note the hero's dizziness and dislike of heights. Edward's acrophobia is an echo of the disempowered and emotionally vulnerable figure of Scottie in *Vertigo*. O'Sullivan (2008, p. 148) identifies Edward's striving and sustaining a career at the top and his confronting of his physical weakness (he lives in a penthouse) as the psychological essence of his vertigo and quotes Bingham's definition 'a fear of – falling down from an exaggerated height of masculinity'.

In fact, this opening scene with Gere negotiating a bewildering system of streets is viewed by O'Sullivan as an early indication of the film's many allusions to Hitchcock's *Vertigo*. O'Sullivan (2008, pp. 143–149) argues convincingly for a raft of references to *Vertigo* in *Pretty Woman* and infers from this that the latter film has an ambiguous tone. This is interesting because there was an alternative and not-so-happy ending mooted for *Pretty Woman* before it went the way of all romantic comedies. Although I had noted some of the correspondences between the two films while presenting papers and working on drafts of this book, Sullivan's article is a comprehensive comparison and well worth reading, especially as she notes the constant interplay between Ovid's narrative and the films in question. Ovid's Pygmalion is the common denominator which enriches the comparison between the two films.

Vivian offers to drive this potential client to his hotel in the hire car he is finding a challenge to control. Edward impulsively invites her into his hotel and fails at the first hurdle to keep her presence discreetly hidden as Vivian exposes her scantily dressed figure before they reach the elevator. Although Vivian is hired for his private pleasure, Edward decides to capitalize upon her striking attractiveness by turning her into an ornamental companion. She re-animates the emotionally scarred Richard Gere who is an amalgam of employer and benefactor to her throughout the film and who uses her for physical pleasure, slowly submitting himself to her capacity for joie de vivre. Edward is a Pygmalion manqué in the first half of the film. The statue is not going to move or act as this 'Pygmalion' directs and he does not know how to be a creative person. In conversation with his business partner, Edward says: 'We don't build anything. We don't make anything'.

Gere is good at playing suave and world weary and suggesting the slow burn of his feelings for Vivian as he submits to the charms of her ebullience and directness. As the prostitute Vivian, Roberts manages to convey a contrived and brittle brightness and, like Edward, she wears protective armour to conceal her uncertainties and disappointments in life. Having no apparent shame about her profession (an unblushing Propoetis) until she is taken away from the familiar territory of the streets, Vivian exhibits vulnerability in the face of the snobbish haute couture shop assistants who ask her to leave the boutique when she attempts, under Edward's instructions, to purchase an evening dress. The obvious reference point for the scene is Cinderella in need of a ball gown so we should not be surprised when the sympathetic hotel manager (Hector Elizondo) plays fairy godmother. Vivian is appropriately kitted out by a dress maker whom he calls into the hotel.

I agree with O'Sullivan (2008, p. 146) that there is a deliberate resonance in the shop sequence of *Vertigo*'s Judy who suffers agonies of discomfort in a high-class emporium. In contrast to the character of Judy, forced to be made-over into a look-alike of a lost ideal, Vivian is only too willing to be bought elegant dresses and suits, but the assistants are contemptuous of her, regarding her as low life and out of place in their establishment. Edward accompanies Vivian on the subsequent trip, which O'Sullivan compares with Pygmalion's wooing of the statue (the dressing of his doll and the presents of jewellery) and as a direct allusion to Scottie's transformation of Judy.

I would add that Edward's comment to the male proprietor that he is unlikely to see anyone as beautiful as Vivian suggests that the hooker is beginning to embody female perfection in the eyes of the Richard Gere character. That would suggest that Edward places a much higher value on Vivian for herself not as an imitation of an ideal. However, O'Sullivan (p. 144) observes that:

> the fact that the refashioning of Vivian into a fully fetishized version of femininity entails the transformation of a Propoetides-like prostitute makes the Pygmalion-like aspects of the *Pretty Woman* narrative more explicit.

I made this point in 2003 and the statue's proximity to the women of Cyprus is a recurrent motif in many of her reincarnations. The virginal girl never escapes her close relationship with the stony women of Cyprus and any one of their number has the potential to be the innocent ivory maiden.

Roberts gives a performance which combines self-doubt with a chirpiness, hiding her lack of confidence. Vivian, like Eliza, finds the etiquette and discourse of high society a challenge. She identifies with and weeps uncontrollably over the fate of the operatic courtesan Camille when Edward takes her to *La Traviata*, an opera which mirrors their story elevated to tragic heights until Vivian breaks the spell and the undercuts her finer feelings by uttering the line 'I almost peed my pants'. Vivian is clear about the rules of her game. For instance, there must be no genuine intimacy between herself and the client, Edward.[21] She avoids kissing on the mouth in her sexual encounters with Edward until the end of the film, when she feels his kisses and realizes her feelings for him (a vivified statue scene). The point is more than driven home that in some aspects Vivian needs bringing to life as much as Edward. She is the statue after all as well as a woman of Cyprus. The first passionate kiss is Edward's moment of realization too. O'Sullivan (p.147) picks up on the reflective aspects of their encounter in that up to this point they had agreed not to kiss. Edward can see they are similar creatures as they both 'screw people for money'. O'Sullivan suggests 'a degree of Narcissism in the mutual attraction they experience'.

In their chapter 'The Newborn Identity', Kord and Kimmer (2005, pp. 17–18) argue that the role of Vivian helped to fashion Julia Roberts' screen persona as a girl in search of an identity. In subsequent films she struggles to find herself as much while ostensibly searching for the 'right man'. In regard to *Pretty Woman* they pose the question: 'Is she a hard core prostitute or an innocent child?' In the context of her screen career they argue that Roberts

> tries on many different identities, many of them ill-fitting and many of them – defined by others. In *Pretty Woman* she encourages first Edward and then the hotel manager to choose a name for her.[22]

The Ethical Implications of *Pretty Woman*

Pretty Woman is still a very popular film; it was voted the all-time favourite romantic movie by a survey done for Valentine's Day in the 2010 February issue of the *Radio Times*. Nevertheless, a significant number of critics find it distasteful and I share their discomfort. This film might be unadulterated fantasy and a myth for modern times to the more mature among us but it seemed to send a message to some teenage girls about the potential glamour of prostitution, that becoming a hooker might be a short cut to romance and riches. Would that Shaw's caveats about imitation without true transformation had been imitated in a cautionary epilogue by the distributors!

In the final scene of *Pretty Woman* Edward woos Vivian from beneath her window. She keeps the (moral) high ground and the superior (goddess-like) position. In *Vertigo* as we have seen, Scottie (James Stewart) attempts to transform his common girl into the ideal woman but Judy, his model, fails to win him over as herself. In contrast Vivian humanizes Edward; he civilizes her but 'fundamentally she does not change. All that is required is a little polish'. O'Sullivan (2008, p.149) concludes that the film telescopes the Pygmalion myth and the incest narrative that follows in which there are 'darker consequences for his descendants'. She speculates upon Vivian's fate after choosing the short-term hedonism of becoming Edward's wife and argues that:

> the darker side of the transformation as experienced by Vivian – and far more explicitly by Judy – gives expression to the 'always otherwise silenced' protestations of Pygmalion's Galatea, and a string of other muted or otherwise 'locked-up' 'living dolls'.

Presumably O'Sullivan is imagining Vivian metamorphosing into one of the Stepford Wives (to be discussed in Chapter 5).

The American dream come true, as a number of the Ghent students characterized the ending of *Pretty Woman*, demands that Vivian finds true love amidst ostentatious wealth. At the end of the film her rescue by Edward is a fantasy fulfilled. She is the damsel in distress and he is the medieval knight on the equivalent of a white horse; but will his arrival derail Vivian's plans to go to college and find autonomy and intellectual independence? (I assume some of the students on the Ghent programme for screening literacy did pick up on this point but it was not recorded as a response to the film in their summary report.) Shaw would no doubt have suggested some alternative scenarios to the hokum of the happy ending but no producer was going to compromise the coupling of two handsome screen icons (one an established star and the other about to enter the firmament).

Educating Rita: Neither Glamorous Nor Amorous

Pretty Woman could be condemned as consumer capitalism striking back at the claims of education to be a liberating and life-affirming experience.

For me the film is a counter blast to an earlier and British make-over movie, namely, Willy Russell's *Educating Rita*, which is also discussed by O'Sullivan. Russell's play was successfully transposed to the cinema seven years before *Pretty Woman*. Lewis Gilbert's 1983 film brought Julie Walters to the screen in the role of Rita, a working class twenty-something with a hunger for education and self-improvement. Michael Caine (like Gere an established star) was cast against type as Frank, her Open University tutor whose main job is lecturing at a conventional campus university. Frank, an accomplished literature tutor, but losing his way in the academic world, has turned to drink and, like Edward in *Pretty Woman*, is a disillusioned man needing to be brought to life. He is shaken out of his cynicism by Rita's thirst for knowledge and is entranced in spite of himself by the heroine's directness and uncomplicated response to the conundrums of life and art.

Rita blossoms or metamorphoses under the influence of her Open University course, but not before she has suffered self-doubt and confronted the uncomfortable challenges of an identity in transit. She is no longer sure where she belongs; in the pub with her husband singing rowdy songs with family and mates, or at her tutor's middle class soiree which she has had not had the confidence to enter. Once again a descendant of Shaw's Pygmalion experiences alienation and struggles to know where she belongs. However, Rita does complete the change, leaving her husband and moving into a new and much more stimulating cultural environment, attending an Open University residential week and finally producing academic essays fit for Frank's pile of undergraduate assignments.

Unfortunately, in Frank's eyes, Rita loses something essential and valuable along the way. It is ironic that as Rita changes and develops intellectually she reverts to her given name, Susan, dispensing with a disguise and a pretension but that this is the very moment when Frank feels she has lost her innocence and spontaneity. Frank as Pygmalion believes he has inadvertently created a monster and compares himself with Mary Shelley, author of *Frankenstein*. Frank (enstein?) feels that Rita has found a different but not a better song to sing. Towards the end of the film they have a confrontation in Frank's study, which has distinct echoes of Higgins and Eliza batting back and forth in Shaw's play. Rita is able to combine her old feisty tone with her new-found eloquence and fight back in the painful exchange she has with Frank but ultimately (and after one last drunken binge has cost him his job) they are reconciled.

Rita sees Frank off at the airport. There is no romantic ending to *Educating Rita* and there is a question mark over the happiness of Frank and Rita as they both embark on new futures. In the downbeat finale, there is one last comic flourish. Rita gives Michael Caine a haircut but teasingly prefaces this by promising to do something that will take years off him.[23] She disappoints any audience expectations that this is going to be their first and last romp in bed. Venus plays no part in their relationship as there is a distinct absence of any erotic passion between the teacher and pupil.

Michael Caine played up Frank's seediness to emphasize the romantic distance between them. In spite of his weakness, self-doubt and self-indulgence he remains, for a large part of the film, a Higgins for the 1970s, a fallen idol or slightly disagreeable deity in his dealings with Rita. The Ghent students mulled over Rita's metamorphosis and the different song she sings. Clearly the film continues to have mixed messages about the fate of a heroine undergoing a life-changing experience and what she gains and loses by being brought to life.

Shaw's *Pygmalion* in a Teenage World

Robert Iscove's 1999 film, *She's All That,* updated Shaw's Pygmalion and changed the location to an American High School.[24] The film starts out as a vaguely critical and satirical study in conformity (especially the female image) and peer group pressure but compromises its message with a predictably soppy ending. The hero, Zack, (Freddie Prinze Jr) makes a bet to transform Laney (Rachael Leigh Cook) into prom queen material as an act of retaliation against his erstwhile girlfriend, Taylor (another significant name, masculine sounding but referencing the iconic Elizabeth Taylor – in fact the actress, Jodi Lyn O'Keefe, resembles swimming screen star Esther Williams). Taylor, prime candidate for the prom queen crown, has ditched Zack for a highly superficial celebrity (a former cast member of MTV's *The Real World*). This new boyfriend of Taylor's proves to be a mindless buffoon with a boundless capacity for self-love and self-image. He reflects the personality of Taylor who in a flashback of their first meeting is shown preening and strutting around the swimming pool, showing off a statuesque figure. Up to this point Taylor has been, as his friends observe, Zack's narcissistic double: 'She's basically you, with tits'. The teenage friends regarded their relationship as a match made in high-school heaven.

Rather than lose face completely, Zack tells his friends that the model girlfriend (in looks at any rate) is easily replaceable. As Zack observes (and once again the concept of the beautiful being embedded in the marble slab springs to mind) 'Take away the surface and any girl is as good'. The mousy student, Laney, is the friends' choice for the transformation project. It is easy to see that the plain Jane character of Laney (Rachael Leigh Cook) is a pretty girl in glasses cultivating an unflattering nerdy or geeky look. It is only going to take a slight cosmetic make-over to reveal her curves and colours.

She's All That has its moments and some of these moments might tempt the classically inclined viewer to bypass the Shavian inspiration and reinsert Ovid into the equation. There is inevitably a 'drawing out' in such films of the girl's beauty and the boy's hitherto suppressed sensitivity and goodness, which gives an echo of Ovidian transformations where inner and outer qualities are brought into harmony. There are one or two interesting reversals of Pygmalion motifs. For instance, Laney's mother has died of cancer some years before. The heroine aspires to be a Bohemian artist and she retreats to her private place at home, the basement studio, to paint pictures of her dead mother in various styles and guises. This does not assuage the grief but it is a method of reconnecting her with a lost one, and giving her image some kind of eternity. From this point of view Laney is an Orpheus figure.

Laney is also interested in experimental theatre. On her first (reluctantly agreed) date with Zack she drags him along to an evening of performances with the theme 'Art is silence; art is love', in which he produces an impromptu act about demonstrating prowess in sport. His performance (not dropping the ball in a tense effort of fancy footwork) is a thinly veiled metaphor for retaining the approbation and adulation of friends, teachers and the world in general.

This is the beginning of Zack's connection with Laney. He has started by ingratiating himself with his prey but of course falls for her fairly rapidly. He persuades Laney to let his sister fix her hair and make-up and dress her for a party, which is to function like the ball of previous Pygmalion stories. Laney references *Pretty Woman* in the make-over scene, delivering the line that she feels like Julia Roberts 'except for that whole hooker thing'. Sadly, even the now gorgeous but still gauche Laney cannot best the Venus figure represented by Taylor and the heroine has a failed 'coming out' moment at a seniors' party where she is humiliated by Taylor for wearing the same sexy red dress. No girl mimics a goddess as Taylor appears, surrounded by a sycophantic circle of her peers.

Taylor's behaviour and Laney's distress prompt further changes in Zack. He has a dream indicating his liminal emotional state in which both Laney and Taylor are 'moulding' him like a sculpture and he is helpless in their hands. After a succession of situations in which Zack shows his blossoming love for Laney and then revelations about the 'make-over bet' drive them briefly apart, the finale of the movie sees them embracing in a romantically lit garden. They have left the Prom night (where, unlike the implied finale of Ovid's myth, they are not crowned king and queen, so at least one cliché is avoided) and Laney has escaped sexual assault at the hands of Zack's erstwhile buddy. Zack's inner mature and sensitive self has now fully emerged and Laney has lost her brittle edge.

A Comic Coda: *Miss Congeniality*

I paused before including this film because at first sight it is only tangential to the Pygmalion myth as told by Ovid. However it does have a mention in the Ghent pedagogical programme and the presence of Michael Caine as the manufacturer of a new look for the heroine is a jokey reference to his earlier role as the intellectual mentor who transforms Rita. *Miss Congeniality* was directed by Donald Petrie and screened in 2000. It is mostly a vehicle for Sandra Bullock's comedic talents. Gracie Hart (Bullock) is a tomboyish and unrefined police officer ordered to go under cover at the Miss United States beauty contest. She saves the contests and contestants from sabotage but during the process changes her judgemental attitude towards the girls she meets in the big parade.

The title, *Miss Congeniality*, complete with sash, is bestowed upon Gracie in gratitude for her heroism but also acknowledges the warm personality, which is a Bullock trademark, even when she is playing a contrary character. She is a congenial presence on screen and her designation as Miss Congeniality conjures up an obliging figure with whom everyone will feel comfortable, not overawed or inclined to genuflect before her. Gracie goes through life not making any effort to add allure to her appearance or improve nature with art. She is primarily concerned with testing her strength, speed and skills of detection in fierce competition with her fellow officers.[25]

Of course, once forced to masquerade as a contestant Gracie like Eliza before her 'scrubs up' well under the tyrannical tutelage of a world-weary fashion guru played with a degree of camp by Michael Caine. (His name is Victor; what else could it be?) Victor despairs of his charge but proceeds to groom her for public exposure. The 'make-over' is played for laughs; it takes place in an air hanger with teams of specialists. Bullock's policewoman undergoes a farcical rebirth during a scene that encapsulates the film's humorous and self-conscious construction of gender. Gracie has already expressed herself graphically when she is squeezed into a revealing costume: 'The last time I was this naked in public was coming out of my mother's uterus'.

So it comes as no surprise that the movements of the new (born) woman are faltering. The film fools the spectator with its slow motion launch of the transformed Gracie into the line up. She looks the part but lacks the poise, tripping over on the cat walk and confounding her name (Grace) in her general demeanour. Those fully steeped in the visual representations of the statue's first faltering steps will recall that Burne-Jones depicted the statue lurching forward from her plinth. Any girl playing a goddess should be careful of her first step down from the pedestal, as Tracey Lord's father cautions her affectionately at the end of *The Philadelphia Story*. [26]

Gracie resigns herself to being on display but she is an awkward off shoot of the ivory maiden and follows in the footsteps of Eliza and Laney in making a clumsy debut appearance. All these made-over women stumble at socially significant moments when the world is watching. There is a further link to Ovid in this respect as the statue comes to life in the context of a ritual and its accompanying festival. The star attraction in Cyprus was, of course, Venus. Gracie becomes the ultimate spectacle and submits herself to the last word in the female body as fetish, by being put on show in a competition for the most beautiful girl in America. However, she cannot let go of her combat skills nor compromise her authenticity and genuineness.

Like Eliza, Gracie almost immediately reveals a talent for making inappropriate statements. When the contestants are interviewed, Gracie talks about tougher penalties for parole breakers before remembering the rule about being as saccharine as possible. She quickly reverts to (stereo) type and utters some rehearsed and anodyne lines about wanting world peace. This is Shaw's winning formula – the statue speaks out of turn and the spectators of the contest find it surprising and refreshing in equal turns. I shall return to the deconstruction of motherhood and apple-pie speak by made-over heroines in the discussion of SIMØNE in Chapter 5.

By the end of the film, as well as saving the day, Gracie has found friendship with other women; getting together with the detective colleague she fancies is almost an afterthought. Victor has been won over and become less jaded about his life in the fashion industry. He is overcome with emotion at Gracie's success in the contest, telling her she is unique and that if he had a daughter, he would want her to be like Gracie. Several strands from the Pygmalion myth might be interwoven into the relationship between Gracie and Victor.

In the weaker sequel *Miss Congeniality 2: Armed and Fabulous* (directed by John Pasquin, 2005) Gracie has to be brought back from the brink of submersion into the superficial world of fashion (where the Head of the precinct has put her to work in the service of police PR and spin) by a reflection of her former self, the sassy (stereotypically so) black policewoman played by Regina King. Gracie's regaining of identity (reversing the metamorphosis of the earlier film) is compromised by the heroine never really reverting to her earlier unlovely state. Instead, she achieves a happy combination of strong, self-willed and smart cop along with a keen fashion sense (armed as much with make-up bag as the dangerous weapons of her trade).

Eliza, Vivian and Laney all start out as post-classical versions of the ivory girl but they do dovetail with other unfortunate mythical females in Ovid who catch the eye of powerful men far above them in the social hierarchy. In *Miss Congeniality* Gracie is controlled by a male dominated agenda at the work place. She also has a crush on a colleague who finally responds to her and then ditches her by the sequel (thus clearing the decks for Bullock and Regina King to develop their partnership at work and on a personal level). Sandra Bullock's *Miss Congeniality* demonstrates that the dream of the perfect woman now entertains another desire.

On the cusp of the twenty-first century Pygmalion's statue supplants (or we could say supplements) the characteristics that render her unsullied, submissive, available and passionate. Gracie relearns the value of human fallibility. She returns to active service in the police force without sacrificing new-found femininity. Gracie remains an assertive, liberated and controlling personality, a girl who can look out for and after herself. The perfect partnership (with a caustic edge and the buzz of rivalry) turns out to be between herself and her previously hostile female colleague.

Chapter 4

She Was Venus All Along: the Statue as Screen Goddess

Introduction

In the previous chapter I concentrated upon the reversal of the statue story, which is the mainstay of many movie narratives. Flawed and sometimes morally or physically degenerate humans are polished up and put on pedestals to be objects of veneration. The process proves that a woman of Cyprus (one of the Propoetides) can be transformed into the ivory statue. However, the myth of Pygmalion is full of potential contradictions of an objective and subjective nature. The Propoetides were forced by the goddess to change their behaviour and to parade themselves in public as common prostitutes. The made-over women of the previous chapters might be for private possession and enjoyment by their creators but they may be commercialized and vulgarized like the prostitutes of the original myth.

Whether the woman is a body to be used or a figure on a plinth, she is a passive object, not an active subject. Either way the metamorphosed creature suffers loss or confusion of identity and risks permanent social alienation. However in the comedy make-over, the heroine acquires a new persona without losing her essence. She proves that it is possible to combine the best of the real and the ideal, that even ivory statues can take control of their own transformations – but only within severe cultural constraints. I have already recommended Kord and Krimmer (2005) in Chapter 2 for an astute analysis of producers, players and consumers of the female image of the 1990s, a flourishing period for make-over movies.

There is also a cinematic tradition of producing apparently empowered and supernatural spirits which are liberated from their solid encasement and step down from their plinths. Shaw drew attention to the godlike nature of Pygmalion as creator. In films about the statue as a goddess or a goddess-like girl from a past age the divine nature of the Pygmalion's ivory girl is revealed and treated with a mixture of intimacy and irreverence.

In the ancient world the implied model for the perfect woman was Venus. Surely artists were subconsciously sculpting the most beautiful goddess when they created statues celebrating the female form, naked or robed? We might assume that cinema in a globalized world has a broader conception and a bigger range of cultural stereotypes when it comes to representing the goddess in the girl. Perhaps we overplay the notion of a classical consensus on beauty. Mary Martin was daunted at the thought of imitating the goddess of love on stage when she was offered a part in the Broadway musical, *One Touch of Venus*, precisely because she envisaged her as a tall, imposing and voluptuous figure. Her husband, Richard Halliday, 'took her to the Metropolitan Museum and showed her that the goddess appears in a great variety of shapes and sizes' (Grant, 2010, p. 5).

Manifestations of Venus

This is the title of a 2000 book by Caroline Arscott and Katie Scott. In the introduction Arscott and Scott make a metaphor out of the way in which Venus sculptures have been found in unexpected places and in parts, evoking a past in pieces (p. 1):

> Indeed, in her blatant imperfection she perfectly personifies the disturbance, the inevitably shattering effects, of desire on the wholeness and wholesomeness of tradition, the very effects with which we are concerned.

A leitmotif of the essays is that the figure of Venus embodies 'the coincidence of art and sexuality' (p. 2) and any representation of her invokes her mythological realm at the same time as heralding her status as a sign of the juncture between the aesthetic and the libidinal (p. 5):

> Artistic allusions to Venus invite us to see art itself as co-substantial with the body of the goddess; seductive in its contours, colour, texture or surface, irresistibly inciting feelings of pleasurable excitation.

The interpretation of the Venus figure in the essays edited by Arscott and Scott book is subtle and wide-ranging, accessing theories of desire and pleasure from the history of aesthetics, Christian theology, the psychological schools of Freud and Lacan and the feminist perspective on the objectification of the female body. Under the heading 'Morality' (p. 19) the authors summarize the approach taken by essays with a focus upon the overlapping Venus:

> In Christian morality a familiar presentation of physical beauty is of the beautiful exterior that hides a corrupt and hideous interior, the mortal shell and the sinful nature. The introduction of Venus offers a different way of approaching physical beauty. Instead of beauty as deceptive surface Venus is understood as substantive beauty, her beauty is not just surface and illusion, it is not subject to decay. Famous for her arbitrary nature, her cruel tricks and wiles she is also a figure of substantive deception. The deception does not undo the beauty.

The multiple manifestations of Venus which emerge throughout the essays in Arscott and Scott undergo a more conceptual treatment than the many guises of the goddess illustrated and discussed in Hersey's 2010 book. His early chapters are an erudite history of human desire for Venus' (Aphrodite's) changing figure from the terra cotta images of ancient Cyprus through Greek and Roman sculpture, Christian statuary and Indian rites of animation up to her present-day avatars, the advanced mechanical doll and the perfect robot woman of science fiction.

When Venus is translated to the screen there is a risk that she will be flattened in more ways than one by becoming a celluloid goddess. However her image's cultural and aesthetic signifiers as identified by Arscott, Scott and Hersey tend to lurk beneath the surface. The artistic designers of mainstream American and European cinema continued to access Western traditions of painting and sculpture when creating their Venus figures. It is interesting that their goddesses combined the ethereal and the worldly, the wholesome and the seductive, and that she remained, like Pygmalion's ivory girl, the 'figure of substantive deception'.

The Venus Statue on Screen

In the 1941 film *Pimpernel Smith* directed by and starring Leslie Howard, the hero plays an archaeology professor Horatio Smith who is courageously smuggling persecuted individuals out of Nazi Germany. He covers his activities by taking parties of students on archaeological digs and towards the start of the film we see him recruiting a team of young Oxford scholars to accompany him – this after he has insulted the one woman in his class and caused her to sweep out of his chauvinist presence. On the way to Germany, his students learn of his dangerous exploits and eagerly fall in behind him. Although the rudeness to his female student has been a ruse, we have already witnessed Smith's idolization of the statue of Aphrodite Kallipygos whom he later claims to have brought back from Lesbos for the university museum. The practically perfect goddess is the only woman worthy of note as far as he is concerned and he is shocked to see her in need of dusting. He gently wipes her shoulders off and remonstrates with the museum's employee. He corrects an ignorant schoolteacher who misnames the statue and then asks Smith to reassure her female charges that this Venus was respectable and only encouraged love in marriage.

Aphrodite / Venus re-emerges later in the film in the form of a photograph the professor carries around with him. He shows this to plucky fighter, Ludmilla, whose father he promises to rescue from the concentration camp. Ludmilla (Mary Morris) is beautiful and one of his students is already besotted with her. Of course, Horatio is head over heels in love with Ludmilla by this time and after celebrating Aphrodite as the only woman for him, he ostentatiously tears up the picture saying that he has become dissatisfied with her. In answer to Ludmilla's question, he admits he would never want the statue to come to life. She is divinely lovely but Smith on his own admission 'tries to supply her mental equipment'. What price narcissism now? When Ludmilla is trapped into betraying Horatio, he reassures her that he factored her weakness in, tenderly telling her 'she is so human!'

Pimpernel Smith, an enterprise dear to Leslie Howard's heart, has a hero not unlike Shaw's Henry Higgins in self-confidence and feelings of superiority. Smith is also given to grand, passionate speeches and he too champions knowledge and culture over blind ignorance. Howard no doubt imported into the part of Professor Smith the characteristics of Higgins whom he had played on screen in 1938. Smith is also a confirmed bachelor and infuriatingly complacent. However, Howard's wartime hero and the film itself have been influential, inspiring the Indiana Jones trilogy, the Steven Spielberg's action movies in which crusty archaeologist Harrison Ford defends freedom and progress against the enemies of civilization. *Pimpernel Smith* has also been praised for its use of lighting and shadows, giving some scenes a film noir flavour and making Howard's professor almost fey, magical and supernatural in quality. He is a hero for his time.

The function of Aphrodite in *Pimpernel Smith* emphasizes that even the goddess needs fleshing out by her adoring lover. The professor realizes that the sculpture has no personality but his own and tears up (symbolically fragments) the photo he carries of her, which is a flat image of her solid image in the gallery. Smith now has his real girl and the cold marble no longer satisfies him. When a likeness of Venus is vivified, and this is the mainstay of the cinematic narratives under study in the next section, interesting aspects of Pygmalion's relationship with his statue are revealed. No wonder Pimpernel Smith responds to Ludmilla with words to the effect that bringing her to life 'wouldn't do at all'. Once again Ovid's text can be revisited with further questions in mind about the ivory maiden's identity. The Venus movies also present us with the spirit of the goddess ready to be released from a temporary marble prison or entombment. They are a reminder of ancient perceptions that continue to be tenacious in a number of belief systems that deities, supernatural spirits, and saints are ready to occupy the images that represent them.

Bringing the Gods Down to Earth

In Chapter 1, I synthesized scholarly arguments in support of the statue's divine identity. The clues Ovid gives the reader about the ivory maiden's proximity to Venus are worth reprising. Although Pygmalion should have no business knowing what the goddess looked like and it is a girl not a goddess he carves, we have to remember that the legend was originally about the king of Cyprus falling in love with a cult statue of Venus. The ritual of the sacred marriage is replaced by Ovid with the union between Pygmalion and his 'real' girl. However mortal lovers of the goddess are not unknown in other mythical traditions and we are reminded of their fate in two films about a Venus statue coming to life. These films under discussion highlight the duality of Venus as immortal and unattainable but also willing to be seduced by men 'out of her league' (no pun intended) beneath her. As these films cast female actors being groomed for iconic stature their Venuses doubles for the movie star. She is lofty and remote but suddenly there she is on screen taking the arm of an ordinary Joe – the male (and maybe the female) fantasy is fulfilled.

In Chapter 2, I focused on Hitchcock's preferences in his projection of desirable images of women onto the screen. Throughout the twentieth century to the present day the entertainment industry has promoted different images of female physical perfection, from curvaceous to gamine, from snowy white to dark and sultry. Increasingly during the twentieth century, it was the entertainment industry that manufactured and maintained a hierarchy of preferences. When movie makers represent female goddesses from Olympus (in a flesh and blood or statue form) they are played by established celebrity beauties of the day or up and coming starlets aspiring for iconic status. These women may come, like representations of Venus, in varying shapes and sizes but there is usually a consensus on costume and coiffure among directors and producers. Goddesses or Muses should arrive on earth in Grecian garb and with a classical hairstyle.

In her interview 'Drat being a Goddess', for the first *Hollywood Album* (1947, pp. 21–22) edited by Ivy Crane Wilson, Rita Hayworth said: 'I'm glad that I'm just a human being. After eight months of playing a goddess in Columbia's Technicolor fantasy, "Down to Earth," I'm sure that the average girl has a much happier time than did the heavenly ladies of legend.' Hayworth was actually cast as Muse of Dance, Terpsichore, in this uninspiring musical directed by Alexander Hall (Winkler, 2009, pp. 93–103) and unwisely remade as *Xanadu* in 1980 (starring Olivia Newton-John and directed by Robert Greenwald). Hayworth complained about wearing a costume of chiffon that weighed exactly four-and-a-quarter ounces during the filming in very chill weather for California. She had to walk on high-wedged shoes (six inches of colourless plastic) to give the illusion of a goddess who did not touch the earth. The elaborate hairstyles (hyacinthine curls, a Greek coronet, or an intricate pompadour) took an hour and half to arrange each morning.

Hayworth was in favour of portraying this glamour goddess with a mind of her own:

> In the old world women were considered simply decorative beings without one grain of sense. Being an independent girl, I'm very, very grateful that I'm living in the year A.D. 1947, for it would be most tedious to be admired for one's looks alone.

We could pass this over with a wry smile as in this and other editions of *The Hollywood Album* the stars themselves and an assortment of directors, producers and photographers regularly contributed pieces on how to approximate to beauty and perfection in form and character. A few female actors managed to insert a dissenting voice in the interviews they gave for these albums. There is no space to explore the rich registers of social and cultural moods movie journals like *The Album* and *Picturegoer* provide but a random trawl through the decades of editions can be very rewarding.

Visualizing Venus (or another divine denizen of Olympus who was an acceptable stand in for her) was still an attractive proposition for moviemakers towards the end of the twentieth century. In 1999 Sharon Stone played the title role in *The Muse* (directed by Albert Brooks) to great comic effect. Her muse is a generic inspirer of Hollywood writers with creativity blocks but she is tyrannical in her demands for the star treatment, capricious in her cravings for special dishes and other luxuries, and generally a spoiled starlet in the guise of an insatiable goddess (Winkler, 2009, p. 93). Nevertheless her unorthodox methods work and she delivers the goods not just for the screenwriter but also for his wife who discovers her true, albeit stereotypical, potential for professional cookery (well, we can't have everything!) and forges a new independence for herself.

The Statue Comes to Life

I have settled upon two films to illustrate the further career of the classical statue on screen: *One Touch of Venus* (1948, directed by William A. Seiter) and *Goddess of Love* (1988, directed by James R. Drake). Both films are based upon F. Anstey's 1885 story, *The Tinted Venus*, in which a sculpture of the goddess of love is accidentally animated by a male mortal. The spirit of the deity seems to come and go from her marble encasement and to be in a state of limbo, or 'shut down' mode when it suits her. Anstey (Thomas Anstey Guthrie, 1856–1934) was a lawyer-turned-journalist. He called his novel a farcical romance but it combines whimsy and satire taking a pop at the debasement of love and repressed sexuality in Victorian society.

The stage musical *One Touch of Venus* transferred the action to 1940s New York and added 'leeringly suggestive dialogue' but 'for all its wisecracking the script has an almost Goethian subtext based on the eternal Madonna / whore theme' (Grant, 2010, p. 3). Grant points out that it contained even more sexual innuendo than *Pal Joey*, which had scandalized critics and theatre-goers a few years before. Marlene Dietrich turned down the part of Venus rejecting the show as too sexy and profane. The theatrical musical still enjoys occasional revivals across America, Canada and Europe, invariably to critical acclaim (and even rave reviews.) Weill had conceived of it as a neo-Offenbachian operetta but his music displays a remarkable mastery of American idioms from light swing to barbershop and hot blues (Grant, p. 5)

The screen version worked within the constraints of the American film censorship system (the Hays code) and was radically different in tone. It sanitized the plot and reduced the score considerably; the result was an unsatisfactory movie on a number of counts with much of the Kurt Weill music and Ogden Nash's acerbic and sophisticated lyrics lost in the transition. The promotional poster pinpoints the film's plus points and is deliberately ambiguous about which 'gal' invented love, Venus or Ava. However, the movie is of interest in its own right especially in its visualization techniques which allow certain Pygmalionesque features to unfold simultaneously reflecting and reversing motifs in Ovid's narrative.

FIGURE 4.1 Poster for *One Touch of Venus* (author's collection)

As well as Pygmalion resonances in a number of its scenarios, it is clearly one of a kind with films that exploit the cinematic possibilities in bringing gods down to earth. Metaphorically speaking this is a double bluff. As Bloom, Mulvey, Stoichita and O'Sullivan suggest (from their distinct theoretical and thematic perspectives) the big screen simultaneously reflects the proximity and the distance of godlike creatures (the Studio Stars). The illusion is given of a palpable presence when in fact the flickering images are no more than modern dreams of moving statues.

Goddess of Love starring Vanna White as Venus also modernizes Anstey's novel transporting the statue and the story to Los Angeles, 1988. It remixes elements from *The Tinted Venus* and *One Touch of Venus* but interestingly introduces a back story for the goddess and explains why she is incarcerated in a marble statue. In *Goddess of Love* Vanna / Venus has been punished with ossification for displaying the very same vices as the Propoetides in Ovid. Like the women of Cyprus whom the goddess changed into prostitutes, Venus in the film is condemned by Jupiter for prostituting herself. In response to her lack of decorum but also her lack of feeling and undisciplined behaviour, Jupiter becomes a censorious Pygmalion figure passing judgement upon an errant daughter, the embodiment of sexual passion, because she has commitment issues and no sense of romantic love.

The Tinted Venus

In 1862 when Anstey was six years old, a marble statue entitled *Tinted Venus* was exhibited by the neo-classical sculptor John Gibson (1790–1866) at the London International Exhibition. Flynn (1998, pp. 118–119) under the sub-heading 'The Warmth of Life: Colour and Controversy' describes how Gibson entered a Pygmalion-like transaction with the sculpted object. Having tinted the marble to resemble warm ivory he believed his Venus was a lifelike and ethereal being. He at moments forgot he was gazing upon his own production and he wondered if he could ever part with her. Anstey would have grown up during a time when artists were experimenting with naturalism to achieve the illusion of a living breathing body. Painting or tinting sculptures of naked bodies was an attempt to imitate ancient Greek practices of coloration which the developing discipline of archaeology had revealed in surviving sculptures. Flynn (p. 116) notes that

> elevated academic theory continued to dictate that such were not the true ends to which the sculptor should aspire. Instead of stimulating the mind of the beholder into pondering more elevated notions, such works, it was felt, all too often excited base bodily passions.

Anstey's comic plot concerning the goddess coming to life after a ring has been placed upon her finger is a pastiche of a medieval narrative. It had been reworked earlier in the nineteenth century by Prosper Mérimée and given a Gothic timbre.[1] In the French novel, things do not end well for the vivifier of Venus. This is one of several nineteenth-century versions of Pygmalion which dissolve the myth's message of optimism in love and art, according to Bloom's subtle studies of Ovid's narrative in literature and its later manifestation in film (2000 and 2003). Anstey creates a more resourceful if rather ordinary Pygmalion who accidentally animates a statue not of his making and who triumphs over the banefully synthetic creature by keeping his sanity against the odds. Far from disintegrating Anstey's hero survives the unwanted attentions of the persistent deity. He is neither nymph nor Adonis and he really does have a happy ending.

Leander is the Victorian hairdresser's name which gives him a classical connection, as Leander was the male of a pair of star-crossed lovers, Hero and Leander, who were separated by an expanse of water. The Victorian Leander is engaged to his beloved, Matilda (Tilly), and no insurmountable obstacles loom on the horizon, until the statue comes on the scene. The hero idolizes his fiancée but admits that 'she wants for a little more liveliness'. While Matilda is away, Leander has been persuaded to join his friend on an outing with two sisters (Chapter 1). In spite of his guilt at being on a double date he becomes slightly infatuated with Ada, the giddier of the girls.

During a stroll in Rosherwich Gardens, Leander and Ada follow a path to a small enclosure and encounter the statue of Aphrodite on a low pedestal. 'The exceptional grace and beauty of the figure would have been apparent to any lover of art. She stood there, her right arm raised, partly in gracious invitation, partly in queenly command.' Ada speculates upon her identity 'as if the sculptor were a harmless lunatic whose delusions took a marble shape occasionally'. Leander pronounces that the sculpture is Afroditty and thinks her 'done from a fine woman'.

Then in a fatal gesture, goaded by Ada who mocks his claim that Matilda's hands are as small as the statue's, Leander puts Tilly's betrothal ring upon the finger of the goddess. However, this is not like the other pale plaster statues but a valuable antique stolen away from a fine sculpture gallery in Wricklesmarsh Court. Leander senses that the hand is warm and almost soft in his grasp but once the ring is on the finger the marble is unyielding and the jewel is immoveable. Leander, always the gentleman, has to escort Ada back to the dance and when he returns the statue has vanished. He has unintentionally summoned the goddess of love from Olympus to Victorian London. Chapter One of the novel was entitled, 'In Pursuit of Pleasure'; Chapter Two is called 'Pleasure in Pursuit'.

This Aphrodite statue may be the genuine article (a classical piece) but she is also a most unappealing creature once vivified, a clunking marble figure who stalks the unfortunate hairdresser, following him to his rented rooms. In Chapter Three, Leander views his visitor as an appallingly massive ghost with spectral eyes and is amazed to hear he has woken a sleeping goddess. Aphrodite has been slumbering through the centuries on Cyprus until the living touch of a mortal hand upon one of her sacred images brought her forth. She is grateful to have life and vision but exasperated by Leander's bewilderment stating that 'a Greek swain would have needed but a few words to divine his bliss'. She might have said 'where is Anchises when you need him?'

Her tenacity of pursuit is what one should expect of an Olympian who has set her sights upon a mortal but this Aphrodite is not exactly passionate about her prey. She seems rather to be invoking a heavenly rule as if it were a legally binding contract, an earthly breach of promise perhaps. This goddess alternates between anger and bewilderment that Leander, a mere mortal, does not immediately fall at her feet in an act of love and worship. Always respectful and mostly bemused Leander has to stave off the advances of the statue and hide this (Aphro) oddity in his lodgings. He exercises the kind of diplomacy we might expect from someone in the hairdressing business and decides to humour his unwanted guest.

So begins the farce involving the thieves of the statue, the detective and assorted females with a claim on Leander. Any reader of Anstey's novel who is familiar with Ovid's Pygmalion will enjoy the paradox of a very unalluring Venus imposing herself upon a mortal with no desire for a divine lover. While the goddess is at rest and back in statue mode, Leander attempts to chip the ring off her finger but makes little impression upon the implacable marble (Chapter Four, 'From Bad to Worse'). The inspector investigating the theft of the valuable statue and the link with the missing ring arrives on the scene and comments on the tools lying around in the living room.[2] Leander pretends to be engaged in producing a work of art, in his spare time.

Anstey's hero has more than a touch of Pygmalion about him in other respects. Once he realizes that the statue is an unbiddable creature in every respect, liable to go walkabout at any time, he decides to render her a little less outlandish. At this point the reader learns that Leander though an apparently run of the mill hairdresser has hidden depths. He really wishes to be a professional beautifier and has started to collect and experiment with various preparations. In other words, Leander is a frustrated artist. Drawing on his 'science of cosmetics', he starts transforming the inert statue as best he can with grease paint preparations from his laboratory: 'He furnished the black eye sockets with a pair of eyes, which, if not exactly artistic, at least supplied a want; he pencilled the eyebrows, laid on several coat of the "Bloom" which he suffused cunningly with a tinge of carnation, and stained the pouting lips with his "Conserve of Coral"'. So far, perhaps, he had not violated the canons of art, and may even have restored to the image something of its pristine hues' (the conclusion of Chapter Six, 'Two are Company').

Leander also puts a wig on the statue and believes he has committed an indefensible act of vandalism. Anstey's Aphrodite is not as discerning as her counterparts on screen will prove to be about new hairstyles. She is pleased with the 'make-over' but privately Leander recognizes that his newly painted goddess 'looks more natural but not half so respectable' and that she needs some sort of covering cloak. He buys the very squirrel fur cape that his human sweetheart, Matilda, had admired in the local shop and drapes it around the statue.[3] Aphrodite receives the gift graciously and is happy with her hues. She misreads the situation thinking that Leander's heart is warming in the sunshine of her favour (melting perhaps like the image of pliable wax Ovid uses of the statue that comes to life in the presence of her lover?) Her approval of animal skin as a covering might remind the reader familiar with classical legend of Venus' occasional impersonation of Diana, the huntress goddess.[4] Indeed Anstey's deity is much more virago like than either of her later screen reincarnations and tends to take on aggressive attributes associated with Hera/Juno especially when confronted or questioned in any way by mortals.

This divine statue never softens in personality or attitude and Leander has to outwit her into surrendering the ring – but not before many misunderstandings and close calls have occurred with the goddess uttering threats of crushing rivals and causing mayhem. Although Zeus does not hear her commands for thunderbolts to strike down Leander and Matilda, Aphrodite swears that she will forever stand between the lovers as a barrier to their happiness 'so shall your days consume away in the torturing desire for a felicity you may never attain'. As Matilde (Tilly) has realized the depth of her feelings for Leander and he has never stopped worshipping at her shrine, the presence of the goddess of love in the form of a statue looming over them is a comic but tender pastiche of the Pygmalion myth. Matilda has come to life and is now facing either death or permanent separation from her beloved Leander. Once the statue has been deceived into removing the ring and has been re-ossified as a consequence, Leander and Tilly are united.

We are told in the conclusion that Leander Tweddle is now running a very successful salon and he has earned the title professor because he is such a creative hairdresser noted for his invention of brilliant and popular hair washes. We also learn that the statue has stayed as a statue to be admired in the new collection of Casts from the Antique, at South Kensington. The official catalogue describes the Cytherean Venus as a copy of an earlier

She Was Venus All Along: the Statue as Screen Goddess 103

FIGURE 4.2 "Did You Want to See Me on—on Business, Mum?"

FIGURE 4.3 She was Standing Before the Low Chimney-Glass, Regarding Herself Intently.

Figure 4.4 "Why Did You not Kneel to Me Before?"

Figure 4.5 "Leader!" She Cried, . . . "I Dont Believe She Can Do It!"

Figures 4.2–4.5 were illustrated by Bernard Partridge for the 1898 edition

work. 'The unusual smallness of the extremities seems to betray the hand of a restorer, and there are traces of colour in the original marble, which are supposed to have been added at a somewhat later period.' Anstey's comedy has a satirical subtext about residues of colour on ancient marble as the tinted Venus has been painted not by the Greeks, nor by the Romans, not even by John Gibson, but by Leander Tweddle, hairdresser.

One Touch of Venus

An ancient Greek setting, the ruins of Athens, occupies the opening shot of the film *One Touch of Venus*. The viewer, given the title of the movie, expect gods or heroes to be strutting their stuff in this Athenian architectural setting, but instead it turns out to be a small-scale model which Robert Walker (Eddie) has designed to advertise the store's latest acquisition, a sculpted Venus. Eddie is the godlike creature in this location at least in terms of size. Shortly after, his girlfriend, Gloria, looks up adoringly at him as he travels up on the store escalator. Eddie is the cooler of the two in this run of the mill mortal relationship but also blissfully unaware that his love-smitten colleague (played by crooner, Dick Haymes, an Orpheus figure perhaps?) is resisting the temptation to woo and pursue Gloria himself. It is very quickly established that Eddie is not ready to settle down while Gloria has marriage on her mind (continuously).

In the presence of his boss, Whitelaw Savory (played by suave Tom Conway), Eddie is flustered and unassertive. Conway has purchased a $200,000 statue of Venus and is very taken with her cool marble beauty. Conway's PA, Molly, a rather wasted wise cracking Eve Arden, caustically comments that both the buyer and his priceless piece have large pedestals, thus pointing up the narcissistic attraction between her employer (for whom she clearly holds a candle) and his purchase, as well as their lack of human responsiveness, their positions of power and their celebrity status. Left alone to adjust the curtains in front of the sculpture (ready for its unveiling) Eddie is so emboldened by some sips of champagne that he impulsively climbs the step ladder to kiss the statue. His lower place in the divine scheme of things is reinforced but he is aspiring to reach the pedestal and his heart's desire, like Burne-Jones' Pygmalion. He has also unwittingly sipped a libation to the gods, an earthly nectar, before approaching the deity.

Eddie kisses the life-size sculpture of Venus, with the words: 'Golly, you are beautiful'. This is a cue for the 'real thing' to appear in an epiphanic moment. Ava Gardner is the vivified statue who taps the amorous mortal on the shoulder when he turns his back to adjust the curtains concealing the plinth. Eddie faints away at the vision of Ava's Venus who glows rather than glowers at the man who awakened her. He reacts to the goddess with the fear appropriate to a divine encounter. From the outset Ava's Venus, with velvety voice and diaphanous dress is all warmth and seduction. Eddie awakes from his swoon to find himself in the lap of the goddess and he looks up at her with adoring eyes. His demeanour reprises Pygmalion's hesitant awe at the goddess's shrine, but this hero also imitates the statue of the original myth coming to life at the touch of her lover.

Eddie is regarded as something special by the awakened Venus 'He's wonderful. Thank you, Jupiter'.[5] She finds him a worthy enough lover and assumes that he has special attributes although he protests his ordinariness. The goddess and Eddie look down from the roof upon the cityscape and she indicates that Eddie can rise above his position as department store manager. The goddess refuses to return to her 'nice warm pedestal' (Eddie expresses concern that the statue will freeze on the balcony in her light Grecian shift) where she can be appropriately worshipped. This Venus (unlike Anstey's Aphrodite) has come into Eddie's life for a purpose. The Olympian gods are in the habit of manifesting themselves (often in disguise) to help a hero when he has reached a crossroads or a crisis in his life.

Initially Venus functions a hindrance rather than a help to Eddie. Like the novel's statue she follows her pet mortal and the standard misunderstandings occur as Eddie tries to keep her existence a secret from his friends, his landlady, the police and his employer. A motif common to book and film is the hero hiding the statue in his apartment, keeping her out of public view rather as Pygmalion does with his miraculously carved ivory girl. In the film the goddess is bathed and dressed in two different sequences. However those who meet her comment on her (super) natural aroma, which puts all commercial perfumes to shame. Otherwise the goddess readily succumbs to the capitalist consumer imperative and embraces the range of 'man-made' fashions and adornments produced in post-war America.

In *One Touch of Venus* the power of love in the form of Ava Gardner is irresistible and infectious, which means that the writers of the screenplay have picked up on the goddess of love embodying and exuding the passion she represents. Not only Eddie but everyone in the vicinity, including Gloria (Olga San Juan) and Joe and the couples in the nearby park, are all in the mood for romance when Venus sings: 'Speak Low', the most memorable tune to survive from the Broadway show. Communal clinching is the coda to the scene and Eddie succumbs to love in her corporeal form. After several misadventures, and the wooing of Venus by Eddie's rich employer who has more of a passion for possessing than for sexual satisfaction, the five main players have had their lives transformed. Conway realizes he loves and cannot do without his PA, Arden, Joe and Gloria become an item and Venus remounts her pedestal and returns to marble. (Like Cinderella she is subject to a curfew and has only a short time on earth.)

When a god or goddess does come into the life of a human being, it is bound to be traumatic but it is not always tragic. In *One Touch of Venus* the divinity has an ultimately fostering role, helping the hero to a better life and a better understanding of human relationships. Ava Gardner's Venus is a mischievous but not unkindly deity propelling a downtrodden little man to happiness (if not to hero status). She is also capable of indulging in capricious behaviour and exhibits a careless disregard for social boundaries and conventions. Once again the Pygmalion plays of Gilbert and Shaw spring to mind. There is, inevitably, given the cinematic genre of romantic comedy (boy meets girl or in this case goddess), an embryonic, not quite fulfilled, love affair between mortal and goddess. Eddie and Venus kiss but any further intimacy is discreetly suggested to save embarrassment and miscegenation all around.

The film resolves the relationship between window designer Walker and gorgeous goddess Gardner by having a facsimile (a dead ringer) for the deity appearing at the end of the film in the guise of a new employee. The mortal Venus mimic or lookalike in *One Touch of Venus* (introduced as Venus Jones) holds out a promise of accessibility and modernity (the surname indicates that she is a kind of everywoman) combined with an expectation of the mystique a high-ranking woman or divinity of the distant past has planted in the mind of the male. Orpheus' own story is an irresistible subtext to a supernaturally engineered restoration of the beloved who seems irrevocably lost. In addition Venus is now truly down to earth (a real girl) and her arrival fulfils the desire of Pygmalion to be blessed with something like the goddess statue as his partner, but not the statue itself.

The reincarnation of the lost love when fantasy shifts back to reality was a device borrowed by the Bing Crosby vehicle of 1949, *A Connecticut Yankee in King Arthur's Court* (based on the book by Mark Twain and directed by Tay Garnett). The hero is catapulted back to Medieval England and falls for Lady Alysande (Sandy). Sandy was played by another studio star, the curvaceous redhead, Rhonda Fleming. Bing meets her contemporary counterpart once back in his own time. This is the best of both (temporal) worlds because the modern Sandy has the added bonus of being a feistier, more flirtatious vision of loveliness, in keeping with the post-war American screen stereotype of femininity.

Goddess of Love

The 1988 film corresponds much more closely to Anstey's novel than the screen version of *One Touch of Venus*. Promoted as 'a fun comedy in the style of *Mannequin*', which really did it no favours, it also carries a warning: 'Be very careful what you wish for!' This is a lesson that several metamorphic victims in Ovid's poem might have learnt and concerns the careless framing of desires, wishes and prayers to the gods, perhaps even the plea uttered by Pygmalion to Venus. On a subsequent viewing I decided I had been far too dismissive of the film which handles the humour of the vivified statue at a good pace. There is a fair sprinkling of clever lines capitalizing on the comedy of a goddess engaging with modern technology and relating these to the powers and attributes of her fellow denizens on Olympus. Just a couple of instances will give a flavour of the interplay. Intrigued by the car, Venus says how much her cousin Mercury would love this mechanical horse power. In the salon she imagines the envy Apollo might feel as Ted can harness the wind with the hair dryers.[6]

Goddess of Love does not reach anywhere near the humorous heights of the screwball genre, the screenplay is not subtle and Vanna White lacks charisma but it keep remarkably close to Anstey's novel and translates the farcical episodes into some successful modern mise en scènes. It is certainly not as charmless as *Mannequin* (more of this movie later.) In the *Goddess of Love* the statue is snatched from its high art setting in the city museum and hidden among replicas of sculptures in the grounds of the Pleasure Gardens' night club. The thieves believe this is an inspired choice for stowing the statue, which will then be ready for collection, to be possessed by the highest bidder. This plotline echoes the novel. The theft first commodifies Venus and then insults her uniqueness by putting her image among cheap copies of valuable artworks. From a different perspective, remembering the myth of the Propoetides and the fact that Venus was patron to the prostitutes and courtesans, why should she be distanced from things meretricious and mercenary? In any case, Vanna White's Venus has been immobilized for bad behaviour and for bringing the Olympic pantheon into disrepute.

This casting brings off screen and on screen personas into an amusing interplay. The film is a lightweight vanity vehicle for the ex-Miss World (this adds another layer to her impersonation on screen of an out of this world beauteous being) but it offers distinct possibilities for teasing out topoi from Ovid's myth, which are not present in Anstey. Vanna / Venus' erotic adventures are put on hold because her father, Jupiter, wishes to punish her for an irresponsible attitude to love. In *Goddess of Love* the principal objections to Venus' attitude are that she has not been taking love seriously enough, and has hardly been a faithful wife to Hephaistus (Roman Vulcan, the unprepossessing, lame blacksmith god).

She has also been busy breaking the hearts of her lovers and inciting wars by inflicting inappropriate passions on others. Jupiter finds this a glaring flaw in her character which needs correction, a perception of the amorous ruler of the gods that is not entirely paradoxical while undoubtedly demonstrating double standards. At first sight this is a somewhat moralizing, Christian characterization of the classical Jupiter who was himself in regular passionate pursuit of goddesses, nymphs and exceptionally well-turned-out mortals with no care for the consequences. However, Jupiter is supposed to keep a watchful eye on the gods and step in if they step out of line. It would seem in some ancient traditions Venus' desire for the handsome Trojan Anchises was in retribution for her bad behaviour.[7]

After the first scene on Olympus and the transformation of Venus into a marble museum piece, the plot of *Goddess of Love* reverts to *The Tinted Venus*. A reluctant Ted agrees to go out clubbing with his hedonistic friend although the hero is now ready to settle down and no longer a party animal. His friend bemoans his new found fidelity and suggests only a goddess would tempt Ted. During the course of the evening Ted slips the ring on the statue's finger in the Pleasure Palace gardens and frees Venus from her frozen state. The pursuit begins.

The cinema in both 1948 and 1988 could not countenance an unattractive Venus figure (the potential for showcasing stars was the motivation for both movies under discussion) but the 1988 film does incorporate the destructive tendencies Anstey's Aphrodite continually exhibits. *One Touch of Venus* allows the goddess metamorphic powers of a light-hearted nature with the temporary transformation of pursuers into owls, the bird sacred to Minerva, which indicates some slippage between Venus and the virginal goddess of wisdom, war and weaving.

Vanna's Venus is a far cry from Anstey's ghost-like marble manifestation. If anything, simply dressed in the generic classical garb of a tunic, the screen statue is a little insipid in appearance. This Venus does not have a commanding screen presence but her threat to crush rivals for Ted's love is taken directly from the Anstey text in which the Aphrodite statue is menacing and malevolent. As in the book Ted has to pretend that his fiancée,

Cathy, is his sister to protect her from the jealous goddess. He is as eager to rid himself of Venus as was the Victorian hero. When Venus arrives at Ted's apartment and solidifies into the sculpture for the night, Ted tries to remove the ring and his attack upon the statue with various tools simply proves its impermeable nature even in a state of rest. Like Leander Ted has to explain the tools lying around in his living room to the detective who comes searching for the stolen statue. This Pygmalion has been trying to fragment the beautiful illusion but has to masquerade as an artist in the act of creation.

Ted decides on a different tactic and takes the precautionary measure of making the living breathing statue a better blend with the world around her. Venus is a willing subject for a make-over as she realizes that modern cosmetics can lend her colour and pulling power in this new situation (where the garish fashions of the 1980s characterize the jet set at play). Ted's skills with lipstick, blusher and make-up generally delight the goddess. The scene in which the mortal and lowly hairdresser tells Venus to put herself in his hands is a classic moment in both senses of the word. Ted becomes Pygmalion to the vivified statue and she declares him a true artist for improving upon the (super) natural. Vanna's Venus, once out in the public domain, is perceived by his best friend and all whom she encounters as a very attractive property.

During the course of her education upon earth in 1980s Los Angeles, this goddess alternates between being a headache and an ornament to the hero. Venus exhibits the same kind of behaviour as her cinematic and literary predecessors on the divine plane as she is engaging and charmingly direct, liable to express affection in public, and invites the attention of the bemused men and women who encounter her. Out of place and time, these supernatural creatures have the potential to wreak havoc in the human social landscape. In *Goddess of Love* the enlivened statue not only neglects the niceties of polite society but when angered or under threat she becomes a liability, setting light to buildings and cars. Ted's salon goes up in flames because Venus hates her permed hair and wreaks vengeance on his hair stylist colleague.

This aspect of the artificial construct, the baneful being brought to life, enters into screen narratives of robot girls who are the subject of the next chapter. Both models of supernatural womanhood can engage in relentless pursuit of the hapless and largely helpless male who has resuscitated them. Things can go either way when gods, nymphs or numinous spirits do not take no for an answer in the world according to Ovid's *Metamorphoses*. Unlike Eddie in *One Touch of Venus* who is present at the epiphany and responds appropriately to the divine encounter, Leander and Ted take some time to understand the power of the inert females they have accidentally animated.

Leander and Ted both find out what Aphrodite / Venus is capable of and why the placing of the ring upon the finger of the goddess's likeness has bound them so closely to the deity in her statue form. In both book and film, the love goddess has a reputation for causing mortals to meet sticky ends – in Anstey a scholarly and somewhat cobwebby old professor enlightens the hero about the actions and affairs of Aphrodite while in the film Ted's friend consults a story book of myth. The dilemma is partly resolved for the 1980s' hero because he follows in the footsteps of Eddie Hatch (Robert Walker in *One Touch of Venus*), and makes love to the statue, yielding to her obvious charms (the later film could convey the preliminary foreplay to couple's night of passion but clearly the 1940s' theatrical version of *One Touch of Venus* was exuberantly explicit in innuendos). Ted, the reformed Lothario, succumbs to Venus but there are a few particles of pity in his lovemaking to this lonely and rather needy Venus. It is the final touch to her education in what it is to be human.

However, in *Goddess of Love* Ted does not fall for the statue – he remains devoted to his fiancée and is prepared to be crushed along with her when the wrathful Venus corners them at their wedding. The hero in Anstey has to deceive the goddess, unmoved, unreconstructed and definitely not modernized, into departing from the human world (the genie goes back in the bottle). In contrast, in *Goddess of Love* Venus softens towards Ted and Cathy, chastened by the proof of true love. This goddess has learnt her lesson and proved to Jupiter that she realizes the power of love. The classical deity must embody love in all its aspects so this is Venus looking in the mirror and recognizing her essential characteristic, but one filtered through modern notions of romance. She releases her accidental suitor, and is probably going to be forgiven her past peccadilloes on Olympus as the film ends. In the meantime, she returns to being a statue and as a valuable sculpture is retrieved by the museum.

Everyone wins and Ted's infidelity with the goddess is airbrushed out as far as he and bride-to-be Cathy are concerned. Cathy is, after all, a smart psychologist who can handle emotionally charged situations and can forgive her lover's infidelity in special circumstances. Ted's love and loyalty to his human girl are not shaken by the encounter with the goddess whereas the appearance of Venus in the earlier film wakes up Eddie (Walker) to his lack of feeling for Gloria. It is perhaps typical of the 1940s' male lead that he chooses the illusion of the movie star statue rather than the reality represented by his less glamorous fiancée. In 1988 the hero has the pleasure of a divine sexual encounter and the security of settling down with a practical and forceful female of the earthly kind. Walker is closer to Pygmalion who is rewarded with a real girl but one designed from an artist's dream, a divine figure but not the divinity itself.

Mannequin: from the Sublime to the Ridiculous

In *Mannequin* (1987, directed by Michael Gottlieb) a girl of ancient Egypt, ready for adventure and with modern notions of independence, is trying to escape the social traps of convention and the prospect of an arranged marriage. Kim Cattrall (who does her best with a seriously unrewarding part consisting of, in essence, a succession of photo shoots and video shorts punctuated by excruciating dialogue) first appears posing in a niche like a mummy in the wall of a tomb. Her prayer to the gods is answered and in a flash forward technique she next turns up in Philadelphia where her spirit invests a mannequin in the making. Evidently in the interim Emmy (her abbreviated name could be a humorous reference to film award statuettes?) has inhabited a fair few facsimiles over the centuries but she is destined to find true love with Jonathan Switcher (Andrew McCarthy), the manufacturer of fibre glass girls. By the end of the film she is finally vivified permanently and her days of inhabiting statues, models and dolls are over.

Switcher (the name has a metamorphic quality but also refers to the succession of jobs he is sacked from) is yet a frustrated craftsman / artist condemned to mass production of models. He loses his position in the store because he has taken six days (the time span suggests he is a small time demiurge) to make one dummy (Emmy) instead of turning out twenty in a working week. Jonathan has been talking to this, his best and favourite creation to date and treating her as if she were real. He is trying to be a sculptor and his artistic aspirations are always to the fore, whether he is employed at pizza topping or topiary. Jonathan's human girlfriend Roxie is materialistic and emotionally cold. Her work colleague is also chasing her and, towards the end of the film, gets her into bed only to despair at her unresponsiveness sexually. He blames Roxie for his impotence declaring 'you are so cold, so unfeeling!'

The metaphor of stone, frigidity, flesh and warmth lingers on through countless statue and robot narratives. One of the thieves in *Goddess of Love* lifts up the cold marble statue of Venus and says she is still less frigid than his wife. In contrast to real girl Roxie, Emmy once vivified will be all warmth and passion. A thunderstorm brings Jonathan's mannequin to life but only for Jonathan's eyes. Their relationship, like Pygmalion and the statue's, is always conducted in private. Emmy tells Jonathan that she liked the way his hands felt as they were putting her together, suggesting that as the mannequin she was sexually responsive and wanting to be moved. Although Emmy is not a sculpted goddess, she does have the supernatural power of changing back and forth from real girl to large doll. In the flesh she is a naïve and knowing creature, characterized by her spontaneity and her happy disregard for conventions. She also hints at having a succession of intimate relationships through the centuries. Jonathan's model is not the first frozen body she has inhabited.

Emmy has acquired other special powers; she believes that together she and Jonathan could design a whole new world and she inspires Jonathan to produce startlingly original shop window facades, which save the ailing store. Hordes of passers-by stop and stare at the imaginative moving tableaux. Emmy has been brought to life as a reflection of Jonathan the artist and to be an architect of his success. As he is the only person who can see her as a real girl both the delusion and the narcissism of Pygmalion lurks beneath the surface of the story (though some would argue there is nothing but surface in the film). There are a number of other set pieces in *Mannequin* that could correspond to the myth of Pygmalion but possibly the most interesting after the central premise has been worked to death comes at the welcome finale. [8]

In the last scene, the real girl Roxie throws mannequin Emmy into the crusher conveyer belt along with other discarded synthetic models and Jonathan only saves his beloved in the nick of time. Roxie is knocked unconscious under a pile of model body parts and regains consciousness as she is being kissed by the mechanical chipper's operator. He has seen Emmy come to life (permanently and publicly at this point) in Jonathan's arms so is busy embracing one mannequin after another in hope that the transformation will be repeated. Roxie, mistaken for a dummy by the eager lover, yells 'Stop touching me!' and the store employee cries out 'It's a miracle!' The last shot of *Mannequin* has Jonathan and Emmy getting married in the store window with a festive atmosphere and the spectators looking on and applauding.

The Dream of the Moving Statue

It would seem that Ovid's Pygmalion motifs refract across subsequent narratives and have a habit of insinuating themselves into the statue's story on screen as well as in art and literature. Refashioning Pygmalion's perfect girl, screenplay writers and directors make assumptions about the identity of the beautiful statue. She is bound to be the goddess of love and a screen goddess is duty bound to imitate her. The remote object of desire becomes flesh and blood within the representational medium but these moving images can never be more than celluloid creatures for the audience (but see Chapter 8 on the construction of perfect men). Hollywood films sell the dream to their audiences. An ordinary mortal meets a star from the cinematic firmament and they work out a way of having a happy ever after. Kord and Krimmer (2005, pp. 27–33) deconstruct the images of celebrity and normality in the 1999 British romantic comedy, *Notting Hill* (directed by Roger Michell and starring Julia Roberts and Hugh Grant), in which the hero cannot believe he is permitted to kiss and then have sex with a screen goddess. However, the image of the whore is never far away:

> The ultimate reduction of Anna (Julia Roberts) to her screen image is performed by a group of men in a restaurant who proclaim that Anna is a prostitute.

Their reasoning is predicated upon the fact that in over 50 per cent of languages, the word for actress in the same as the word for prostitute.

Falling for a goddess (Olympian or Thespian) is fraught with pitfalls even when the feelings are mutual. A divinely beautiful image coming to life fulfils the male (and the female) fantasy. Going on a date with a deity is a delusion that any of us can have a gorgeous celebrity on our arm outside the fictional space of the picture house. Rita Hayworth commented ruefully on the fact that 'every man I knew had fallen in love with Gilda and wakened with me'.[9] The goddess girlfriend points up the tensions in wanting your idol to be accessible and approachable while retaining special star status. This is the dream that desires a combination of ageless beauty and charming imperfection and vulnerability.

The Venuses on film turn out to be a positive thing for the hero as they actually assist his re-integration into society and because they strip away inhibitions and pretence in the humans around them; they also restore relationships to closeness, warmth and sincerity. This is the irony of the living 'statue', the ancient and culturally displaced spirit, and the synthetic and cybernetic being or the computer graphic girlfriend introduced in the next chapters. All these creatures of myth come to life without artifice and shows just how dissembling and constructed social identities can be. In short, the statue (as in Gilbert's play) teaches those around her about being human. The alien being can see where alienation has set in.

Chapter 5

Pygmalion's Robots: the Horror and the Humour

Introduction

In the penultimate chapter of his book *Falling in Love with Statues: Artificial Humans from Pygmalion to the Present* (2009, p. 132), George Hersey identifies four present-day forms of Pygmalionic (his adjective) artificial life. He lists automata and robots, dolls and action figures, puppets and marionettes, and 'synthetic biomorphic beings' or cyborgs (cybernetic organisms). Hersey's foray into artificial life as the modern location for the vivified statue supplements Stoichita's exploration of dolls as another legacy of Pygmalion's life-size synthetic girl (2008, 195–198). For my next three chapters I have selected screen stories that feature robots, cyborgs and dolls and also computer-generated images which take on a life of their own. My cinematic and television texts have been chosen for their correspondences (some conscious, some coincidental) with Ovid's myth on a narrative and figurative level. The fascination with artificial life makes Pygmalions of us all and the emergence of synthetic beings (real and imagined) causes cultural and ideological tremors across the study of myth and of science.

In his fanciful conclusion (Chapter Nine, 'The Primacy of Artificial Humans') Hersey asks whether humans are or have ever been needed and suggests we come to terms with contemporary evolutions towards robots made of living tissues or molecular circuits replacing silicon (p. 161). Human beings seem to be moving closer to machines and using them as extensions of their minds and bodies. Sophisticated prostheses mimic the multiple functions of limbs and an individual's identity may be preserved and prolonged through mechanical devices when the physical body has become frail through disease or ageing. Remarkable advances in medicine and the biological sciences could be viewed as a whole raft of mythical metamorphoses from Ovid's imaginative poem finding their way into modern life.[1]

Hersey (*ibid*) goes on to pose the theory that 'real life is just an optional subroutine of artificial life'. Power in his 2010 review of Hersey's book dubs these 'far out enjoyable musings on the potential modes of artificial life suggested by fractal mathematics and self-replicating systems called cellular automata'. This reviewer judges Hersey's last two chapter 'too discursive, their links to Pygmalion and ancient statue love too notional'. Power laments the lack of a reference to the film, *Blade Runner* and the absence of Chris Cunningham's 'transcendent video for popular singer Bjork's "All is Full of Love" which features twin Bjork cyborgs seducing one another'. To my mind, Power has pinpointed the problem of making Pygmalion the literary progenitor of all narratives (artistic, scientific, fictional and factual) about artificial life in any form. Is this a bridge too far for the potent myth?

It is worth noting that Liveley's critical and stimulating engagement as a classicist (2006, pp. 275–294) with Haraway's work, especially the 1991 chapter 'A Cyborg Manifesto: Science, Technology, and Socialist-Feminism in the Twentieth Century' only mentions Ovid's vivified statue in passing. Liveley has published elsewhere (see Chapter 1) on the Pygmalion myth in the *Metamorphoses* and developed strategies for reading the narrative of the artificial girl from a feminist perspective. Although Liveley (pp. 278–281) maps an alternative history for the cyborg (which entails moving away from the fixation upon nineteenth-century literature for the genesis of this figure of science fiction) she does not focus on the statue as an early automaton.

Instead, she relates the ancient legendary stories of golden robotic slave girls designed by the blacksmith god, Hephaistos (Roman Vulcan) for his workshop on Olympus (Homer, *Iliad* Book 18, 373–379) and the miraculous tripod automata serving dishes at feasts of the gods (humorously alluded to elsewhere by Liveley as 'glorified hostess trolleys').[2] It is worth noting, I think, that the lame blacksmith god looked to the future in designing robots to help him overcome his disability.

Liveley reassesses the nature of the bronze giant Talos described by Apollonius of Rhodes in his epic poem *Argonautica* (Book 4, 1635–1688) as he fits Haraway's model for the cyborg more closely.[3] Talos is an animated metal humanoid. Self-propelled but 'coded' for the single purpose of guarding Crete against all comers, Talos in the Apollonius narrative is part god and part man, the last survivor of the bronze race of humans born from ash trees (Liveley, p. 280).[4]

Liveley (pp. 281–282) suggests that Haraway's cyborg genealogy which is indebted to gender-free (or post-gender) utopias of feminist science fiction and the psychoanalytical writings of the French feminists might also be traced back to the classical mythographers from Homer to Ovid.

They too, to quote Liveley quoting Haraway, 'knew how to write the body; how to weave eroticism, cosmology and politics from imagery of embodiment – from imagery of fragmentation and reconstitution of bodies'. Liveley does acknowledge that by 1997 Haraway was invoking the myth of Pygmalion and Galatea for theories of 'masculine parthenogenesis' (Haraway, *Modest Witness*, p. 253) and was writing about 'classical myths that were crusted like barnacles' onto popular representations of cyborg figures.

Haraway appropriated the cyborg as a site for deconstructing and reconstructing feminist theory whose champions have naturally been suspicious and hostile towards gynoids created for the pleasure and servicing of males. She offered a critique of American feminists who promoted the organic against the technological, demonstrating the interchangeable qualities of the natural and manufactured (1991, pp. 161–162). In declaring 'we cannot go back ideologically or materially. It's not just that "god" is dead; so is the "goddess",' Haraway cautioned against the restricting aspects of an oppositional ideology based on female technophobia. She argued:

> But there are also great riches for feminists in explicitly embracing the possibilities inherent in the breakdown of clean distinctions between organism and machine and similar distinctions structuring the Western self. (1991, p.174)[5]

However, the production of a sentient robot which looks like a human figure and is fully articulated and articulate remains such stuff as scientific dreams are made on. The mechanical and electronically driven creature capable of mimicking anything other than the simplest function of the human brain or more than a few fluid physical movements is still way beyond the reach of human engineering and computer science. Robot 'workers' tend to be one trick ponies; they are mono-functional and frequently dysfunctional. On *Start the Week* (24 January 2011) anthropologist Kathleen Richardson observed that science had replaced the image of a robotized human workforce with the metaphor of the machine. She was supported by the scientists on the programme in her statements about the crudity of mechanical humanoid robots, the regularity with which they broke down and the way in which video clips on the internet idealized them, massaging their screen movements into perfect replicas of the body.[6] The automaton that is indistinguishable from a human subject and able to operate with sophisticated spatial awareness is a thing of smoke and mirrors, as much a creature of myth as the ivory statue who metamorphosed into a real girl.

If the truly integrated organism and machine posited by Haraway must remain in the realms of the fantastic, it does not detract from the fact that science fiction scenarios, like mythical ones, are good to think with. The female science fiction writer has managed to divert the notional mechanical woman (so frequently demonized) into a new locus of empowerment. Rafaella Baccolini (2000, pp. 140–153) follows in Haraway's footsteps when she celebrates Deirdre, the heroine of C.L. Moore's *No Woman Born*, as a post-modern metaphor for the complex, multiple feminist subject. Destroyed in a fire and reconstructed with durable materials, the heroine Deirdre accepts her liminality and her multi-faceted nature as a cyborg.[7]

Living the Dream: Robots as Real as the Statue

Apart from *Metropolis* and *Cherry 2000* I have side stepped film versions of futurist fantasies in which a whole species of high-functioning robots or biologically hybrid cyborgs characterize a technological or digitalized society.[8] My main interest is in the fictional one-off automaton, whether this is a mechanized robot, a Frankenstinian fusion of human tissue or a graphic image that steps out of the machine. These are a closer match to Pygmalion's perfect woman as such phenomena are wondrous works of technological or digital art, ahead of or out of their time. It could be argued that Ovid's metamorphic landscape is an *Ortloskeit* (unidentified society) in the fairy tale and science fiction traditions. To a certain extent this would invalidate my marginalization of fantasy genres where lifelike robots are part of everyday life.

It is also true that in some texts, for instance the novel *The Holy Machine* (yet to be filmed [9]) and *Do Androids Dream of Electric Sheep* (which became the SF cult movie, *Blade Runner*, directed by Ridley Scott and released in 1982), one of many mass-produced synthetic creatures becomes a distinct and desired individual in the eyes of the hero.[10] However, the Pygmalion aspects of *Blade Runner* have been discussed by Brown (2005) and also O'Sullivan (2008). I would struggle to add anything illuminating or philosophically profound to their interpretations. The following exploration of robot 'women' that share attributes with Pygmalion's statue has examples of the demonized and the idealized female manufactured for pleasure and pain, for practical and psychological purposes.

The Serious Stuff: Pygmalions Producing Pandoras

In his contribution to *Femspec* (2004), 'Menacing Technologies: Counterfeit Women and the Mutability of Nature in Science Fiction Cinema', Albert Anthony noted the prevalence of the cyborg as a hypermasculine and hypermuscular warrior in the 1980s. Anthony summarizes female critics' responses to science fiction's fetishization of masculinity on screen. The patriarchal attempt to re-empower men by endowing them with the exceptional powers of advanced technology is a two-edged sword. Masculinity is revealed as artificial and constructed, depending on props for performance and only able to sustain super strength and authority when the male body becomes fused with electronic circuitry and mechanical hardware. Anthony is interested in exploring the nature of artificial females on film whose images seemed to have been temporarily eclipsed by the advent of the cyborg action hero and anti-hero in the Terminator mould.

His cinematic reference point is *Metropolis* (directed by Fritz Lang, 1927) but he recognizes that the *Maschinemensch* as female can be traced back to nineteenth-century imaginative fiction. He quotes Huyssen (1986, p. 70) on the gendering of the machine as woman once it was perceived as demonic, threatening and a harbinger of chaos and destruction. Fear of the female reaches new heights if that female is a prototypical bionic woman combining in one body the female affinity with untamed nature (the call of the wild) and the mechanical parts provided by male-driven technology. Such a constructed woman is at first sight much more like Pandora in her destructive potential than Pygmalion's perfect girl but in a number of texts the motive for her making and the image in which she is made to combine elements of Orpheus' loss of Eurydice and the sculptor's acquisition of his dream wife.

Fritz Lang's 1927 film is a landmark for cinematic visions of a dystopian future. Set in the early twenty-first century, it depicts an architectural miracle city with skyscrapers where a leisured class enjoys the high life (in both senses of the word) while beneath the ground workers toil away like slaves on the vast complex of machinery owned by Metropolis' Master, Joh Frederson. The narrative like the spectacular sets is disjointed but it concerns the political and ethical education of Frederson's son as he realizes the inhuman exploitation and dangerous conditions of the city's workers. Frederson's son, Freder, suffering from love at first sight, has followed the beautiful Maria, champion of the underground people, down to the living hell beneath the city.

The Master in the meantime asks his old rival in love and an exceptional scientist and inventor, Rotwang, to help him find out more about the workers' female leader and nip any independent thinking and resistance in the bud. Accessing the labyrinthine catacombs, the two men spy upon Maria preaching a sermon of hope to the entranced workers in which she prophesies the coming of a Mediator who will unite the classes for a better future. Rotwang agrees to give his latest invention, a robot, the face of Maria and send her to the workforce where she will disillusion them about the real Maria and destroy their faith in her message. However, Freder's son believes that it is his destiny to be the *Mittler* (the German for mediator which bears an uncomfortable rhyming resonance with Hitler[11]).

Rotwang creates the robot Maria to be an agent provocateur and launches her onto the effete elite before rousing the men and women underground to acts of mindless vandalism, which very nearly destroys the foundations of Metropolis, unleashing a great flood beneath the city. Rotwang's interpretation of Frederson's instructions motivation was not altogether clear until the piecemeal recovery of missing footage from the film. The latest discovery (Argentina, 2008) and restoration of some poor-quality negatives have clarified the motivation of the robot's maker, Rotwang, in programming his invention to be both sexually provocative and politically nihilistic.

The metallic body, which takes on Maria's face and form, was going to be a copy of the dead wife of his employer, Frederson. The inventor has an Easter Island sized bust of Hel, the dead wife, hidden behind a curtain with a placard accusing the Master of stealing her from the embittered engineer. Lang and von Harbou's choice of back story is clearly indebted to E.T.A. Hoffmann's *Der Sandman* and Villiers de L'Isle Adam's *The Future Eve* but it is also a daring transference of their personal off screen love triangle into the cinematic fantasy world. The retrieval of the dead wife and the creation of a Whore of Babylon to supplant a virginal and angelic creature yet again remix the ingredients we find in Orpheus' account of Pygmalion.

The embittered Rotwang determines to have his revenge upon Frederson for stealing and possessing his ideal woman. He transforms the robot woman into something brittle and baneful, capable of bringing Frederson's empire to ruins. Robot Maria functions as a heartless and soulless Pandora fitting for the uncaring and mechanized capitalist world she is destined to disturb. Anthony (2004) notes that the transfer of Maria's features to the robot's *tabula rasa* is achieved cinematically as if Rotwang has within the film magically accessed a camera technique to give the empty visage its new identity. The sequence lays bare the reproductive process of film and according to Kracauer (1947, p.149) 'the creation of the robot is detailed with a technical exactitude that is not at all required to further the action'. The moment of the robot's 'birth' is now iconic as mechanical Maria epitomizes the film's vision of the dialectic (destructive and creative) between machinery and humans, innocence and experience and the real and the representational.

The function of robot Maria is to cause general mayhem in Frederson's mechanized conurbation of Metropolis. The cyborg is presented to the parasitical class on the surface of the city (they live in skyscrapers) as a highly sexualized cabaret dancer (at the Yoshiwara club). She inflames her audience with her provocative movements, representing the antithesis of the modest Maria she is impersonating. She is also a travesty of Rotwang's idealized beloved (whom he has lost a second time because the robot he would have made into Hel's mechanical likeness has become the property of Frederson). The real Maria, a modest and gentle girl fighting exploitation and injustice, is saved to take her place alongside Frederson's son as a mediator between the workers and Frederson while her robot Doppelganger is burnt (effectively melted down) as a witch by the crowd she has duped.

Until Freder and the real Maria bring the Master and the people into a harmonious hand and heart union, the workers are treated as cogs in the complex of machinery that creates and sustains the cityscape above. Elsaesser (2000, *BFI* screening notes, p. 1) comments:

> Generally recognised as the fetish image of all city and cyborg futures, the once dystopian *Metropolis* now speaks of vitality and the body electric, fusing human and machine energy, its sleek figures animated more by high-voltage fluorescence than Expressionism's dark urges.

Anthony sums up the critical consensus that Fritz Lang's cinematic visualization of a dystopian and divided society is stunning and ground-breaking while his ideological message is an anodyne compromise with capitalism and its dehumanization and alienation of exploited labour:

> Yet by allowing the cyborg figure to carry the weight of the film's critique of technology and capitalism, *Metropolis* ultimately displaces its distrust of technocratic industrialism onto a more manageable distrust of feminine sexuality.

Solving a Problem Like Maria: *Eve of Destruction*

Anthony (2005, pp. 7–10) discusses the film *Eve of Destruction* (directed Duncan Gibbins, 1991) in which a robot double of Dr Eve Simmons is created and programmed by the scientist herself as part of a military project. The robot's name, Eve 8, suggests failed and discarded models before this version is tested out in combat. A bullet to the body causes a malfunction and Eve 8 becomes an aggressive terminating machine with the added complication of sharing the doctor's memories of sexual abuse and her suppressed physical desires. Robot Eve presents herself as promiscuous, dressing provocatively and picking men up in bars, only to castrate and generally mutilate the males who fall into bed with her. She is the antithesis of the demure doctor but also plays out the real Eve's potential for vengeance upon her father and her teenage fantasies about being sexually rampant.[12] There is an atomic bomb where her uterus should be and she seems indestructible but Dr Eve Simmons finally dispatches robot Eve under a train in the subway.

Anthony argues (p. 8) that the film engages with many of the issues raised by *Metropolis*.

> *Eve of Destruction* produces an ambivalently misogynist spectacle in the image of the evil and highly sexual cyborg female, but because the film ascribes her misconduct to 'malfunction', rather than to the machinations of the evil scientist, the film functions as a paternalistic cautionary tale about a world in which men dictate the behaviour of neither woman nor machines.

He also finds the probing of robot Eve's interior a way of making a female body thoroughly and profoundly visible, using the camera to construct the ultimate spectacle for the 'scopophilic pleasure of a masculine audience', as Mulvey argued in her seminal essay of 1975 (Antony, pp. 9–10).

Bould (in the same issue of *Fem Spec*) introduces his interpretation of *Eve of Destruction* by noting the tendency of science and science fiction 'to confuse the categories of Woman and World, to propose them as enigmas, as objects of masculine epistemophilia' which gives 'unsurprising prominence to the female (as) cyborg, a figure which collapses woman/world and subject/object distinctions' (2004, p. 18). Bould puts another trio of films under scrutiny and quotes a humorous description of *Eve of Destruction* as *Marnie* replayed as *Terminator* (p. 20). He makes the telling point (p. 28) that strong (cyborg) females should not necessarily be equated with pro-feminist or pro-woman models. Bould draws upon Ien Ang's critique of Soap Opera to remind us that empowered females on screen are still Disneyland fictions not reflections of reality. He would apply a large dose of irony to the reception of such sexualized cyborgs as 'a Marianne, a Liberty, to symbolise and inspire gender revolution'.

In conclusion (and conscious that I have strayed some distance from Pygmalion) the classical provenance of *Eve of Destruction* is a tenuous one, although it could be argued that the two Eves represent the modest and the immodest, the passive and the active aspects of Pygmalion's statue. Eve Simmons has certainly displayed narcissistic tendencies in producing a succession of reflections, exact copies of her own form. The Pandora factor is probably uppermost in this film, however, as the scientist designs a creature which will be both volatile and highly dangerous to men, letting evils out of the box that is her own body. It is possible that the Eve story of not just a mechanical but a militarized woman manufactured to serve the American military was inspired by the 1960s American comedy series, *My Living Doll*, of which more later.

Cloning for Romantic Purposes

In the now little known and little shown 1953 British film *Four Sided Triangle*. the concept of cloning an ideal woman through an electro-magnetic process looks back to the Gothic horror genres in literature and cinema but also has premonitory shades of the cyborgs in *Blade Runner* and the duplicating machine in *The Prestige* (2006, directed by Christopher Nolan). *Four Sided Triangle* was directed by Terence Fisher later of Hammer Studios fame and was his first foray into science fiction. In the movie, two close friends and colleagues, Robin and Bill, invent a machine called 'The Reproducer', which can clone any object. The theory is that a heavy dose of radiation (intensive X-ray treatment) will force mass to migrate into the energy of electrons and then be reconverted into matter. It does not do to enquire too deeply into the laws of physics in this explanation, but the first experiment with live tissue does produce a second identical but short lived guinea pig.

In the meantime, the beautiful Lena (played by Minnesota-born blonde bombshell Barbara Payton), a childhood playmate, reappears in Robin and Bill's lives and supports their experiment as a 'ministering angel', a woman who inspires them (and makes the tea). She unintentionally comes between them as both engineer scientists want her as a wife. She chooses Robin, and Bill after suppressing his jealous rage begs Lena to submit herself to the

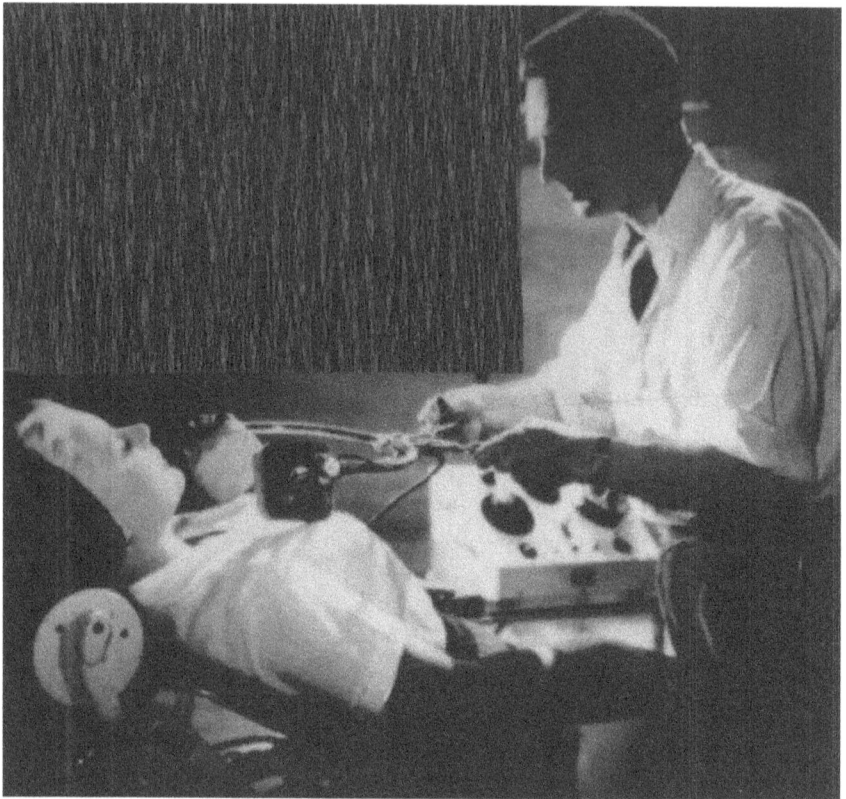

FIGURE 5.1 *Four Sided Triangle* still (author's collection)

Reproducer so he can create an exact copy of the woman he worships. *The New York Times* reviewer (quoted in the 2005 DVD Viewing Notes) described the duplication of Barbara Payton as 'the most delectable trick of the year'. Bill in a sense brings alive a dream on screen that men or women in the audience might share if they envy the possessor of the beautiful star and wish they could supplant the actor/hero she chooses. Barbara Payton does have a look of *Vertigo*'s Madeleine (Kim Novak) about her.

This plot development reprises that of a closely contemporaneous film, also directed by Terence Fisher. *Stolen Face* premiered at the Plaza in the West End in May 1952 and is defined in the 2005 DVD Viewing Notes as a Pygmalion meets plastic surgery melodrama (see Chapter 2). A surgeon (Paul Henried) operates upon a disfigured convict, Lily, to give her the face of Alice, the woman he cannot have. As Alice is a concert pianist and devoted to her fiancé this movie mixes up motifs from *Mad Love* and *The Orlacs Hände*.[13] The story was written by Alexander Paal and Steven Vas.

Paal produced *Four Sided Triangle* and clearly he and Fisher shared a fascination for the Gothic reworkings of the Pygmalion myth which had their heyday in the literature of the nineteenth century.

Four Sided Triangle moves from a biological make-over to an electromagnetic cloning moment, which is also successful on the surface. Lena's double is called Helen, a name with an obvious classical association and, as it proves, an ominous one. At first all seems well. The second Lena opens her eyes, sees her lover and he helps her to start breathing and pulsing. Bill believes he will be blissfully happy with Helen and takes her away for a holiday so they can get to know each other. They are only ten days into an idyllic honeymoon trip when his newly awakened wife exhibits discontentment and psychological turmoil. She has started to have feelings for Robin. Helen is as likely to stray away from her 'husband' as her ancient Greek namesake was because she has retained traces of Lena's emotional make-up and memories in the physical cloning process. The replica is so unhappy in her bereft state (she has lost her true love) that she demands the right to die. It is interesting to speculate what Pygmalion would have done if his vivified statue had not found him attractive or was pre-programmed to love another.

The melodrama moves on relentlessly with Bill deciding to repeat the cloning experiment and pressurizing Lena to help him. She tells him he is not god but agrees to suffer the machine one more time. Bill hopes he can remodel Helen and eradicate Lena's personality and romantic preferences from her inner psyche. However, the two bodies on slabs have more than a suggestion of corpses at a morgue. The Reproducer over heats and Bill dies in the conflagration. Only one of the two Lenas survives, saved by Robin. There is a vampiric resonance as Robin checks his wife's neck to see if she is the real or the replica Lena. (The American title of the film was *The Monster and the Woman*.) The auto injector would have left two scars on the back of Helen's neck. On finding her blemish free, he seems satisfied that he is holding the original Lena as she opens her eyes and smiles at him, but she has lost her memory. It remains ambiguous whether Robin has been left with a *simulacrum*.

The film is a curio. In terms of its science fiction content and how this is realized, according to Hearn and Rigby (DVD viewing notes, 2009), *Four Sided Triangle* harks back to German classics but also prefigures *The Fly* (1958).

The creation sequence, in fact, is impressively staged, given the film's paucity of resources, and, with its abundance of shadowy, long-angled close-ups, plays rather like a low-rent parody of Universal's *Bride of Frankenstein* (directed by James Whale, 1935).

The same notes conclude that director Fisher was always

> much more interested in the human drama than in the science fiction nuts and bolts of it – the film ends with some salutary advice from Emerson; 'You shall have joy or you shall have power, said God; you shall not have both.' No such qualms disturb the Pygmalion figures of my next feature film, *The Stepford Wives*.

The Pliable Plastic Woman

Bryan Forbes' 1975 film *The Stepford Wives* brought Ira Levin's novel with its cynical vision of male desire to the screen.[14] The men who move to Stepford are prepared to eliminate their attractive and intelligent wives and live with mechanical copies. In other words, they wish to exchange their free thinking, fallible human partners with ciphers, mechanical dolls with no desires other than to please their men. As Forbes observed (1998, p.vii) 'Levin wrote it as a savage comment on a media-driven society which values the pursuit of youth and beauty above all else'. The apparently enlightened husbands who join their men's club in Stepford have been easily persuaded to commission robot versions of their partners as they harbour deep resentment towards their wives' independence, their attempts to resume careers, to pursue their own intellectual interests or, less ambitiously, to enjoy outdoor activities in which they excel.

The film stayed fairly faithful to the book in which it slowly emerges that the men's club in the quiet suburbia of Stepford is more than a bonding place for the local husbands. The members of the club have found a way of turning the clock back to an idealized era before the women's liberation movement. Levin's book was written during a period when the feminist movement was making significant advances in exposing and challenging patriarchy in the economic, social and cultural spheres. His 1970s husbands crave women who will pander to their every need, so they eagerly agree to robot replacements for their wives. The robots are modelled on their individual partners but their personalities are flattened into stultified housewives whose goal in life is to cook, clean, care for the children and massage their husbands' egos.

The heroine, Joanna Eberhart, and other recent arrivals to Stepford have been deceived into entering an established community of robot women, the Stepford wives.

The real women find their female neighbours amusing and exasperating. Joanna and Bobby (Roberta) Markow who becomes her best friend belong to a class and income bracket that had benefited from the women's liberation lobby and the piecemeal economic and social gains part conceded and part wrested from capitalism from the 1960s onwards. In contrast, the resident wives of Stepford seem positively old fashioned in their obsession with recipes and waxed kitchen floors.

The sinister truth is slowly revealed. Disney designed automata with a full set of working parts and communication skills confined to pleasantries and practicalities have been built to replace the creative and vibrant females the men of the Stepford suburbia have married. The real wives are, we presume, murdered and incinerated. The enterprise has been masterminded by men involved in the film industry (making Disney models) who have devoted their skills of animation to this monstrous project. At the end of the film the heroine Joanna suffers the same fate as her friends and neighbours. In the book, beautiful bosomy Bobby, the robot replacement for Joanna's scatty and slovenly best friend, comes towards her with a knife and the reader is left to assume she has done the deed. Forbes' decision to have synthetic Joanna as the assassin of her real-life counterpart in the movie underlines the twisted nature of this distorted Disneyland scenario.

In terms of suspense, Forbes' change does not leave so much to the imagination as Levin but as a cinematic moment it does drive home the horror of meeting her Doppelgänger. Katherine Ross in the part of robot Joanna presumably had to be made over into the physically flawless and implant enhanced starlet narcissistically admiring herself in the mirror. The copy then turns on her less glamorous, dishevelled and terrified original with the knife. Forbes chose to present a scene symbolic of the fate of actresses who do not want to conform to images of femininity that the cinema studio industry continues to privilege and peddle nearly 40 years on. It is the reflection, the *simulacrum* that kills her human model and this is a metaphor for the movie construct triumphing over the real (albeit ultimately fictional) Joanna.[15]

We should remember that in the book and the film we witness Joanna's camera skills. She is a talented photographer who is beginning to realize her true potential for capturing vibrant human personalities (particularly children at play) on camera. In the book when she confronts her husband Walter with her suspicions, Joanna accuses him of lying to her (about his pride in and support for her work) from the moment she took her first picture. Joanna represents the creative cognition of the artist while the Disney men can only produce sterile *simulacra* even if their technology is far more advanced. The creativity of the female and its inevitable suppression is reinforced in the final scene of the book when we see robot Joanna in the supermarket from the point of view of Ruthanne, the latest newcomer to Stepford.

Ruthanne is a middle-class black woman and a successful writer and illustrator of children's books. She too is an artist with an apparently supportive husband but the fateful 'weekend away' is already being planned for her. Ignorant of her imminent demise and supplanting by a robot double, she is still unsettled by the sight of Joanna as an immaculate and curvaceous Barbie figure neatly stacking her trolley with slow and deliberate movements. In the film the camera pulls back to reveal the Stepford wives shopping almost in unison and on auto pilot with the dulled expressions of housewives on Prozac.

The Robot Woman as Farce

In the 1949 Bernard Knowles' film *The Perfect Woman* starring Patricia Roc, the heroine's uncle (an absent minded professor) makes a mechanical likeness of his adored but over-cosseted niece, Penelope whom he has attempted to protect from all perils and especially the attentions of young men. This storyline was essentially a reworking of Coppelia. Miles Malleson took the part of the dithering genius. The professor's housekeeper Buttercup (played by Irene Handl) is unimpressed by Olga the robot, calling her the professor's great big beautiful doll and accusing her employer of thinking more of his invention than he does of 'miss Penelope'.[16] Penelope, the long-suffering and usually biddable niece, wonders why 'he made it like me'. To add insult to injury, Penelope and Buttercup are given the task of fitting out Olga with a wardrobe that is much more sophisticated and more revealing than anything the professor's niece is permitted to wear.

Sitting in the dress department of the store the two women make barbed comments about the costumes and the girls modelling them. Live models talk back of course and one of them (played by a young Dora Brian) reprimands the customers for being insensitive to her feelings. Penelope in particular is sarcastic about the nice outfits Olga is to wear and wittily rejects a rust colour gown for her mechanical twin. Another evening dress has 'too many bones in it'. The discomfort and lack of enthusiasm Penelope shows set up an intriguing similarity with the purchase of a suit and evening gown for Judy in *Vertigo*. It would be difficult to argue for this correspondence to be anything other than coincidental given that it is a cinematic genre scene based on middle class customs of the times, but both episodes pinpoint the

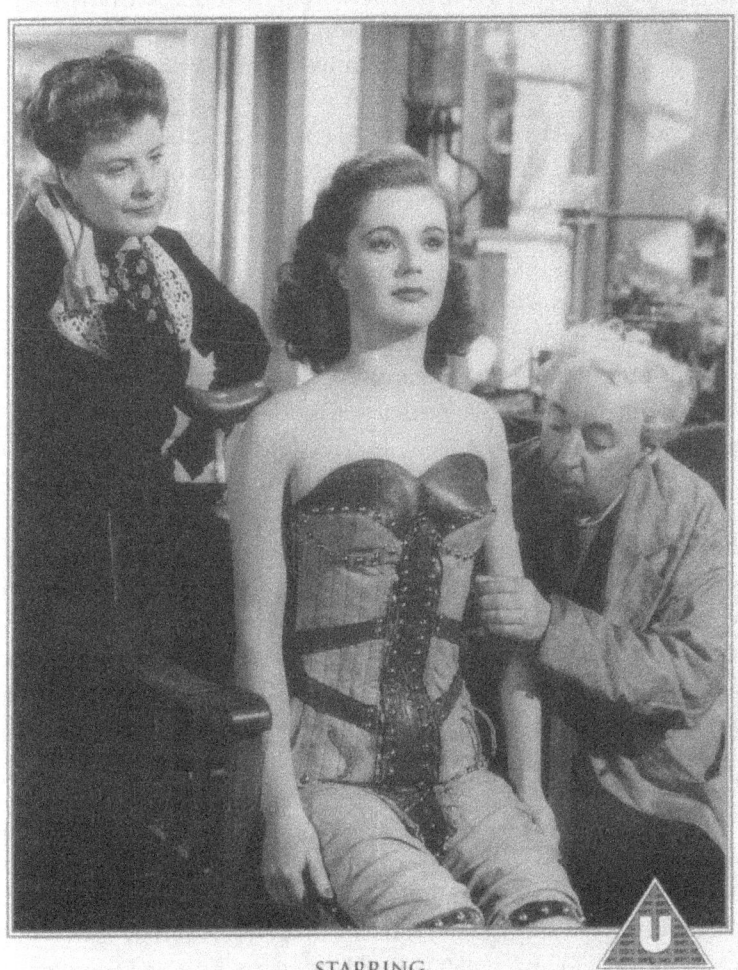

FIGURE 5.2 Full frontal of robot Olga (author's collection)

resentment of real women being asked to dress or be dressed as illusory creatures they resemble.

In the meantime, Miles Malleson (the professor) hires an impecunious gent, Roger Cavendish (Nigel Patrick), who comes complete with a valet, Ramshead (played by Stanley Holloway), to test out Olga the automaton in public before the professor shares his exciting invention with the scientific community. They take on the task with some trepidation as the dotty scientist and the explosions emanating from his laboratory are unmistakeable signs that they are entering the territory of the horror genre. The cinematic allusions are played for laughs and continue with Malleson's obvious pride in his creation. He calls her the perfect woman (although he points out that, strictly speaking, she has no sex) and claims that no other man has managed such an achievement, a mechanical model of femininity.

The professor celebrates the fact that this electronic dummy does as she is told, does not need to eat and does not talk. She responds to key words and has been wired to act on every verbal prompt so Olga's escorts should avoid the idiomatic and metaphorical use of phrases denoting movement. Olga will also go into a combative defence mode if the word 'love' is uttered in her presence. This sets the scene for the slapstick situations that follow.

When the disorganized professor realizes he has double booked his own evening and has to disappoint his niece Penelope by cancelling their attendance at the university ball, Buttercup contrives a Coppelia-like strategy for the niece to masquerade as her robot double, Olga. In this way Penelope can leave the house with the handsome escort she has seen from the window, before making her way to the dance, which is the unexciting but only social highlight of her year. The plan is that Buttercup, the housekeeper, will bring Olga to the hotel where Cavendish's valet has booked the bridal suite as the only available set of rooms. Olga will be swiftly and secretly substituted for Penelope. The ruse will also enable the niece to wear some of the fashionable and flattering outfits Penelope and Buttercup have bought for Olga.

Penelope takes up position under the dustsheet in her uncle's laboratory. The comedy duo (Cavendish and Ramshead) arrive and they search for the robot, uncovering an arm and a pair of legs before finding Olga. Paintings of the artist's studio with its half-finished sculptures may have inspired this scene of a room of incomplete robotic body parts. There is certainly an element of ritual in the unveiling of this modern equivalent of the statue.[17] The two men admire her facial features and the 'lovely wobbly bits on the backs of her legs'. Their sense of awe in front of a model of perfection, a mechanical work of art, does not stop them touching and prodding what they believe

FIGURE 5.3 Unveiling of Penelope (author's collection)

to be a miraculous automaton. Patrick in particular is almost immediately besotted with Olga, predicting that no home will be without one.

Penelope is able to react to their careless and colloquial conversation (for instance 'she's a real slap-up job!') with appropriate movements. Playing the robot programmed to obey instructions literally enables her to discomfit the men and is the mainstay of the comedy for much of the film. The articulate woman who has to impersonate a voiceless but voice-activated dummy manages to manipulate the situation without saying a word. Penelope is as resourceful as Ovid's Echo in finding ways around a lack of autonomous speech. Pat Roc plays the role with her usual mixture of the minx and the modest maiden (she was evidently a lot racier off screen than the parts she tended to be given on screen). Her masquerade as the robot is slightly satirical in suggesting the concealed power superficially subservient and silenced females of any variety possess.

Penelope must pretend that she cannot eat, drink or speak, so the evening in the bridal suite is hardly an enjoyable experience. By the time that Buttercup has reached the hotel with Olga the game is up. Roger and Ramshead have taken off Penelope / Olga's dress and laid her on the hotel bed where Roger's interfering aunt, shocked and sceptical at his insistence that the girl is a robot, sticks a pin in her. She screams and cries and the revelation that she is flesh and blood delights the hero. Penelope and

FIGURE 5.4 Pat Roc and Holloway relaxing on set (author's collection)

Roger exchange chaste on-the-cheek kisses in these last scenes, which are punctuated with more misunderstanding and knockabout comedy.

Penelope makes the first move and a pleasantly surprised Roger has a delayed reaction: 'You kissed me'. Pygmalion's statue would never have been so bold. In *The Perfect Woman* the invention of an unfeeling and unthinking robot allows a real rather repressed girl to find freedom from seclusion and be handled by men who admire her body aesthetically without desiring it sexually. There is a sting in the tail for the feminist spectator as this leads rapidly to romance once the girl feigning to be an inert *simulacrum* reveals herself as a living creature. Masquerading as the robot she has fallen in love with the hero.

When the 'real' robot, Olga is stabbed by the aunt, still determined to demonstrate her ability to feel, her circuits start to go haywire and Roger's declaration of love to Penelope sends the robot rampaging through the hotel. The automaton has been designed with a built-in chastity mechanism or has it? Uttering the word 'love' sends Olga into overdrive and she rushes wildly about rather like a Bacchante. Olga's resistance to erotic overtures recurs in a much later screen robot, namely, April in Season Five of *Buffy the Vampire Slayer*. It is paradoxical that love, the embodiment of Venus, proves a trigger for the perfect woman to show her powers not of seduction but of destruction. In this respect, Olga is a true heir to the mechanical Maria, the agent provocateur in Fritz Lang's *Metropolis*, although she is not programmed to be consciously psychotic. Olga is not the first or last female automaton to display unpredictable and Pandora-like characteristics, after appearing to be modelled on the myth of Pygmalion's statue. In *The Perfect Woman* there are no apocalyptic consequences of her malfunction apart from a classical pillar being toppled over in her wake, which is probably not symbolic of anything in particular!

A Sophisticated Spin-Off from Olga: Julie Newmar as a Living Doll

The comical robot girl reappeared in the 1960s, in an American series *My Living Doll* (created by Bill Kelsey and Al Martin). This had a relatively short run (26 episodes from September 1964 to September 1965) but was highly rated at the time. It lost out in the viewing stakes to soap operas like the Western series *Bonanza* and tensions between the main stars, Julie Newmar and Bob Cummings, also contributed to its earlier than expected demise. Surviving episodes suggest that while the comedy was inventive and well paced, it was highly situational and had limited capacity for plot or character development.[18]

In *My Living Doll*, Dr Carl Miller (Henry Beckman) has designed a prototype robot for the US Air Force. He sends Rhoda the robot to his friend, the psychologist Bob McDonald (played by Robert Cummings) as he wants her kept out of the hands of the military, at least for the time being. Julie Newmar took the part of the robot girl. When Rhoda is first introduced to the audience she is naked under a blanket in Cumming's bachelor pad and he has to pass her off as his sister to visitors. The unveiling of Rhoda (a surviving clip) is slightly reminiscent of the dust sheet scene in *The Perfect Woman*. Newmar had to play naïve and sexy simultaneously. Bob is supposed to be completing her education so she can be the perfect woman (there is a scene in which she plays the piano) and this echoes the acquiring of social and artistic accomplishments by Eliza in Shaw's play.

The push buttons on her back (her control panel) are disguised as beauty spots (moles) and she is on the surface a shapely secretary who is super-efficient at her job. Her catch phrase 'It does not compute' when faced with illogical or unknown situations or statements has become part of SF repertoire. The humour springs from the grooming of the robot to become the sort of woman who is always willing to serve men at work and at home. Being laconic and direct is definitely one of her virtues in the eyes of admiring males. Bob's neighbour falls for her and a smitten business client proposes to her while she is performing as the perfect secretary in the psychologist's office. Cummings has to extricate his robot girl from the entanglement. She may not be a destructive Eve but like her artificial sisters across the cultural spectrum she is liable to attract attention with her combination of directness and distance. Rhoda is subservient but her servility is spiced with an unpredictable quality. As she is emotionally remote, the men who desire her tend to detect in her the slow burn of a passion she cannot possibly feel. The male supplies the warmth and is happy in his delusion!

The Robot Wife as Rom Com

The Pygmalion premise is significant in the film *Cherry 2000*, which deserves attention for this and other mythical resonances incorporated into the storyline. However, *Cherry 2000* is partly predicated upon the much darker *Stepford Wives* in imagining mass-produced robot companions in an America of the future. The first scene of *Cherry 2000* introduces a facsimile of an ideal wife, presenting her as caring, cooking and coquettish in rapid succession. The hero arrives home with flowers and a twentieth-century American soap opera appears to be underway. Cherry is designed to display a happy fulfilment in satisfying her man's every need, and is the kind of partner that supplanted real women in *The Stepford Wives*. She does have a limited capacity for absorbing 'interesting facts' from the television but intellectual engagement is beyond her programming. In Levin's book and in Forbes' film, Joanna realizes the truth when the replaced women no longer recognize words like 'atavistic' as it was not on the list they were asked to record unwittingly for the voice patterning and core vocabulary of their robot replacements.

Cherry, the robot wife, short circuits as she and her male owner have spontaneous sex among the soap suds on the kitchen floor. Her distressed husband Sam Treadwell (played by David Andrews) takes her to the robot repair shop but only the chip with her programming is salvageable. Sam does not want any of the modern models on display and the owner of the robot repair shop is very understanding. The Cherries are rare and valuable, a product of a bygone age when perfection in craftsmanship still existed 'and each one of those honeys had their own special magic and romance'. Nor can Sam accept the solace of flesh and blood women and he rejects his friends' efforts to tempt him with transactional sex at the after work club. He returns to his apartment and lies next to the inert Cherry whom he has placed carefully and lovingly beside him on the bed.

Cherry has reverted to statue state, frigid and unresponsive but Sam is mourning her as if she is a dead wife. In spite of the difficulties this futuristic Pygmalion decides he must find another Cherry model. Orpheus never seems far from the surface in the robot partner scenario. Certain, and by now I would hope, familiar correspondences with Ovid's myth rapidly emerge in the film. At home the hero has led a sheltered and secluded existence with his perfect woman who combines the characteristics of cheery American housewife, bustling about her domestic duties while preserving inexhaustible sex appeal and eternal allure. When Cherry reverts to an inanimate toy, Sam does not want a new and improved automaton, which is in itself interesting and shows the attachment he has formed to an outdated stereotype of womanhood in the form of Cherry.

For Sam in *Cherry 2000*, there is no real woman or wife acting as a blueprint for his robot partner although we do meet a human ex-girlfriend later in the film, one of several who did not fulfil his dreams and desires and was ultimately rejected. The artificial love of his life has technically died and so Sam contemplates a heroic journey to bring back Cherry. There is a remote possibility that this obsolete model might be found in the Las Vegas robot 'graveyard' (a warehouse of old parts and mannequins in a now deserted and dangerous complex of dilapidated buildings). The territory is controlled by psychotic gangs in a vaguely Mad Max world (Maltin, 2010, p. 239).

Outside of Sam's cocoon, his private paradise with a soap opera wife, the social fabric has broken down and he will need a tracker to see him safely through lawless and hazardous territory to the abandoned pleasure dome. So he goes to a Wild West bar to hire a sharp shooting mercenary willing as a guide to the 'graveyard' where he may be able to retrieve a Cherry 2000. The recommended gunslinger, E. Johnson (played by Melanie Griffith; the character's surname is significant as it is American slang for the male member), turns out to be a rough and plain-speaking antithesis to the domestic goddess, Cherry (Pamela Gidley).

After some hesitation, Sam hooks up with E and embarks upon a quest which Holtsmark (2001, in Winkler, ed.) views as a classic katabasis, the descent to an unknown sphere, a motif that crosses cinematic genres from the Western to Film Noir. Thus Sam, as both Pygmalion and Orpheus, teeters between the living and the mechanically dead, the civilized and the barbarous.

The film then metamorphoses into a road movie with Melanie's masculine skills and deportment providing a vague nod towards the female cowboys who outshoot Howard Keel in *Annie Get Your Gun* and *Calamity Jane* (see Chapter 4). At one point Sam reprises Bill Hickok's (Howard Keel) exasperated suggestion to Calam (Doris Day) that she does something about her dishevelled and dirty appearance. To which E responds contemptuously that real women cannot be glamour pusses 24 hours a day. Unfortunately Melanie Griffith as E. Johnson (incidentally the name of her ex-husband in real life, Don Johnson) gives a fairly flat and listless performance as the girl taught to be tough in a futuristic world. To be charitable this may have been a deliberate or directorial decision.

In contrast, Cherry (even the mark two model briefly brought back to life and providing actress Pamela Gidley with a second 'cameo' appearance) comes across as more animated if conversationally limited by her programming. The Melanie Griffith's character develops feelings for Sam and begins to discover her feminine side while managing some contemptuous and partially jealous imitations of the adoring robot wife along the way. Johnson (Griffith) conceals the Cherry chip in her pocket when Sam drops it in the first violent confrontation en route to the old robot factory. Griffith does have a good line in sulky expressions and smoulders in her first kiss or clinch with Sam, which is spoilt by the Cherry's voice chip going off in her jeans pocket. The sexual tension does not evaporate but constant attacks from the gang community prevent it from re-igniting until the end of the film when Sam has to decide which of the two women in his life (shiny Cherry or grubby 'E') to save from the psychopathic Lester and his henchmen.

Cherry 2000 is about the transformation of a man into a less superficial human being who by the end sacrifices his retrieved robot wife to rescue his real girl companion, realizing that he prefers the roughly hewn, morose and fierce fighter to the helpless and chirpy Cherry. This is corny stuff of course and the message is hardly profound but *Cherry 2000* does show a Pygmalion figure revived and redeemed, realizing that a life of unalloyed pleasure with a passive partner is far less interesting than trouble shooting with Johnson. He is also an Orpheus fit for a fairly bleak dystopian future but unlike Ovid's bard he confounds the myth by jettisoning his re-functioning 'wife' and keeping the female tracker Melanie Griffith on board. At least she does not put on a dress and presumably Sam never looks back.

Chapter 6

Bathos and Pathos: a *Simulacrum* among *Simulacra*

This chapter is devoted to a particularly significant mechanical girl, the robot April. I decided it was worth making this a 'stand alone' case study as the episode and the season in which it appears need a fair amount of contextualization. The artificial girlfriend of Season Five has a multi-functional role and is important to several story arcs in the series. In this respect, April remains one of the most versatile robots to be found on screen. Like her predecessors and indeed like Pygmalion's statue, April in the critically acclaimed American television series, *Buffy the Vampire Slayer*, has distinct affinities with Maria, Olga and Rhoda. With a pliable material covering the circuit board which is her midriff, she is not a cyborg but a programmed and propelled body whose production has been motivated by one man's need for a devoted girlfriend. April corresponds closely to Pygmalion's statue, for her sole function is to satisfy a range of physical and emotional needs for her creator. He is the producer and the consumer and he does not intend to start an industry or display April as the technological work of art she clearly is. This uncanny creature does not require a divinely assisted awakening but her movements and responses are at the mercy of her creator's needs and desires.

'I Was Made to Love You'

Buffy the Vampire Slayer Season Five, Episode 15.

I indicated in the introduction that Joss Whedon's series following the fortunes of a petite and fashion-conscious female vampire slayer became a cultural phenomenon and continues to be discussed at conventions and academic conferences. The online site, Slayage, boasts an ever-expanding bibliography of papers, articles and books on the many layers of *Buffy*.

From 1997 to 2003, avid viewers followed the fortunes of the chosen one, the initially reluctant hero figure, Buffy Anne Summers, from her arrival at Sunnydale High School, a fictional suburbia of Southern California. She is forced to accept her role as the Slayer of vampires and demons as Sunnydale and specifically Sunnydale High is built over the Hellmouth, a geographical fault line which allows the undead as well as other monstrous phenomena to leak into the apparently normal 'pleasantville' above.

Whedon's whimsical worldview (the Buffverse) comprised a rich pick and mix of science fiction and fantasy, folk lore and mythological motifs with a similarly eclectic choice of philosophical themes situated within a generally subversive and constantly questioning ideological framework. Belief systems from the major religions to the cult of Wicca and modern paganism were regularly enmeshed within storylines where the supernatural was both real and metaphorical at the same time. An important premise of the show's setting was that teenage years at an American High School could not just feel like but actually become a Hellmouth. Demons of self-doubt and the nightmares of peer group pressure jockey for position with flesh and blood monsters and apocalyptic close calls emanating from the ancient forces that regularly break through the surface of suburbia.[1]

With the support of a talented team of writers and co-directors, Whedon accessed and refashioned a fascinating and sometimes bewildering variety of genres, literary, artistic, musical and cinematic to represent the transformation and 'graduation' of his characters with Buffy as the fulcrum of this heroic journey.[2] In Season One, fellow students (Ale) Xander Harris (Nicholas Brendon) and Willow Rosenberg (Alyson Hannigan) join teenage Buffy in fighting evil. Buffy's watcher (a mentor, trainer and ultimately a father figure) is an English librarian at the school. Rupert Giles (Anthony Stewart Head)' respectability and generally stuffy but endearing demeanour hides an unconventional past. Middle-aged Giles is now an authority figure, one of the Watchers' Council, but his experience and strength comes from a rebellious adolescence and forays into the dangerous territory of magic and the occult (to say nothing of his abiding aspiration to be a rock star). He can wield weapons against supernatural forces as well as conducting research into their origins, powers and apocalyptic tendencies.

Buffy's team are her emotional support network with Xander as a dependable and loyal friend always half in love with the Slayer. He has no special slaying talents but he does become a skilled carpenter when his friends go onto college. He is capable of sudden psychological insights and acts of bravery beyond the call of duty. In fact at least one commentator has made a persuasive argument that he is the Holy Fool figure of the series, always ready to sacrifice himself to the cause and to saving the world.[3] This is generally Buffy's province – she does it 'a lot' (the epitaph her friends have inscribed on her gravestone) but Xander brings his humanity and wisdom to comfort the group at crisis points. In contrast, Willow is a high-flying student and academically astute, expert in computer technology. In later seasons she proves adept in 'the magics' and her exceptional talents as a witch very nearly corrupt her irrevocably. During her time at the local college she becomes romantically involved with Tara (Amber Benson), a shy and gentle but very perceptive practitioner of Wicca magic.

There are also two vampires with whom Buffy has intense relationships; in the earlier seasons Buffy falls in love with Angel (David Boreanaz) whose soul has been restored. After a temporary lapse into his evil persona, Angelus, in Season Two, which causes great grief for the Buffy team, he moves to Los Angeles (to fight evil in his own spin-off series). The second significant demonic lover for Buffy is Spike (aka William the Bloody, so-called because of the bloody awful poetry he used to write as a repressed Victorian youth in his human and prelapsarian existence). Spike (James Marsters) is less brooding and tortured than Angel, the older vampire who centuries before sired Spike's beloved Drusilla (Juliet Landau). Dru made Spike into one of the undead so this trio are very much 'family' falling in and out of alliance with each other and demonstrating sexual tensions with incestuous and homoerotic undertones. Spike sees himself as The Big Bad since Angel's reformation and functions as Buffy's arch-enemy (or at least the most persistent one) until he realizes in Season Four that he has a passionate craving for her.

Spike's erotic obsession horrifies Buffy and it is not until Season Six that the traumatized Slayer summoned back from her grave by Willow's spell embarks upon a sado masochistic sexual affair with Spike (thus finally fulfilling the fantasies of fansites associated with the series). English Spike is a wonderfully comic commentator on Buffy, her friends and the demons they spar with and slaughter. Rendered harmless (also in Season Four) by a chip in his head (an operation carried out by a covert government operation in Sunnydale, a militarized scientific outfit called the Initiative) he starts attacking his own kind for sport and excitement. Hence he becomes an unpredictable and not always welcome sidekick of the Slayer and her team. By Season Four Anyanka (Emma Caulfield), an ex-vengeance demon, who has lost her powers and been reduced to a normal young woman, has attached herself to Xander and she too is a humorous foil in the Slayer circle. Anya struggles to understand the conventions of modern American society and she can be startlingly and hilariously astute about its values and hypocrisies.

April the robot takes centre stage for just one episode in Season Five.[4] Early in the episode, she emerges from a car telling the driver she is in search of true love. Petite and pretty in a demure kind of way (her skimpy dress might be provocative if she did not have such a wide open and childlike face), she stands out in Sunnydale from the moment of her arrival. On first appearance, she is an innocent and very likely to become a victim in this unusual American suburbia, which has so many sinister and supernatural creatures lurking beneath its surface. In fact, Sunnydale is akin to Ovid's numinous landscape in the *Metamorphoses* and April has all the characteristics of a victim, a ready prey for the vampires and demons who stalk its streets by night. She could be a carefree classical nymph courting danger and the guy she has hitched a lift from is clearly concerned that she is letting herself loose and on her own in a now notoriously weird environment.

April very rapidly proves she is able to look after herself. She is single-mindedly looking for her boyfriend Warren Mears (Adam Busch) and chirpily asks perfect strangers (including two of the Slayer's 'gang', Anya and Tara) if they have seen him or know where he is. Her search takes her to the college campus bar where Buffy and friends witness her super strength when she throws vampire Spike out of the window for propositioning her. April has a combat mode worthy of the mechanical psychotic, Eve in *Eve of Destruction*. April's aggression is also triggered by anyone making sexual advances to her. She may not be virginal but she preserves herself for one man, her maker Warren. Once the danger is passed (and the danger is anyone who threatens her relationship with Warren), April readily reverts to a naïve and direct way of engaging with those around her. Buffy and the gang quickly conclude that the new girl in town is a robot and start researching into possible owners. Clearly April is a loose cannon and could do serious damage in her obsessive search.

April turns out to be Warren's creation. A computer genius, he has produced a mechanical miracle in designing a living *simulacrum* that is perfect in every detail, and programmed to offer him unquestioning devotion. Britney Spears was considered to play the part of the automaton, which would have compromised April's cultural anonymity. On the other hand, it would have made sense that Warren might model his artificial girl on a current celebrity. Shonda Farr took on the role and made it her own; as a lesser known actress she was a better fit for the slightly dated air and demeanour April displays throughout the episode. April needs to be a cultural stereotype rather than a stereotypical star. She is also closer to the statue by having no obvious model but being in her fictional context a composite from Warren's imagination.

When Buffy tracks Warren down and confronts him as April's creator he insists that his robot was not a toy but that he had made a girlfriend. He is surprised that April is readily recognizable as a robot, which suggests that he does have some pride in his talent as a modern-day mechanical sculptor whose facsimile is so compellingly real on the surface. Warren confesses to Buffy that he left April in his dorm room, assuming her batteries would run down and never imagining she would come after him. He has abandoned his artificial girlfriend for the independent, unfussy and liberated Katrina (Amelinda Smith). Katrina is in his engineering class at college; she makes models and she is entertaining and funny, keeping Warren on his toes. She has a mind of her own and 'edges to her' and while giving Warren 'a hard time', seems to be bringing him to life, socializing him in a way that April could never do. He tells Buffy that his robot 'was exactly what I wanted, and I didn't want her'.

Warren's creation of a perfect girlfriend for private consumption (he does not want to share or publicize this brilliantly crafted technological miracle) is very reminiscent of Ovid's mythical sculptor. There are certain refinements to Warren's design that raise questions about the ethics as well as the aesthetics of creating a creature for private pleasure. Warren has wired April to feel electric shocks if she is at all tardy in obeying his commands. This may seem a far cry from Pygmalion's solicitous treatment of his statue girl but the ivory maiden would have had very little room for manoeuvre when she awoke to his embraces in the secluded boudoir. Warren most definitely parts company with the Pygmalion figure because he is tired of perfect and accommodating April once he finds a real girl to go out with. Pygmalion was more than satisfied by his creation once she was vivified by the apparent intervention of Venus.

Warren has fallen in love with Katrina but such information is likely to send April into meltdown. In the meantime Katrina, already a little perturbed by the arrival of the comely Buffy as she is leaving Warren's house, encounters April in the Sunnydale playground. April asks her usual question about the whereabouts of Warren and Katrina replies in no uncertain terms that she (Katrina) is Warren's girlfriend. She prefaces this dangerous declaration with a question of her own 'How many of you are there?' April's response 'There's only me, April' means more than Katrina could possibly know at this stage. The meeting of the constructed and the natural girl, both rivals for Warren's affections, points up the contrast between them. Katrina looks strong and assertive. She is casually dressed in trousers and T-shirt and wears no visible make-up while April seems younger and more fragile in her pretty pink dress and with her slightly plastic expression.

However (and this comes as no surprise to the viewer), Katrina's statement goads April into an assault. A true heir to Anstey's marble Aphrodite and Vanna White's Venus, Warren's creation likes to crush and she takes her rival's throat into a vice-like grip. Buffy and Warren discover April holding Katrina up by the neck asking if she is broken. The real girl dangles rather like a rag doll or an automaton while robot April looks anxious and perplexed. Once the still breathing Katrina has recovered, Buffy insists Warren tells April the truth and 'does it right'. As Warren attempts to reason with her, we see April's internal programme files listing positions for sex and other erotic functions with just a few directions about emotional support and comforts she can provide her godlike maker. April has knitted Warren five sweaters in his absence and is all ready to give him a neck rub. She cannot accept that Warren has made a mistake or that he no longer cares for her.

Warren then pretends he loves Buffy to distract April. He runs after a shocked and disgusted Katrina with the comic reassurance that his robot was not just for sex.

Buffy now has to face the incensed and jealous robot which Warren has programmed to growl prior to combat and crushing. Once again the perfect girl of post-classical invention shows herself to be partly bestial to complicate an already unstable combination of human, divine and mechanical. Buffy fights April in the playground and in broad daylight finding her harder to beat than the vampires she disposes of regularly at night in Sunnydale cemetery. Significantly she does not intersperse her martial art fighting techniques with her usual wordplay and fun puns about her foe's imminent defeat. Instead the fight with the robot is a close call until Buffy manages to damage her circuits. April finally starts to malfunction ('I can't crush, so tired') and there is a cut to a tranquil scene. Buffy sits next to April on the swings and now that the battle is over attempts to save her feelings.

The bereft robot asks why Warren has gone again. She has checked everything and she was a 'good girlfriend'. In response to her question 'if I can't love him, what do I exist for?' Buffy says 'It isn't fair; he wasn't fair to you'. The 'what's to become of me' lament of past Pygmalion girls is implicit in April's disturbed ontological status.

April gives voice but still without choice to the silent statue in Ovid – she condemns Warren out of his own mouth, expressing his narcissism and his lack of imagination in producing a real girl. The robot can never have edges to it and Warren has given her mostly comforting clichés to utter: 'Every cloud has a silver lining. When life gives you lemons, make lemonade'. The Stepford wives' restricted discourse is brought to mind. By this time April is shutting down and her voice deepens reminding us that she was only ever an extension of Warren.[5] And yet she still elicits our sympathy as well as Buffy's when she notes that it is getting dark and it is so early to be dark. April or her batteries seem finally to be 'dying'.

The scene counterposes the myth in Ovid. The statue is brought to life and sees her lover against the light of the sky.[6] The ivory girl gazes upon Pygmalion who desperately desires her. April closes down abandoned with a frozen smile of hope on her face, as the light fades for her. The camera draws back so that Buffy still and pensive and the inert robot are viewed from above. They could be two teenage girls in naturalistic poses on the children's swings, emphasizing innocence perhaps, but also placing Buffy in a location associated with nostalgia and emotional regression.[7] Like Ovid's text, Whedon's television is rarely straightforward or without narrative angles.

For instance, Warren is destined to reappear in Season Six with delusions of grandeur and with an even greater propensity to play god. In Season Five, he is a comical and pathetic Pygmalion figure but he returns in the next season with a much more darkly misogynist agenda, attempting to destroy Buffy and control events in Sunnydale with sidekicks Andrew and Jonathan. His ethical demise is not my focus here but it is significant that he attempts to superimpose April's compliant nature upon Katrina whose independence and humanity he had once valued. In Season Six, he seeks out Katrina and with the help of a mind control mechanism (a magic ball) briefly compels her to call him her master and to be sexually submissive to him. The consequences are tragic when the effects wear off. A disgusted Katrina justifiably accuses him of rape and attempts to leave. Warren strikes Katrina and she falls and dies. Hers is the fate we might have predicted for April when she first came into view. Katrina is the victim not of a male deity but of a man with a temporary strength to control and abuse her, one who uses his power without any reference to a moral compass.

The Robot Girl in a World of Constructs and Illusions

The April storyline of Season Five continues to resonate across a number of narrative arcs. It would appear that as things fall apart for April at the end of 'I was made to love you,' for Buffy they fall into place. From the beginning of the episode, Buffy has been thinking of dating again but has decided this requires her to be more accommodating and girlish, to be what men want. The superstrength that is the core of her slayer persona has been a factor in the break down of her previous intimate relationships. She is also worried about brittleness and a lack of feeling as obstacles to 'true love' and wonders if her inability to show her feelings to her recently departed boyfriend Riley is part of the self-obsession or narcissism that comes with the territory of being a chosen hero. Listening to April 'made to love Warren' and hearing her agonize over what she has done wrong, Buffy realizes that she too has been attempting to be what pleases a potential partner, conforming to the stereotype, wanting to be a good girlfriend. She has fallen into the trap of thinking she must have a man to define her.

If 'I was made to love you' had been a stand-alone episode designed solely to send a message to Buffy about getting to know yourself and avoiding the stereotypes of femininity, it would not come across as particularly subtle. However, followers of the whole series recognize that the brief appearance of April gathers up and simultaneously develops several storylines, lending psychological shading to the main characters. I am reminded of the Ovidian technique of transforming the reader's perceptions and disturbing the equilibrium of narratives like Pygmalion by repeating and counter-posing motifs appearing in previous and subsequent myths. Buffy is connected to April on more than one level but April also forms part of a complicated thematic in Season Five concerning constructed creatures, invulnerable deities and human mortality.

Glory (Glorificus) is Season Five's 'Big Bad', a seemingly unstoppable chaos god whom Buffy will die defeating. When April appears in Season Five, viewers have already been introduced to Glory played by Clare Kramer.[8] Kramer does a delightful pastiche of a mean girl / blonde bimbo whose devotion to tight dresses and high heels belies her enormous physical power and divine stature. Buffy complains in exasperation that she 'is tired of strong little women who aren't me!' when April comes onto the scene, suggesting that both god and robot are reflections and rivals to her identity. A further irony of the April episode is that the personable and sensitive young doctor Ben whom Buffy is considering as a boyfriend shares his body with Glory through some quirk of the colliding dimensions that have catapulted the god through Sunnydale's Hellmouth. When Buffy rings to cancel her tentative coffee date with Ben, Glory picks up the message and says rather ruefully to her minions 'The slayer turned us down?'

In the 'normal' run of things, Glory is stalking Buffy and has started persecuting her friends because the Slayer is hiding and protecting the mystical key the god needs to return to her own universe (the hell fires of home as Glory puts it). The key has been sent to Buffy in the form of a younger sister, Dawn. During Season Five, Dawn has to deal with the discovery that she is not a real girl and that she is in fact a shaft of bright energy, which if used to open demonic portals will cause dimensions to bleed catastrophically into each other. Potentially a Pandora figure, Dawn has been accepted as an annoying fourteen-year-old by Buffy and her friends even when they find out her true nature and realize their memories have been tampered with. Dawn is a construct but like normal teenagers she doubles as a bundle of adolescent hormonal energy searching for an identity. Her integration into the loving but strange social world of the Scoobies is what ensures her transition to humanity and allows her sham past as Buffy's sibling to become authenticated.

April, then, is not the first or last artificial or uncanny creature to highlight human characters in Sunnydale whose own nature proves illusory or liminal. Even Anya's comment upon April's rather stilted speech patterns and strangely direct questioning is ironic in that Anya, the ex-vengeance demon, also tends towards the aberrant and inappropriate in conversation and behaviour. She too is wearing her humanity as an alien form. April also inspires the character of Spike to commission an exact replica of Buffy from a reluctant Warren. Although robot and slayer on the swings has been set up as a satisfying finale and certainly shot cinematically as if the credits were about to roll, there are several subsequent scenes.

Buffy celebrates her new-found self-worth with Xander and we see Spike visiting Warren and handing over a box of specifications so that his robot will be a true image of the slayer with all her physical attributes and slayer skills. Having discarded the crudely made model of Buffy he keeps secretly in his crypt, Spike commissions an exact *simulacrum* of the Slayer with which he can play out his erotic fantasies. (They will beat each other up and then have sex.[9]) Even this scene is a false finale and the episode ends with Buffy returning home eager to find out how her mother's date with Brian, a nice new man, has gone. Seeing a lovely bouquet in the hallway, she utters the line, 'still some guys getting it right' and then enters the lounge to find her mother dead on the couch from an aneurism. Although Joyce Summers, played by Kristine Sutherland, has tragically died of natural causes she is laid out like an automaton. At the beginning of the next episode 'The Body' Buffy has a brief fantasy moment that she has resuscitated her mother before the terrible realization that there is no coming back for Joyce.[10]

The tragedy of Joyce's sudden relapse after an apparently full recovery from her operation is heightened because she has found a nice and cultured man to go out with and has been discussing what to wear and how to behave with her daughters at the beginning of the episode. She teases Dawn and Buffy about losing her bra and is once again full of life. Later in 'I was made to love you', Dawn refers to an incident of some years before (from Season Two, an episode simply called 'Ted'[11]) when Joyce found a perfect boyfriend in Ted (played by the late John Ritter) her first romantic attachment since her divorce.[12] Ted won over everyone except Buffy who did not buy into this caring, cookie-baking paragon of virtue. Her friends and also Giles and Angel assumed that Buffy was displaying typical teenage angst and jealousy about a replacement for her father.

However, when the manipulative Ted struck Buffy and she retaliated with her slayer strength, accidentally 'killing' him, he turned out to be a robot, like April. He had once been human but had mechanized himself to survive beyond the 1950s. A modern technological Bluebeard (or Stepford husband) he had been working through a succession of women, discarding them as they aged or if they disappointed him. Joyce very nearly became the victim of a Pygmalion with a twist as Ted kept his ideal woman by his side by replacing his models regularly. He made over and transformed himself into an artificial being who could be effortlessly and eternally efficient and dissembling. Ted took on the guise of a liberated and enlightened man in his search for a suitable woman in the 1990s, but he could not sustain this sham as his chauvinist values and expectations had been set in stone for five decades.

Further Pygmalion resonances of April re-emerge two episodes after Joyce's death. The finished Buffy robot has been completed and provides some welcome light relief in the eighteenth episode *Intervention*. The robot is ready for Spike at the same time as Buffy is taking a trip to the desert to explore her origins and identity as the slayer. In the opening scene of *Intervention*, we see the real bereaved Buffy confiding in Giles that she feels she has been 'shutting down'. Giles tries to comfort Buffy by immediately praising her resilience and strength but she points out that these are words for hardness and that for some time, before Joyce's death, she felt as if she were 'turning into stone'.

While Buffy is encountering the spirit of the first Slayer from primeval times and receiving the cryptic and gloomy message that 'death is your gift', her replica back in Sunnydale is programmed to slay and cheerily starts patrolling the cemetery after satisfying Spike with various sexual acrobatics. Seeing the robot slayer straddling Spike in the cemetery, Buffy's friends are bemused by their friend's behaviour and put it down to a form of grieving. They are totally fooled by Warren's robot, even though they had recently identified the artificial sheen and demeanour of his earlier automaton, April. Of course, April had no obvious model but it is still surprising that the Buffybot deceives the gang so easily.

This robot is evidence of Warren's improved engineering and computer skills and convinces because of its uncanny resemblance to the real Buffy. Even when the two Buffies meet in the Summers' house, the gang do not realize what has happened. The real Buffy is not best pleased that her close friends could not tell her apart from an automaton and reminds them of that thing Warren made. It is worth noting that Buffy's touching moment with Warren's sad mechanical girlfriend on the swings has totally faded from her consciousness. She does not name April and she contemptuously refers to her own double as 'skirt girl'.[13]

The reflective relationship between human and robot Buffy is not at an end although the Buffybot is damaged at the end of the episode and the Scoobies put her into cold storage. Thomas (2006, p. 202) observes that when Buffy imitates her own robot *simulacrum* and visits Spike (to ascertain what, if anything, he told Glory under torture)

> a statue just behind her may remind us of Buffy's confession to Giles earlier in the episode that being the Slayer is turning me into stone.

When real Buffy impulsively kisses Spike for not betraying her and Dawn, it is the vampire's Pygmalion moment. His true beloved has come alive, exposing the second best that was the programmed Buffybot. As Buffy says to Spike, the robot girlfriend was gross and 'not real'.

The Buffybot is given another outing by the Scoobies at the end of Season Five to help defeat Glory. At the beginning of Season Six, this replica robot replaces Buffy (who sacrificed herself to save Dawn and the world) in all her roles at home and out and about in Sunnydale. It has been noted by Calvert and Thomas that the Buffybot functions as an object to be loved as well as being programmed to care and to love itself. It is also crucial that the Buffybot deceives the demons and vampires into believing that the Slayer is still alive and kicking. Sarah Michelle Gellar performs her part as robot Buffy with a real joie de vivre during the first double episode of Season Six ('Bargaining' 1 and 2).[14]

The relentlessly cheery Buffybot functions as an idealized version of the slayer, restoring something of the human Buffy's youthful chirpiness and being used as an emotional substitute by Dawn who actually lies down on the bed next to her as if she were the real thing. Soon after, the Buffybot is torn apart by a demon biker gang, just as buried Buffy is clawing her way out of her grave, compelled to leave her peaceful heavenly dimension by Willow's summoning spell.[15] This is a Eurydice moment except that Buffy 'comes back wrong' or at least psychologically traumatized. Much of Season Six focuses upon Buffy's inability to cope with being back in the world as she tries to hide her emotional distance from her friends and her weariness with her mission.

The resurrected Buffy suffers from feelings of liminality and displacement which the ivory of Pygmalion's statue symbolizes for so many subsequent synthetic constructs of womanhood. Anya describes the resurrected Buffy as 'broken'. The relationship between the living and the dead is always complicated in *Buffy the Vampire Slayer* because vampires are the undead and Buffy herself 'dies' twice during the course of the show. Once again the statue as corpse and the revenant as replicant seem to be reasserting themselves in a storyline. Buffy reveals the truth about the heavenly dimension she was torn out of by her friends in the musical episode of Season Six, 'Once more with feeling'. In this episode, a Hades figure, Mr Sweet played by Hinton Battle, is inadvertently summoned up by Xander and this king of Hell infects the inhabitants of Sunnydale with a compulsion for bursting into song and dance (and then spontaneously combusting). During their forays into various musical styles (from Rogers and Hammerstein to Rock and Heavy Metal) Buffy and her friends reveal their secrets and their inner-most traumas.

The opening song is Buffy's confession to a chorus of vampires that she has been 'going through the motions' of feeling and fighting. By the end of the 'show' Buffy can no longer conceal from her friends her horror at being back in a garish and violent world. As the credits go up she falls into a clinch with Spike and soon after starts a clandestine relationship with the vampire. Their intense and violent sex staves off the numbness of her existence. So Buffy re-enacts the role of the Buffybot but it is Spike who is now the sex toy. When she finally addresses her addiction and breaks off her secret liaison she expresses remorse in a speech to Spike. 'I am using you and it's killing me. I'm sorry, William.' It is significant that she calls the vampire by his human name.

Reprising the Role of April

Jane Espenson who wrote the episode about the robot girlfriend does not acknowledge Pygmalion as a source or inspiration in the DVD voice-over feature. Thomas (2006) assumes that the episode still has the mark of Whedon upon it and the cinematic references it does contain emanate from him. I found it intriguing that Espenson had chosen the name April for Warren's robot and that she was aiming to give a festive and vernal ambience to the episode set in the Spring break. The robot's floral print dress epitomizes April as Spring itself. April is Venus' sacred month in the Roman calendar (Ovid's *Fasti*, Book Four, lines 85–92,) and if April's uncomplicated personality is a breath of spring air and a hymn to simplicity and artlessness, her super strength puts her on a par with a goddess. Technically she could be an immortal; roaming the suburbs of Sunnydale she has the qualities of persistence and self-assurance that mark out an Ovidian god in pursuit of an object of desire. She has a remarkable run on her batteries after all. April has come to Sunnydale for True Love but she is an embodiment of True Love herself and her presence summons up the Pygmalion statue and his patron goddess simultaneously.

Clearly April and later the Buffybot are designed as fetichized females – no change there then from Pygmalion and his elegiac and compliant mistress – but the modern day mechanical maidens go beyond the raison d'être envisaged by their creators. They certainly teach some of the mortals who meet them important lessons about feeling, suffering and the meaning of life. Warren learns nothing by playing Pygmalion and seems to forget what he found lacking in biddable April. Artificial or synthetic copies of human beings whether made up from pieces of ivory, hewn from marble, or manufactured from plastics or pixels should force us to focus on what it is to be human or even superhuman. Through such uncanny creatures we reaffirm our identity, our independence and our socially determined moral compass. This is what happens to Buffy when she realizes that April only exists to give unqualified devotion to her creator.

Chapter 7

Virtually Perfect: Hi and Lo Tech Gals of the Computer Age

Introduction

This chapter focuses on *simulacra* that take shape from computer programmes but there are two exceptions to this category. They are included because both the artificial creatures under scrutiny appear in recent films and have some unexpected affinities as well as polarities with the constructed 'microchip' women who form the basis of my penultimate discussion. Dren, the genetically engineered organism in *Splice* (2010), and Bianca, the silicone doll in *Lars and the Real Girl* (2007), are in different ways two of the most up-to-date descendants of Pygmalion's ivory girl the twenty-first century has produced. Dren is biologically complex to the point of magic realism (a truly metamorphic creature) and Bianca is from a psychological viewpoint a sophisticated 'statue' substitute (in spite of being a crudely designed plastic facsimile of a real girl).

However, I shall look first at a computer generated being from the distant past in the history of television, the computer-generated Andromeda. She is the first in a line of superior imitations who, in their materialization out of virtual reality, enjoy the peculiar advantage of metamorphosing into flesh and blood. Such artificial beings emerge fully grown just as Athena did from the head of Zeus. They become completely 'biological' but a machine gives birth to them.

A Gift from the Gods: *A for Andromeda*

During October and November 1961 millions of television viewers tuned into Fred Hoyle and John Elliot's serial *A For Andromeda*, which was produced by Michael Haynes and Norman James. After a dip in audiences by Episode Two, the story took an intriguing turn as the mysterious radio messages from outer space are decoded by a brilliant young scientist, John Fleming. He realizes that the communications (later identified by the radio telescope as emanating from the Andromeda constellation) are a do-it-yourself kit for a super computer. When Fleming and his team have constructed the machine, it helps the scientists to develop a synthesized living organism. The serial kept audiences on their toes as it combined the concept of a not-too-distant and exciting scientific future (it is set in 1970!) with international industrial and political intrigue.[1]

Fleming is the Promethean figure who starts to suspect the agenda of a computer that masquerades as a bestower of beneficial knowledge from a higher intelligence. The scientist embodies both aspects of the Titan, Prometheus, in being himself a gift giver but also having the forethought (the meaning of the Titan's name) to detect the danger in developing the creature of the computer. In constructing the machine Fleming is praised for bestowing a significant scientific gain upon humankind but he recognizes the menacing nature of the body it has prompted the science team to gestate. Nevertheless, he is pressurized to make a direct link between the machine's electrical supply and the embryonic biological organism it has produced. This is the monster of Episode Four and it is appropriately nicknamed the Cyclops.

Once Fleming realizes that the 'gift' he has accessed for humanity from an alien planet (a modern equivalent of Olympus complete with the designation of the classical figure of Andromeda) is deceptive and destructive he angrily pleads with his superiors to reject it. His fears are justified; the machine manages to compel the young lab assistant Christine (to whom Fleming is attracted) to immolate herself on one of its exposed terminals and then proceeds to copy her likeness onto the synthesized being. Thus a biologically human but essentially a gynoid is born as a replica of Christine.

Julie Christie in an early role as Christine and then Andromeda was part of the drama's winning formula, especially when the laboratory assistant with her plain white coat and short black hair is transformed into the enigmatic and blonde Andromeda. Christine is described as 'a young postgraduate student, serious and pretty in a rather striking Baltic way'. Christine exhibits a certain amount of coolness and emotional detachment but Fleming behaves in a heartless and careless fashion towards her. He was written as 'a forceful and unconventional young man of thirty whose brain is better disciplined than his emotions'. However Christine's innate and very human vulnerability will seep through the sinews of the artificial woman who supplants her.

The stage directions state that when Andromeda is first revealed 'Her eyes are shut and she is breathing peacefully, as if asleep. She looks like a purified version of Christine'. Philip Purser wrote in his review for *The Sunday Telegraph* (12 November 1961) that 'Andromeda is a master stroke, attractive, sexy (the actress is Julie Christie) but more than that, a catalyst to make the plot fizz at last'. Previous reviewers had judged the plot so far a bit messy and characterization clichéd. With the vivification of the creature, named Andromeda by the scientists, the replay of the myth of Pandora is complete. Controlled by the alien computer and of highly advanced intelligence Andromeda becomes an object of scientific desire for all the stakeholders. Her ability to design a rocket capable of intercepting and destroying space satellites makes her hot governmental property and Fleming's disquiet and warnings about the alien machine's true agenda continue to be ignored.

The scientist sets about trying to sabotage the machine by subverting and challenging its control of Andromeda. The scene in which Fleming attempts to arouse a sensuous response in the cool now Nordic looking creature of the computer (close to a Hitchcock blonde) has a seductive air. It is one of the few surviving sequences of this historic production. Fleming treats the Pandora figure as if she were Pygmalion's unresponsive ivory girl and this reminds the reader that the manufacturing processes of Pandora and Pygmalion's statue have distinct correspondences. This is one of several subtexts in Ovid that tends to become the text when the myth is modernized. Fleming suppresses his irascibility and shows more patience, care and commitment in his relationship with Andromeda than he had managed with her human prototype. Once again the artificial woman prompts her creator to change and become emotionally involved.

The accompanying novel uses an interesting metaphor to capture the moment on screen when the scientist teaches Andromeda to feel:

> She looked at him solemnly. She might have been a statue with her fine carved face, her long hair and her arms hanging limply down beside her simple pale dress. 'Please be careful what you talk about', she said. Quietly and deliberately he pinched her arm. 'Ow!' she stepped back with a sudden look of fear in her eyes and rubbed the place where he had hurt her. 'Nice or nasty?' he inquired.

Fleming then strokes her cheek to show her what 'nice' means. This twentieth-century Andromeda, a distillation of a distant planetary system, is compared with a sculpture. This simile is the very one used in Ovid's *Metamorphoses* to describe how Andromeda appeared to Perseus, who stars in the legendary cycle the poet has condensed as a mini epic and narrated across Books Four and Five. In Book Four, lines 675–678, Ovid takes Perseus's perspective as he flies across the ocean upon the winged sandals he has borrowed from the divine messenger, Mercury. The Ethiopian princess had been chained to a rock as a sacrifice to appease the sea goddess Thetis. In the eyes of Perseus were it not for her tears and the wind ruffling her hair, Andromeda could have been a marble statue.

The hero, fresh from killing the gorgon Medusa (whose glance turned all things to stone), was so entranced at the sight of this beautiful maiden awaiting the sea monster that he forgot to flap the wings on his sandals and froze in mid-flight. Perhaps Fleming has finally discovered his heroic status in rescuing Christine/Andromeda from the fetters of her programming and the living death she is experiencing as a machine in a mortal body. Thus we can see (if we are inclined to) that this mythical moment in Ovid's *Metamorphoses*, which Classical scholars have interpreted as part of the persistent stone to flesh motif throughout the epic was re-forged in the pages of the science fiction novel.

The television serial ended on a cliff hanger with the episode, 'The Last Mystery', with the audience unsure if Andromeda had survived after helping Fleming in the defiant act of sabotaging the computer. (The penultimate episode, 'The Face of the Tiger' is the only one completely restored.) *A for Andromeda* was followed by *The Andromeda Breakthrough*, starring a young Susan Hampshire as the humanized heroine fighting against her programming and against the destructive capacity of the computer. By this time, it is putting its covert long-term plan into action, namely to strip away the air from earth and suffocate its peoples. Viewing figures remained healthy at around 6 million and in later years the two series were regarded as at least as significant in the history of science fiction on television as Nigel Kneale's acclaimed Quatermass productions.[2]

A 90-minute dramatization of *A for Andromeda* (shown on BBC 4 in November 2005) had none of the ambience of the earlier black and white serial. Viewing monochrome television in the twenty-first century has a novelty and nostalgia value that, along with echoing studio sound and the occasional shaky scenery, lends these now 50-year-old programmes an appropriate other worldliness. Better special effects and colour is no substitution for suspense and characterization.

A Home-Grown Pandora: *Splice*

Splice, a Canadian-French science fiction horror, premiered in 2009 (at the Sitges Film Festival) and had a generally positive response from reviewers. It picked up a special effects award and was nominated in the best film category at the Sundance Film Festival (Utah). Directed by Vincenzo Natali and produced by Steve Hoban and Guillermo del Toro, it enjoyed only a brief distribution in the UK but was more widely shown (through Warner Bros) in the United States during 2010. The film taps into fears about producing life through biological cloning and, as the title suggests, 'splicing' the DNA of different animals to create hybrids. The following synopsis comes with a Spoiler Warning.

The Nucleic Exchange Research and Development pharmaceutical company (NERD) have funded a team of genetic engineers led by Clive and Elsa (Adrien Brody and Sarah Polley). In order to isolate the gene that produces a 'magic' protein for use in curing disease, Clive and Elsa have grown two hybrid creatures (Fred and Ginger), which are biologically programmed to procreate. The hybrids are blobby chrysalis-like formations of tissue with long leafy tongues that reach out to each other in a love-at-first-sight moment when we first see them.

Elsa is the driving force in taking the cellular experiments forward while the company is cautious about any further genetic engineering and instructs the scientists to concentrate on isolating the key proteins from Fred and Ginger. In other words, the funders put a brake on future DNA blending. However Elsa and Clive continue their experiment in secret and another hybrid is created. This creature looks unpromising and frail from the outset but it grows at an accelerated rate after escaping from its tank. It develops as a foetus would (but outside the 'womb' of its incubator) and it becomes increasingly human and female in appearance apart from a tail with a toxic sting. Elsa names the hybrid Dren when at a child stage of development she spells out NERD from scrabble letters. Elsa and Clive discover that Dren is amphibious after Clive holds her under water.

Within months Dren is a fully grown girl, sentient and intelligent but unable to utter anything other than primitive sounds. Elsa and Clive hide Dren on Elsa's late mother's farm. Only Gavin, Clive's brother and one of the team is aware of the Dren experiment. Otherwise, her existence is kept secret especially since the early hybrids, Fred and Ginger, slaughter each other bloodily in a public presentation at the shareholders' meeting. The female has metamorphosed into a male so these experimental creatures are now mutually hostile instead of potential mates. Dren, in contrast, has grown into a nubile young woman and both Elsa and Clive encourage her to exhibit feminine behaviour. She responds to Elsa's maternal feelings and enjoys being dressed, made up and told she is beautiful.

However, Dren becomes restless in captivity. Spelling out 'tedious' to describe her imprisonment inside the barn, she disobeys Elsa and Clive and escapes through a sky light. High on the roof ridge she generates retractable wings. Although coaxed back down by Clive, Dren proves increasingly unpredictable (like a recalcitrant teenager). When she exhibits sudden aggressive and violent behaviour, Elsa removes her toxic glands and her stinger. Elsa then takes the tissue back to the lab in order to isolate and to synthesize the vital protein, which was the whole point of the original research.

There have been plenty of hints that Dren is potentially a Pandora figure, a first of her kind with a mystique and strange attractiveness that occludes her bestial attributes and appetites. (On arriving at the farm, she takes off into the woods, tears a rabbit apart and eats it raw.) She is seductive enough to arouse Clive erotically when he returns to the barn and tries to comfort her after Elsa's mutilating operation.[3] Elsa surprises them having sex and rushes off in disgust. Both Elsa and Clive realize that they have crossed boundaries in science and morality, and are out of their depth with the child they have created. They return contritely to the barn to find Dren apparently dying in her tank of water. They sorrowfully bury her placing her doll upon the grave.

The pace of the film then significantly quickens with a resurrected Dren (she was regenerating to her next phase not dying) attacking Clive, Elsa, Gavin and the manager of the pharmaceutical project in the woods. Gavin has brought the boss to see the hybrid but both are slaughtered by Dren who then dives into the lake and metamorphoses into a male. Elsa manages to smash Dren's head in but not before the creature has raped her with the hoarsely articulated words 'Inside you', and killed Clive with a newly grown stinger tail. In the final scene set in the company office the female Head (Simona Maicanescu) pledges to take care of a pregnant Elsa and hands over a large sum of money in exchange for her silence and for taking the experiment to the next stage. Elsa is clearly closed down emotionally and it would seem to me she craves a similar anonymity to Myrrha in Ovid's *Metamorphoses* as both women, viewing themselves as monstrous and uncanny wish to be excluded from the realms of the living and the dead.

The Mythical Process of Movie Making

Splice cannot be categorized as a Pygmalionesque narrative in any conscious and sustained sense. In the DVD interview, director Natali cited films in the horror genre, singling out the work of James Whale and the Frankenstein movies as important influences (as well as cinematic versions of *enfant sauvage* stories). [4] Natali developed the narrative and the screenplay of *Splice* (his collaborators were Doug Taylor and Antoinette Terry Bryant) with a vision of a creature that was plausible and appropriate for the twenty-first century, a monster that would mutate beyond the Mary Shelley paradigm and its Gothic successors. He did not mention Pygmalion's statue but he did allude to the ancient provenance of the fantasy that mortals could fall in love with creatures who are subhuman or superhuman, for instance, mermaids, sirens and angels.

Natali talked about *Splice's* long gestation and its fraught financial and production process in terms of a painful birth. The film took on a life of its own and was indeed a splicing of many skills by the time it reached the final stages. He delineated his care in creating Dren on screen using the language of metaphor and the imagery familiar to students of the Pygmalion myth. Fine art designers were employed to sculpt Dren's appearance from 'birth' with the facial contours of actress Delphine Chanéac (the adult Dren) in mind. Chanéac was their real girl model for the infant and the grown 'girl' while the special effects team moulded the alien aspects of Dren's body around the artistic conception. For Natali Dren had to be perfect and authentic. Chanéac infused her with humanity and soul after many talented creators had achieved a dramatic evolving of the body as if there was an artistic connective tissue between each stage of Dren's cinematic realization.

The imaginative creation of Dren on screen results in a mythical hybrid that would find more than one niche in Ovid's *Metamorphoses*. She is the result of a Narcissus complex in that she is a reflection and a daughter of Elsa who has avoided conventional motherhood. Some of Elsa's DNA is fused with animal cells to produce Dren but the two of them also have an emotional correspondence. Elsa justifies her mutilation of her 'child' with the accusation that Dren is unstable but Elsa herself is a maelstrom of conflicts and issues about her own identity and relationships. Dren also hovers between the perfection of the statue and the monster of assembled body parts. She is at once Beauty and the Beast.

Dren is a miracle of science, conceived as a complex organism and in many ways biologically more advanced than her human progenitors. Her wings give her a supernatural as well as a biblical appearance. (The scene on the roof is almost epiphanic.) Her amphibious attributes make her nymph or naiad-like and her capriciousness is a characteristic she shares with dangerous and numinous creatures of nature in Ovid's mythical landscape. Dren's final metamorphosis under water and her emergence from the pool as a freshly made man (the voice is uncertain and only just deepening into a male pitch) could almost be a visualization of Hermaphroditus' traumatic change in Book Four of the *Metamorphoses*. The unwilling boy has become the 'sex which is not one' (Nugent, 1989, pp. 164–169) because the gods have answered the nymph Salmacis' prayer mischievously. She desired to possess Hermaphroditus sexually and they were fused together biologically.[5]

Finally, in impregnating his 'mother' Elsa, Dren has broken human taboos and placed himself irrevocably outside the social norms. The act is one of bestial survival but it is also a reintegration with the person who gave him life and nurtured him. Dren has to die as there is no place in society for such a creature. (Clive has shown remorse at creating something they could neither control nor protect, the age-old dilemma of those who play god.) The story of Myrrha as an extension of the myth of Pygmalion seems to have come to the surface here. Although Natali has planned no sequel (he likes to leave his audiences guessing and supplying what might happen next) the heavily pregnant Elsa will, we assume, give birth to a child as exceptional (perhaps even as beautiful) as Adonis.

The Ghost in the Machine: Lightening the Mood

Dren is entirely biological but Christine/Andromeda paved the way for the mixed materials that make up the cyborg species in *Blade Runner*.[6] The formation of these hybrid creatures is scientifically fudged, a fusion between virtual and material reality. The 1985 film *Weird Science* (directed by John Hughes) posits the emergence of a virtual woman from a computer but only with the help of a real small-scale doll, the surface appearance of which has to be in some mysterious way assimilated into its circuits. The creators are two nerdy teenage boys (Anthony Michael Hall and Ilan Mitchell-Smith) who despair of ever getting laid (even in a morgue). We first see them as voyeuristic viewers of the girls in the gym class. They wonder what it would be like to shower with them. In designing their programme for the perfect woman, the heroes, Gary and Wyatt, are keen to move away from the Frankenstein model (they have been watching the 1960s film) and avoid using 'dead girls' for blueprints and body parts. Their composite will need a brain (to play chess) but most importantly must live, breathe and aerobicize.

After scanning in pictures of glamorous women, they bring their small-scale model girl close to the computer. This sequence (like the rest of the film, more manic than comic) is strangely ceremonial and involves Gary and Wyatt wearing women's brassieres on their heads. It is significant that the vivification of the ivory girl's equivalent continues to need a festive and ritual ambience, albeit laughable, to deliver the goods. Causing an electrical storm and local mayhem, the boys succeed in bringing forth a fully grown, gorgeous 'computer-generated fairy godmother' played by Kelly Le Brock. I can confirm (on the basis of anecdotal evidence) that the film or more accurately Le Brock made an impression upon teenage boys at the time who now in their thirties fondly remember its appeal as fantasy fulfilment. As Kelly Le Brock comes through the blown off bedroom doors, the boys cry out 'She's alive', a homage to near orgasmic exclamations uttered by the scientist in previous Frankenstein films.

For present-day viewers, spoilt for choice when it comes to special effects, this may not be a very exciting moment. The constructed girl's arrival is, however, in the traditional manner of a classical goddess who should sail effortlessly through the portals of a machine. Epiphanies, Greek and Roman style, generally entail doors opening spontaneously in the presence of the divinity (The Türöffnung technique). If gods gate crash through, it is usually to make a statement and it does seem as if this feisty and fashionable female has actually been summoned out of the machine not created by it. Kelly comes equipped with supernatural powers; she is able to transform the people around her. She metamorphoses Gary and Wyatt into snappy dressers for a night on the town and their car number plates change to add to the super cool image.

Brought into the world to do the boys' bidding, she is clearly in control while appearing to be compliant to their desires. Asking 'what would you little maniacs like to do with me first?' the as yet unnamed vision agrees they can all shower together, which has its ritualistic flavour. This will, after all, be an aphrodisiac activity. Gary names their 'creation' Lisa (after a girl he used to like) and she teaches him to kiss, complaining that his lips are like rigor mortis and he should learn to relax. This is a *Some Like it Hot* replay with Le Broc as Marilyn Monroe warming up Tony Curtis. It also reverses the Pygmalion process with a forward and sexually mature statue bringing her teenage creator to life.

When Gary and Wyatt wake up the next morning assuming the events of the previous night are a dream, Lisa is making them breakfast. Thus her first full day in the world begins with the fulfilment of a young male fantasy – a sexy woman playing mother. Lisa really is a fostering deity in a sparkly outfit, reminiscent of Ava Gardner, Kim Cattrall and Vanna White who played goddesses and ancient spirits turning around the lives of the heroes. Pygmalion's statue in her benign reincarnations reinforces the Ovidian subtext that Venus takes on the form of the vivified to vivify those who create or summon her *simulacrum*.

This is not to say that Lisa is all hugs and puppies. She performs some punitive transformations, making her a metamorphic deity (as object and agent) in the Ovidian mould. Wyatt's bullying older brother is taught a lesson by a brief spell as a downsized monster (Jabba the Hut style). There is a near nuclear and localized apocalyptic fall out when Gary and Wyatt try to duplicate their experiment. Creating the perfect woman in the age of advanced technology tends to bring a trail of destructive phenomena in its wake and the Pandora factor (the fearful female cyborg) comes with the territory. Fortunately the 'original' Lisa if she is potentially a baneful synthetic superwoman is also ephemeral (as both Venuses proved to be in the statue films discussed previously). Her part is played out once the teenagers are taken out of their isolation and socialized into the real world. Gary is given self-worth by having Lisa on his arm and also because she reprimands his parents for never praising him for anything. Her message to both boys is 'be liked for what you are'.

Gary starts dating Deborah (Debs) a girl of his own age. He is able to produce a fine line in flattery by telling her that if he ever again produces a perfect woman it will be like her. Agreeing with Debs that Lisa is so beautiful and has a gorgeous body, he explains that Lisa is everything he ever wanted in a girl until he knew what he wanted. This is the cue for Kelly le Brock's departure. She does not quite utter the cliché 'my work here is done', but tells the teenagers that they have what she wanted for them – it is hurtful to be no longer required but she would not have it any other way. She kisses them goodbye and goes up in or disappears into a large puff of smoke. For veterans of *One Touch of Venus* it is no surprise to see her reincarnated in the final shot of the film as the new gym teacher, leading a class in callisthenics. The illusory woman has a habit of coming down to earth in the world according to the movies.

The Ghost Stays in the Machine: simøne Or Simulation One

The 2002 film, SIMØNE was written and directed by Andrew Niccol who had won critical acclaim with his scripting of *The Truman Show* (directed by Peter Weir) in 1998. SIMØNE did not receive a wide distribution in the UK nor did it prove popular with American audiences. Izod (2006, p. 155) notes that the movie received mixed reviews 'from delight to downright hostility' and that its North American box office returns show it falling rapidly out of the top twenty. SIMØNE is an acquired taste. Leonard Maltin (2010, p. 1255) is disparaging about its central premise:

> One-joke idea about a desperate filmmaker who, fed up with temperamental stars, creates his new discovery on a computer – and then can't get anyone to believe she doesn't exist. Alas, no one in the film is real, which makes it hard to accept, even as satire.

This is a paradoxical critique of a screen narrative that is deliberately drawing attention to artificiality and constructed images in the movie industry and how this might 'infect' the human players operating in a cinematic environment. Izod (pp. 155–156) observes that all satire has a distancing effect and agrees that SIMØNE undermines our engagement with the 'live' fictional characters. His explanation of the story's alienating effects on real audiences points up the irony of the total and unqualified embracement of the pixel persona of Simone by the mass of movie-goers within the film's fiction. Izod's analysis of the film is masterly and the following interpretation owes a great deal to his insights. Kate Stables' *Sight and Sound* review (November, 2002, p. 56) will also figure in my discussion. Like Maltin, she is unimpressed with the film's leaden satire and the portentous treatment of what is at bottom an old-fashioned and derivative movie:

> Like all "she bot" movies from *Metropolis* to *Stepford Wives*, SIMØNE's axiom is that female weakness (in this case, the insane demands of cinema's leading ladies) can be surmounted only by creating a faultless artificial woman.

The plot of Niccol's film is as follows: Los Angeles-based director Viktor Taransky is facing a career on the rocks. His temperamental star has walked out, his ex-wife and head of the studio, Elaine Christian, has fired him and the movie he hoped would restore his reputation, a Bergmanesque reflective piece, *Sunrise, Sunset* is going to be shelved. Taransky's fairy godmother/saviour appears in the form of Hank Aleno, a wizard of computer programming who offers him a software package guaranteed to produce a made-to-order virtual actress.[7] Hank is dying from a brain tumour and is eager to gain immortality through his brain child. Izod believes that Taransky has been rescued by the trickster (pp. 140–141) and reflects upon Hank as a shadowy character. Hank is already between the living and the dead. He is also blind and could be viewed as a prophetic figure like Tiresias as such seers in classical time tended to suffer with this disability. Second sight is balanced up by the removal of normal sight (frequently by the gods but in Hank's case his devotion to the computer screen and the subsequent damage to his eyes are self-inflicted).

Viktor invents a composite of past female stars to manufacture his elaborate fraud on cinema-going audiences along with film critics and journalists. Simone (Rachel Roberts) fulfils the Hitchcock stereotype with her pale complexion, fair hair and Scandinavian air. Her acting style (obviously she is voiced over by Viktor with a touch of the huskiness of a Lauren Bacall) is languorous, even vacuous, but the viewers see her as intense and enigmatic. Viktor's own family – Elaine, his wife, and Lainey, his teenage daughter – is fooled by the new leading lady. His ex-wife assumes that Viktor is romantically involved with Simone. Then, the nation embarks upon a love affair with the image the director has created and only desires her more when she exhibits remoteness, mystery and a Garboesque propensity to be left alone. In a classic line about filming her scenes separately from her co-stars, Viktor has Simone say pretentiously 'I relate better to people when they're not actually there'.

However, Viktor manages to fake live video interviews, the odd out and about appearance (using photo stills with a mannequin) and even a stadium show to launch Simone's singing career, all done by a hologram projected onto the stage. Viktor himself communes with the image of Simone on the computer screen in the seclusion and privacy of a guarded room on the studio lot. He confides his anxieties to this *simulacrum* of himself about her runaway success and his own monumental deception upon the world outside. This cinematic sculptor of a perfect woman is not exactly fooled by his own invention but she does function as both a suppressed conscience and a mirror of his psyche.

Viktor decides that his virtual actress has turned into such a powerful icon she will destroy his work and scupper his chances of winning back his wife and daughter. He attempts to ruin her reputation by placing her at the centre of a short autobiographical work, 'I am Pig' in which the image of Simone eats at the swine trough and besmirches herself in the mud. The critics adore her more. The desperate director then has her give an interview in which she (or rather Viktor) voices shocking, politically incorrect and ideological neo-fascistic views while chain smoking, all the time with a sunny smile. Audiences go wild at her refreshingly honest fallibility and her popularity soars. Viktor finally stages her death (infecting the file of the virtual Simone with a virus simultaneously) but a besotted reporter sees him deposit a trunk off the jetty. This contains the corrupted Simone files on disc.

Drowning the *simulacrum* is a symbolic act and gives Viktor's closure an air of ritual. Izod interprets the watery grave of Simone as an appropriate submersion of the now negative anima. It might remind a classicist of the birth of Venus from the waves and point up the paradox of the screen goddess's death by drowning. However, in this film you just cannot keep a good *simulacrum* down! The journalist, suspecting foul play, reports Taransky's actions to the precinct and the police force open Simone's coffin at the funeral. It contains a cardboard cut out of the actress, which looks to the amazed spectators like an insulting and sick joke from a deranged director who has murdered his starlet.

Viktor is put on trial for murder but Lainey, his computer genius daughter, discovers the deception when she and her mother Elaine enter the locked studio. Lainey restores Simone's programme and with his family re-united and in on the great deception, Viktor issues an interview tape for television showing a revivified Simone and their son, Chip (another hologram). Her disappearance and the director's reticence are explained as a bid for privacy, this to the satisfaction of the authorities and the devoted fans. Simone suggests that she will be fighting for a better world for her (cyber) baby to grow up in!

Actual and Metaphorical Allusions to Pygmalion in SIMØNE

Izod begins his chapter on 'The Case of SIMØNE' with a synopsis of Ovid's Pygmalion. Early in the film, Lainey[8] (Evan Rachel Wood) is seen reading the myth and we have a brief, over her shoulder, glimpse of the Burne-Jones illustrations (discussed in the Introduction and Appendix). This is the only direct allusion to the classical story about creating a compliant and perfect woman but a later sequence when the constructed star portrays herself in a pig sty (in a short film she calls 'I am Pig') is an unmistakeable joke about her artificial status and her true identity as the Pygmalioniesque director/designer, Viktor (the name immediately evokes Frankenstein) Taransky.[9]

Izod (p. 139) argues that the film follows Shaw's play in mocking the stereotypes of creative genius and of Hollywood as a political minefield: 'In Hollywood, art and industry politics go hand in glove, so it is no surprise to find that Viktor's creation of his ideal woman cannot long remain untouched by industry and public expectations. She too becomes politicised'. SIMØNE encapsulates the way in which a star might be born in the digital age. Stables remarks that 'More Prometheus than Pygmalion, Viktor surely represents a consoling fantasy for old Hollywood that Art in the person of the director can win out over ever-encroaching science as film becomes increasingly a digital domain'. Izod (p. 141) takes issue with the vision of the triumph of art as a message and reframes it as the essence of the director's delusion.

Stables finds the director's orchestration of his *simulacrum*'s every move a technological absurdity, scoffing at the device of a simple keyboard button marked MIMIC, which 'magically renders his actions as her performance'. For Stables, the ease with which Viktor manages to manufacture his screen star takes the film into the realms of fantasy. In an irritable if astute response to the movie's failings, Stables comments: 'Ignoring the nerdy, labour intensive algorithmic realities of creating synthespians, the months of code-crunching needed to achieve a set of simple facial expressions, SIMØNE paints digital creativity as equal parts alchemy and auteurism'.

Izod (p. 143), in contrast, buys into the suspension of disbelief as he finds the simulation package uttering Viktor's words through Simone's mouth as a replay of the myth in which Echo repeats the phrases of Narcissus: 'Indeed Pacino plays these scenes like just such a lonely, self-obsessed man as Narcissus, with a persuasive blend of vain gloriousness (Simone endlessly praising his work) and pathos (at those times when she becomes his sole confidante)'. Ovid engineered the relationship between Pygmalion and Narcissus by altering the story of the sculptor and suggesting he too desired a *simulacrum* that was a projection of himself. Izod's citing of the Narcissus myth places Viktor firmly in the long cultural line of post Ovidian Pygmalions. He is narcissistic and selfishly obsessed with his own art, unable to commit to relationships with those closest to him and very much in the business of creating illusion and playing god. Izod assumes that Viktor has been emotionally rigid in the past and this has led to the failure of his marriage.

It becomes all the more fascinating that Simone soon outstrips Viktor in fame and accolades so that his identity becomes submerged into the uncanny creature he has designed but no longer seems able to control. Stables' insertion of Prometheus into the equation prompts the obvious question about Simone's status as Frankenstein's monster. It also allows the mythological figure of Pandora to intrude into the movie's meta-narrative with Simone's seductive persona and distinctive voice imitating the gifts the gods bestowed upon this constructed woman. Taransky's simulated actress presents as much of a challenge to his artistic recognition as his previous petulant leading lady, Nicola (Winona Ryder), had been.

Simone's performances outshine the art house films in which she appears, nor can Viktor their director, take any credit for the screen charisma of his other self. The only compensation for this unexpected turn of events is the return of a chastened Nicola wishing to audition for Taransky not just because he is suddenly successful again but because she has been inspired by Simone to enter into the part and bring a newly discovered authenticity to her acting. She moves Taransky with a reading of warmth, sensitivity and feeling.

This scene in the film is neglected by Izod although the change in Nicola moves Taransky and demonstrates that in the form of an artificial woman he has imparted something about the soul of acting to his superficial ex-star. The softening of Nicola as well as Viktor would fit well with Izod's focus on Simone as an 'anima', a projection of the self from the semi-conscious realms of the mind, which can play a positive psychological role in a time of individual crisis. The anima can manifest itself as 'a supple, bewitching and endlessly transforming wraith' (p. 142). Simone might also double for the goddess as helper who appears before a troubled hero in order to guide him out of a real impasse. Sharon Stone's Muse has some affinity with Simone.

Izod, then, detects a more profound symbolism in the film than Maltin and Staples. He uses the Jungian theory of enantiodromia to illuminate the central tensions of the screen narrative (pp. 147–149). Jung argued

> that every archetype, every psychological extreme, contains the seed of conversion into its opposite ... the creation and subsequent destruction of heroic or godlike figures can be comprehended within this cyclical pattern. [10]

Izod applies the theory to the 'accelerated cycle of elevation and desecration of celebrities in the tabloids'. SIMØNE features a press fronted by journalist Max Sayer 'orchestrating devotion to the star and doing all it can to dish the dirt on her' (p. 149.) However the screen goddess, Simone, desecrates and deconstructs herself in 'I am Pig' (clearly a reference to herself or to Viktor as Pygmalion) and in her infamous interview, both actions predicting and pre-empting 'the downswing in press favour'.

The critics see the short film as bold and experimental 'theatre'. Her many fans elevate her further for revealing the slutty side of her celebrity personality on 'live' television. Simone's followers have relished both her refined elegance-at-a-distance pose and her cigarette smoking slut act, which suggests that the cinema audiences respond with a collective Pygmalion consciousness to the dual aspects of their star. Harking back to *Vertigo*, Simone is both the Madeleine and the Judy for her fans demonstrating that opposing stereotypes of female allure (available, unobtainable) can exist in one woman. Viktor's presentation of Simone has unintentionally called the bluff of a puritanical and prurient press with the connivance of its consumers.

Obviously the finale of the film which shows creator and created with their newly born child gives the public another metamorphosis to enjoy, the sight of Simone as a caring mother and also one willing to enter the political arena when the time is ripe. The virtual star, spawning a virtual celebrity child, will exercise her influence as a virtual politician, which is indeed a scary note for the movie to end upon. Izod (p. 154) comments: 'Is this the monstrous gestation resulting from the union of Viktor and Simone as quasi-incestuous muses to each other's narcissism?'

For the Ovidian scholar, the union of the modern movie 'sculptor' and his disembodied 'statue' reprises the rapid coupling of Pygmalion and the ivory girl. The birth of 'Chip' is a sudden revelation to the media and the public and this near 'royal' babe is like his mythical counterpart, Paphos, a telescoped narrative event. The union between Viktor and Simone also references Myrrha and her father and the product of their miscegenation, Adonis. Izod concludes that Viktor is now doomed to split his 'anima' or newly restored and integrated persona across a private and public manifestation as his reconciliation with real wife, Elaine, can never be common knowledge.

In conclusion there are plenty of Pygmalion factors in the film. Perhaps the most telling is a linguistic one, the fact that Simone comes out of a 'software' package and is as plastic and yielding as the wax screen she inhabits. Yet the film itself is a metaphor for the myth. Critics found it brittle and did not think that any of the characters came to life. SIMØNE was perhaps too successful in laying bare the artificiality of the entertainment business and the fact that identities are distorted in a world where the image is everything and the substance has transmuted into the elusive shadow. Eccentric though it may seem, the second half of this chapter culminates in a study of a film which showcases an all-too-palpable present-day version of the statue, which is not a recognizably real girl in any respect. Nevertheless she takes her place at the heart of a community, reveals its humanity and cements it socially.

Hello Dolly! Answering a Need

In *Private Eye* (n. 1273, 29 October 2010), in the 'Funny Old World' section, the case of an infatuation with a silicone doll was reported. The maker of life-sized dolls, Diego Bortolin of Treviso, told the journalist that a customer had been ditched by his girlfriend and dating other women was just not the same. He commissioned a doll just like his ex-girlfriend but with bigger boobs. Speaking from his workshop (Tentazioni / Temptations) Bortolin said the wealthy client paid top Euro for something as lifelike as possible, so the manufacturer took extra care to replicate every bodily part from photos but followed instructions to give this smiling blonde bigger breasts and a curvier backside.

> The doll is fully flexible, and automatically warms up to body temperature when switched on. Everything works just like the real thing, and she can take on any movement or position a human can. As far as I can see, she is now the perfect girlfriend.

It may be helpful to demarcate dolls as descendants of the ivory statue from her other cultural avatars through the centuries. The anecdote above demonstrates that that full-sized articulated (but not articulate) mannequins are alive and kicking in Europe. Alongside the discreet workshops (how one wonders if these look like Pygmalion's studio) there is also a manufacturing industry of mannequins in California and from their internet sites the silent and acquiescent partner can be packed off to the purchaser – satisfaction guaranteed. The social implications of the American factory where workers craft hyper-realistic women (in 2005 the asking price was $6000) featured in a thought-provoking and at times unsettling exhibition, Guys n Dolls held in Brighton (UK) in April 2005. The accompanying exhibition catalogue has contributions from doll makers, photographers of the dolls and also analyses of the different roles dolls of all sizes play in religion, therapy and art. The doll figures as a psychopompus (a guide to the realms of the dead, helping the deceased to cross over) in a number of spiritual belief systems. Notorious and maligned as an artefact of witchcraft it is a powerful symbol in religious ceremony and rituals from Vodoo (known to the Western world as Voodoo) to the Akua'ba fertility doll, a replica of adult size and appearance, which is part of the religious traditions of the Asante people in Ghana.

Ovid's story of Pygmalion is summarized in the introduction (p. 11) but it is seen as just one facet of the doll's function in human history. In this broader context the myth reflects the male desire for a passive, silent and compliant woman as well as establishing the statue as a cultural model for substitute companions carried on into adulthood. Elena Dorfman writes in her essay 'Still Lovers' (p. 60):

> What began for me as playful curiosity – how to photograph men having sex with 125 lbs of a perfectly-formed synthetic female – rapidly turned into a serious exploration of the emotional ties that exist between men

and women and their dolls. This exploration forced me to evaluate my own notions of love and what it means to value an object – a replacement human being, in effect – as real.

Dorfman goes on to relate her meeting with Jerry and Adriana in the UK who kept five dolls hidden away from the children and friends. Adriana collected these 'girls' to represent different parts of herself, lover, child, friend, toy and intellectual partner.

However, Dorfman has no illusions about the male desire for the doll in a historical and contemporary cultural context, believing that most newly made *simulacra* of woman invariably reference the biblical Eve and the Greek Pandora. The first woman

> starts out as a creature of perfection made by the gods for the pleasure of men. But as soon as she comes alive and exhibits her thirst for knowledge, she becomes a source of suffering and death. Men, afraid of the impulses women inspire, set about to rectify this by creating their own women: statues, mannequins, dolls that function for sexual pleasure.

This truly absorbing book indicates just some of the psychological complexity surrounding dolls and human attempts to accept and objectify fractured identities with their help. It also explores the significance of familiar figures (creators and created) in what Gaby Wood described as the quest for mechanical life. The Brighton exhibition teased out issues raised by Gaby Wood in 2002, and an engagement with it might have enriched Hersey's discussion of doll culture in his work, *Falling in Love with Statues*. Any scholar researching into the afterlife of Pygmalion's ivory girl is bound to brush up against the question of life-size dolls in human culture. Indeed, as Hersey notes (2009, p. 138), Lactantius, the early Christian writer, criticized the Roman satirist, Persius, for not realizing that gold and ivory statues of the Olympian were merely big dolls.

Stoichita (2008, p. 195) introduces Barbie dolls into his discussion of *Vertigo* to clarify the psychological infantilism of Scottie's obsessive condition. In 2009 Barolsky and D'Ambra wrote a short article (cited in Chapter 1) suggesting that Pygmalion was child-like in his need for a plaything and that Ovid drew his inspiration for the Pygmalion story from the well-crafted toys made of ivory and enjoyed by the small daughters of the wealthy at Rome and in the provinces. The relinquishing of the doll upon marriage was a rite of passage, the putting away of childish things. Moving from the sublime (or symbolic) to the ridiculous, Barolsky and D'Ambra's exposition resurrects the conundrum of the statue's ivory material and whether the replica of a fully grown girl could be completely constructed out of this substance. Ahl's suggestion that we could visualize both Pygmalion (Pygmy) and the ivory maiden in downsized form is possibly the way madness lies, although in terms of the myth's reception, there is a tradition of creating miniature moving and lifelike beings in cinema narrative. (We see moving dolls in Whale's 1935 *Bride of Frankenstein* and a small assassin, a pint-sized Pandora, in the form of a charming ballerina in Todd Browning's 1936 film *The Devil-Doll*.)

The introduction to the Brighton exhibition book by the editors, Suzie Plumb and Jackie Lewis, surveys the fictional and factual creation of dolls from Olimpia as a substitute for Clara in Hofmann's *The Sandman* (1817) to Oscar Kokoschka's facsimile of his former mistress, Alma Mahler, commissioned from puppet maker, Hermine Moos, in 1918 (pp. 14–15). Quoting an earlier 2004 article from Peers, one of their contributors, they trace the negative associations between dolls and the female sex, the former being symbolic of 'women as objects of sexual desire, vulnerable victims, vacuous and easily manipulated'. Peers concluded that the doll was 'a clear unmistakeable sign of women's limited intellect, passivity, frivolity' and that

> ironically essentialism's key stereotype is that woman is neither fixed nor stable but false and empty, constantly shifting, a chimerical illusion, a performance of carefully judged and confected surfaces and maquillage. When the male edits and re-orders the world he is an artist, when the female edits and re-orders – principally herself – she is a doll. (Rogers, 1999, pp. 92–94)

The successful replacement of real wives with robots was the shock revelation of *Stepford Wives*. The impulse to convert real women into biddable dolls or puppets without any independent movement but in total thrall to a puppet master has propelled a number of horror films. A strange 1964 British movie called *Devil Doll* (not to be confused with Browning's 1930s film), directed by Lindsay Shonteff and starring Bryant Halliday, is judged by Maltin to be 'an exquisitely tailored, sharply edited sleeper' in the traditions of the mystery genre (2010, p. 350). It concerns a ventriloquist with the power to hypnotize. He has already transferred his assistant's soul into his dummy and wishes (rather inexplicably) to do the same with the beautiful brunette he is vigorously wooing.

The heroine who does escape having her feisty personality submerged into a doll was played by the striking looking Yvonne Romain. There are shades of *Corridor of Mirrors* in the narrative, the atmosphere and the ambiguous chemistry between the Halliday and Romain characters but the narrative coherence is not strong. It is definitely a movie where form surpasses content. On the other hand, *Devil Doll* does demonstrate the way in which a disturbed and psychotic hero might blur the boundaries in his relationships between the human and the synthetic to justify the eternal entrapment of his rival and the immortalization of a desirable woman.

However, the doll as therapy and its use as a positive strategy in uncovering trauma and setting the psychologically damaged on the road to recovery is also a pertinent feature of the Plumb and Lewis exhibition and book. A doll with a therapeutic function but also one which invites comparison with Ovid's myth of Pygmalion is at the core of my final case study in this chapter.

Why Retro Is So Real: Bianca as the True Heir to the Ivory Girl

I had originally intended to demarcate dolls firmly from robots and to finish the book with the most perfect illusion, Simone. After pondering the failure of the film to impress either as comedy or as social satire, I decided a better candidate for my penultimate chapter was Bianca, the mail order doll in the 2007 movie, *Lars and the Real Girl*. Although this film also suffered from a limited distribution in the UK, the few critical reviews I have read (and comments from family and friends who have caught up with it since) confirm my response to it as a warm and life-affirming story with a plastic doll at its heart. Set in the American mid-West, *Lars and the Real Girl* relates the touching story of a shy young man who keeps even family at bay through a fear of loving, losing and being hurt. His brother Gus and pregnant sister-in-law Karen finally coax him over for a meal (he lives in their garage apartment) only to find he has purchased a life-sized silicone doll and that she (Bianca) is to be his constant companion.

Seeking the advice of the local doctor, Dagmar Berman, they are advised by her to accept the doll ('Bianca's in town for a reason'). In the meantime the perspicacious doctor starts therapeutic sessions with Lars under the pretence that she is keeping an eye on Bianca's health. Dagmar discovers Lars' aversion to being touched and his deep-seated anxieties about Karen's condition as his mother died in childbirth. The visits to the doctor tie in with the elaborate fiction Lars has invented for his fiancée by giving her a handicap (she is in a wheelchair) and a past full of good works in children's orphanages abroad. Bianca is characterized by altruistic acts, fulfilling expectations of the fostering female. In spite of her robust plasticity, Lars has built disability and fragility into Bianca's synthetic frame.

The community rallies around Lars and his family at every level from workmates to the local church activists. Bianca is involved in volunteer work, becomes a governor at the school and embarks upon a social life separate from Lars, including nights out with other women and doing part-time modelling. She is encouraged to show off 'that darling figure', and she spends time having her hair done.[11] Lars becomes anxious and jealous at her increasing independence although he is beginning to show his attraction to a bubbly work colleague, Margo, whom he has always kept at arm's length. He is clearly unhappy when Margo dates another co-worker, in the belief that Lars will always be faithful to Bianca. However, Lars indicates to the doctor and to Gus and Karen that Bianca's health is failing. News of Bianca's chronic illness becomes public and the grieving community prepare for the worst. Lars' brother and wife discover him weeping and embracing her (as ever) lifeless body down by the lake where he played as a child. A funeral is held for Bianca with an acknowledgement that she touched everyone's lives and was truly an exceptional person. Lars and Margo leave together at the end of the service with Lars agreeing to go for a walk. A little smile plays around his lips.

In her insightful interpretation of the film as a Pygmalion myth for modern times, Bazzoli (2009, NCA convention, Chicago) suggested a framework in which this screen text of the twenty-first century can be compared with a 2000-year-old Latin narrative, namely, Ovid's *Metamorphoses*. Drawing upon the work of Barkan and Grassi, Bazzoli defines Ovid's poem as focusing upon explanations of creation, human personality and the organization of society through the image of change with the gods or more generally the divine effecting and affecting transformations in the broadest sense. I am very much in agreement with Bazzoli's expansive approach to the Pygmalion effect as the myth brings in its trail many other motifs and figures from Ovid's epic. Modern narratives with resonances of the sculptor and his statue invariably conjure with the Latin poet's comprehensive view of metamorphosis and the transparent and opaque connections between victims and beneficiaries of transformations, both physical and psychological.

Bazzoli looks back to Ovid's distinct version of the Pygmalion legend in the light of Lars' phobias and social inadequacies. The ordering of Bianca from the internet is a cry for help but Lars exhibits genuine excitement when his girlfriend arrives. Unlike Pygmalion, he has not created this image but he has chosen the form she will take (as his workmate says, 'yes, you can customise everything – you can design your own woman'). With blow-up dolls, the purchaser is given the part of breathing his spirit (anima, the breath of life) into the artificial being but Bianca is silicone from top to toe (with all anatomical parts correct as Karen and Gus are disturbed to discover). Lars, so prickly and phobic about physical intimacy, is tender in his touching and lifting Bianca. He may have commissioned a sex doll but as Bazzoli observes he sees himself as a courteous and caring companion to her, a support worker in love with a disabled angel in constant need of dressing and general attendance.

Any reader of this book who has made the journey thus far will readily recognize the reassertion of Ovidian themes in the film. Lars is the awkward and stilted figure, shunning the company of others, who ultimately desires to be enlivened and integrated into society. Bianca is the statue that will achieve his release from rigidity in demeanour and personality. At first Gus feels that the doll is further evidence that Lars has faulty wiring in his brain, that he is not functional and needs fixing: 'he's in love with a lump of silicone'. In the end, the presence of Bianca ('God made her to help people') brings the whole community together notwithstanding initial concerns from some of the less enlightened Christians that engaging with her is idolatry 'like worshipping a golden calf'.

Bianca is material and palpable in a way that hologram Simone could never be but she has none of the mobility and speech Viktor's creation can boast. The frozen expression of the silicone doll never changes and all who meet her are confronted with her inflexibility and the fact that she is to all intents and purposes a mannequin. Lars has to bend her into a limited repertoire of positions and we have to assume that she does not have the special features Bortolin claims for his creations. Lars in an elaborate fiction also gives her a mixed parentage of Danish and Brazilian, which can explain her inability to converse through a lack of English. There is also a combination of the cool Nordic with the hot Latin American stereotype lurking here perhaps, but the erotic attributes of Bianca are never to the fore.

Bianca's purity as constructed by Lars should counterpose her to the Propoetides, those tarnished models of womanhood. Bazzoli (p. 8), in discussing Bianca's role as an unachievable puritanical idea, concludes that

> the modern telling of the tale picks up some vague nuances of Ovid's text as the statue in the myth is set up as a contrast to the female Propoetides, a group of impious prostitutes.

Stables (*Sight and Sound*, April, 2008, p. 66) who is much more favourably disposed towards this film than she was towards SIMØNE writes of the close-ups on Bianca that

> manage to get the maximum mileage from the ineradicable and discomfiting contrast between her lifeless come-hither features, frozen into a blowjob-ready rictus, and Lars' solicitous whispers in her ear.

Stables interprets the styling of Bianca's hair by Lars' female friends as a metamorphosis of her hardcore streetwalker wig into a pretty girl-next-door look. This suggests that it is not just Lars who wants to refashion a

Propoetis into the pure ivory maiden. The women of the community are keen to keep her image untarnished.

This relatively crude representation of a real girl is a recognizable contemporary cultural artefact (such dolls do exist and become beloved companions) as opposed to the refined robot of the future or the computer-generated facsimile, which fools everyone. Bianca very quickly becomes a real force in the community and the humanity which Lars and those around him invest in her and invest her with puts this artificial construct into a league of her own. Bianca comes to embody an almost utopian vision of collective care, love and sensitivity in small-town America, a much more positive message than her literary and screen forerunners who easily outdo her in sophistication. The cinema audience can empathize with the response of the townsfolk although watching this singularly unattractive doll on screen we are distanced from the impact of Bianca. I am not sure we are ever won over by her. Like the adoration of Simone, you would have to be there!

There is another way of signifying the appearance of this ultimately unprepossessing mannequin. Within the fiction of the film, Lars' doll gains reality by being less directly representational of an actual girl. Those around her have to supply her with the gifts of warmth, speech and allure. Far from being a descendant of Pandora waiting to be endowed with human qualities, Bianca is at least a little like the magical effigy in ancient beliefs discussed in Kris and Kurz (1979, 79). As Keen (1982, 125) points out 'the stronger the belief in the identity of picture and depicted, the less the concern to make the work of art as "life-like" as possible'. My point is that the community constructs an exceptionally pure spirit for the doll and draws closer to her day by day. Bianca's lack of correspondence to a living being is therefore not a problem.[12]

Bazzoli sees the role of the community as similar to a divine council. She makes a persuasive argument for their agency in bringing Bianca to life and interprets the abstract power of love as a replacement for the gods in general and Venus in particular as far as the vivification of the *simulacrum* is concerned. Bazzoli singles out Karen as a Venus figure. Throughout the film, Lars' sister-in-law represents the warmth and the fertility of the goddess of love and her creative and nurturing aspects. If Karen is the heart of the community then one could pose Dr Berman as the rational principle orchestrating the therapy strategies to a successful conclusion. Berman is childless and Lars tells her during one session, she is like Bianca who always listens and always understands him.

Bianca tends to be a site of displacement, a repository of the qualities Lars perceives, admires but will not articulate about Karen, Dr Dagmar and Margo, his co-worker. Margo is 'the real girl', as Bazzoli points out. She is warm and exhibits a sweetness combined with a sense of humour that draws in the viewer. She also has an air of innocence which Lars recognizes and responds to. When her teddy bear mascot has been 'hanged' by the boyfriend she has rejected, Lars gives the toy mouth to mouth resuscitation. There is a childlike aspect to the blossoming relationship between Lars and Margo. The viewer must breathe a sigh of relief when Bianca, having fulfilled her function, is put to rest, and Margo and Lars are free to walk off (not quite into the sunset) together.

There are probably a number of correspondences between the Lars narrative and the myth of Pygmalion still to be explored and it is very likely that different conclusions could be drawn about the motivation behind the motifs we find in the film. For instance, the death of Bianca in or by the lake summons up the ritual washing of the statue as well as the birth of Venus from the waves. It also reprises the scene from *Vertigo* when the non-existent persona of Madeleine (in the very real body of Judy) is rescued from near death in San Francisco Bay by Scottie. It could even be a reference to Simone's watery grave. Lars' decision to 'kill off' Bianca is a more humane and justifiable act than Warren's attempt to terminate April in the Buffy episode. Herein lies the problem of casting a classicist's eye at the modern screen without acknowledging cinematic and televisual filters.

For this reason, I commend the conclusion of Bazzoli (2009, pp. 20–21), which I found both refreshing and reassuring. In celebrating the achievement of *Lars and the Real Girl* as joining 'the ever-evolving myths of our culture' and identifying 'things about its own society's identity', she urges us to 'not only to observe interactions with timeless and universal themes but conversations and even debates between voices of the past and the present'.

As the final film to be put under scrutiny in this chapter, I would add that *Lars*, like my other choices of screen texts with a flavour of Pygmalion, encourages us to explore Ovid's myth for further aesthetic and sociological implications within its original context. The statue's cultural trajectory has seen her alternately privatized and commercialized, abstracted from and integrated into human society, remythologized, rationalized and historicized while teetering between the model and the copy, the living and the dead, the all-too-material and the fleeting image. For my concluding chapter I shall revisit the question I asked in my 2003 article when I claimed that the ivory maiden possesses the potential to be all the synthetic creatures that have been made or made over in subsequent Pygmalion narratives. Is Ovid's statue truly 'all that'?

Chapter 8

More Myth Making at the Movies

In Pursuit of the Perfect Man

In calling my 2003 article 'She's All That', I set up expectations for myself as well as for the reader that Ovid's Pygmalion narrative contained the seeds of all its future variations. I concluded that in keeping the statue faceless Ovid simultaneously limited and liberated her post-classical copies. He may not have envisaged her future empowerment but he certainly suggested her ambiguity and potential to delude by his choice of ivory for her substance. It is fascinating to observe Pygmalion's *simulacrum* overturning and critiquing her passivity and purity as she is continuously transformed in literature, art and on screen. She might even supplant Pygmalion as the one who desires an ideal or even creates a male equivalent to the ivory girl.

There are strong and sexually predatory women in the *Metamorphoses* but the statue is not one of them. They tend to be goddesses or at least nymphs, and these models of feminine forwardness do seem to have integrated themselves into Pygmalion's story when it is retold. Salmacis is a pertinent instance of a woman in pursuit of a perfect man.

In Book Four (lines 285–388), one of the daughters of Minyas tells the story of Salmacis and Hermaphroditus. The latter (at first unnamed by Ovid) is of divine parentage, the son of Aphrodite (Roman Venus) and Hermes (Roman Mercury). Hermaphroditus, the lovely virginal adolescent, stumbles into Salmacis' glade and she is smitten with lust. He blushes at her flattering and wooing words and his flushed face is described as the colour of apples in an orchard, like painted ivory or resembling the eclipsed moon. We see him through Salmacis' eyes. The young boy spurns the advances of the erotically aroused nymph but foolishly leaps into the inviting lake, which is the naiad's element and therefore her other self. In other words he has submitted to her seduction in her elemental form while refusing her in her corporeal form.

The sight of the boy's body in the water enflames the nymph and the storyteller (a virginal female) describes his translucent flesh as resembling lilies or ivory figures under glass. Pygmalion's statue is prefigured in the ivory simile. The nymph and the boy struggle in the water, and Salmacis prays for them to be permanently united. The gods hear her prayer but unfortunately, the two of them become one; male and female are tightly fused into a bisexual body. Instead of a frenzy of sexual congress Salmacis becomes submerged into what she desires and will forever suffer the frustration experienced by Narcissus.

Hermaphroditus is now given the name that denotes his parentage and also describes his hybrid state. In fact these two, semi-divine boy and self-regarding nymph, are in the same situation as Narcissus except for the fact that the boy never desired Salmacis (any more than Narcissus' reflection could return his feelings).[1] Until she set eyes upon Hermaphroditus, Salmacis was very much in love with her own image in the water. Hermaphroditus curses her pool in which she enveloped him both with her body and her watery element. The voice of the hybrid creature that emerges from the water is still that of the male, but it is a no-win situation all around. The pool is later described as *obscenus*, 'polluted' in the lengthy speech of Pythagoras (*Met.* 15.319) whereas before it was crystal clear. (Perhaps Ovid intends us to think back to the Propoetides with this re-application of the adjective Orpheus has used to describe the 'foulness' of sexually active women.) Hermaphroditus prays that Salmacis' waters will enervate anyone who enters them from that moment on. The now presumably murky pool is all that is left of Salmacis.

In the Venus statue films under discussion in Chapter 4, goddesses are entranced at the sight of a comely male mortal. Myrrha's child Adonis grows up to be the lover of Venus and he is described as a flawless beauty. There is no gainsaying the goddess of love when she herself is in the throes of passion. As my focus in this book was the pursuit of the perfect woman I did not stray into the territory of the artificially constructed man, but this gender reversal of the myth has appeared on the screen. The Pygmalion formula works just as well in delineating the pleasures and pitfalls of capturing an elusive (male) ideal.[2]

There is a poignant Pygmalion undertow to Woody Allen's 1985 movie, *Purple Rose of Cairo*. In this film, downtrodden Depression-era housewife, Mia Farrow, is brought to life and out of her shell by the miraculous manifestation of a screen idol (Jeff Daniels) who materializes among the cinema audience. It is his film persona or *simulacrum* as distinct from the real actor/star that makes the Mia Farrow character feel special but the fantasy is short-lived. It is a cruelly conceived scenario with a heartbreaking resolution and benefits from superlative performances by Jeff Daniels and Mia Farrow.

Jeff Daniels' character springs out of the screen[3] to bring glamour into the humdrum life of his adoring fan, the mousy Mia Farrow, but he proves unable to feel or be more than a cardboard cut out and does great emotional harm before returning to the celluloid plinth he has vacated. Farrow's character realizes that this is the only place where heroic men and movie stars rescue and woo lesser beings – pace *Pretty Woman*. She stoically returns to the cinema to see her illusion back where he belongs. Ironically, Maltin states that the film is successful in spite of a 'coldly clever script' by Woody Allen.[4]

The 1999 British film *Virtual Sexuality* (directed by Nick Hurran) decided to play a two-in-one Pygmalion game (there is even a statue scene at the start) by transforming a 17-year-old Justine (Laura Fraser) into the gorgeous guy she has created on a Narcissus make-over machine at the technology fair. This remarkable occurrence is triggered by a freak explosion in the booth and hologram Jake – Justine as a young male, played with jeu d'esprit by Rupert Penry-Jones – emerges from the rubble. Unlike Salmacis, Justine still exists in her own body so in theory she can possess her dream man at last. It has been her priority since the start of the film to lose her virginity but she has rejected available partners at her school. Of course it cannot work; her clone, charming though he is and with a sensitive side, is Justine in male form and does not think of his creator in a sexual way.

Eventually it all works out and Justine decides that her geeky friend Chas will do as the deflowerer. Jake is absorbed back into the Narcissus machine and the lesson for Justine is spelt out: she did not want the perfect man, just an ego extension. The perfect man was all about her as the perfect woman. However, she retains aspects of Jake (his physical strength and talent for baseball) who will always be a part of her, proving that she has gained from being in touch with her masculine side![5]

The 2003 film version of Neil LaBute's play *The Shape of Things*, directed by the author and starring Rachel Weisz and Paul Rudd (who played the leads on stage) has a geeky male college student falling under the spell of a charismatic art major.[6] She remoulds his personality and appearance but the make-over treatment is not out of any affection or to transform him into a suitable boyfriend as he believes. At the end of the film he is displayed in public as a successful project proving how readily an autonomous human being can be reshaped to a stereotype and willingly become all show.

The play was judged as brittle and disturbing and the sight of a male statue figure being 'sculpted' by a female elicited comments about art for art's sake being distorted into art with no moral boundaries. Kate Bassett in *The Independent on Sunday* (3 June 2001, p. 6) concluded that 'The aesthetic debate grows into a really provocative row about modern artists and moral decency'. Susannah Clapp, in *The Observer Review* (3 June 2001, p. 10), wrote:

> There is no curtain call: quite rightly, for this is a piece that requires an audience, who have been thinking about the thin line between life and art, to consider themselves as actors.

When Myth Meets History

But my dear, how can you call my statues dead? When I'm alone and rather tired, think what it means to me to have my statues with me, to know that they'll always be lovely, never grow old and never walk out with sailors.

These lines are uttered by actor Alan Mowbray in Alexander Korda's 1941 film, *That Hamilton Woman*. He plays Sir William Hamilton in this historical drama, which traces the love affair between his much younger wife Emma (Vivien Leigh) and Horatio Nelson (Laurence Olivier). This is played out against the backdrop of the Napoleonic wars at the turn of the nineteenth century. Miller (1988, pp. 208–209) elaborates upon the theory that the Pygmalion myth has two main avenues of interpretation, the mystical and the historical.[7] However the 'historical' versions of Pygmalion are illustrated by the sort of 'realist' fiction found in Shaw's play where no magic or supernatural machinery intrudes upon the action. The true story of Emma Hart (later Lady Hamilton) has been viewed as a Pygmalion drama predating Shaw. Emma arrived in London with her mother and embarked upon the kind of work a poor and uneducated country girl might expect to find in the big city.[8] To use a cliché she was a lady of easy virtue.[9]

Emma was strikingly beautiful and very quick at acquiring the accomplishments associated with women of the upper class. By the time she was 18, Emma had been painted by George Romney; there was also talk of her performances in risqué tableaux and for her Dance of the Seven Veils. She was mistress to several men including the baronet Charles Greville (nephew of Sir William) who in the film narrative has promised to marry her. In the film no punches are pulled about Greville 'selling' her to Hamilton in return for the paying of his debts and a princely sum of £5000. William Hamilton refined Emma further (Greville had started her education) and she learned to sing and speak French and Italian. Small wonder Hamilton has been described as the Higgins to her Eliza.[10]

However Emma had learnt a great deal from posing for the painter Romney (sometimes in the guise of a mythical heroine or a Greek goddesses) and she herself was the architect of the tableau vivant in which she performed 'Attitudes' from classical legend and Greek tragedy. She also imitated images of femininity found on the walls of Pompeii! The tableaux became extremely popular first in Naples (where Sir Willliam was envoy) and then across Europe where Emma's shawl dance according to anecdotes caused a storm of approbation. British ladies performed Emma's 'Attitudes' at dinner parties. As Emma could strike 150 poses in 90 minutes, the 2010 Radio Four programme compared her concept of a rapid succession of postures with the camera effects of early silent cinema. Emma was a movie star well before the movies.

By this time she was the wife of Hamilton. Blundell (in her 2008 presentation) quoted Horace Walpole, one of the many sons of Robert, and known as a wit, scholar, letter writer and designer of Strawberry Hill, who tartly commented that Hamilton had 'married his gallery of statues'. This brings me back to Korda's gloriously photographed film in which Vivien Leigh's stunning looks were seen as a distraction from the cinematic narrative – at least as far as the *New York Times* critic was concerned.[11] It is true that the camera adores her. Whatever liberties were taken with the historical fact and however much aspects of Emma's life had to be sanitized, this movie is a remarkably close fit to the story of Pygmalion and the ivory girl in Ovid – and not just because of the Shavian 'make-over' element.

When Emma shows her distress at not bidding Horatio goodbye, Sir William muses upon his reactions as a deceived husband. He coolly categorizes the sort of man who is born to be deceived, the sort who does not know and the sort who does not care. Emma adds a fourth type, the hard husband who is empty and gives nothing. She accuses him of only wanting her as an ornament and that for him, she is just as dead to him as his statues. Hence his cynical and barbed riposte quoted above. It seems that in reality William Hamilton willingly accepted the ménage a trois with Nelson, which would suggest that he regarded Emma as an artistic asset rather than a wife. However, in the film he is also shown as feeling affection and concern for her to the end and in real life, he was not necessarily a cold Pygmalion figure, needing to be brought to life.

The film portrays Hamilton from the outset as a collector of beautiful things. The French ambassador cannot believe that the Romney painting of Emma that Hamilton possesses has a real woman as a model. He insists it must be an ideal conjured up by the artist as no woman ever lived with such colouring and godlike simplicity. However when he hears of Emma's ethereal beauty and of her disreputable past, he questions the wisdom of Hamilton's welcome to this tarnished creature however lovely she is. Hamilton shows him a beautiful classical bust and utters a speech about such a wonderful sculpture lying in the mud for 2000 years.[12] He says 'what of its past? It changes hands every year until someone understands its beauty.'

The message of the film is more equivocal and less charitable. The first scene of *That Hamilton Woman* (itself a pejorative title) is of Emma, drunk and dishevelled, showing the ravages of time and telling her story to the women in the Parisian cell (a prison for the Propoetides?) The flashback is signposted by Emma doubting the truth of her own life and her famous beauty and saying she looks in vain in the mirror for her former face. Taking all these facets of her story on screen together, the cinematic Emma embodies the identity of Pygmalion's ivory girl as statue, as whore, as goddess and as *simulacrum* in the sense of a dead thing and an illusory ideal.

Ironically the film lovingly dwells upon and enlivens the image of an historical Emma whom we can only admire in paintings but does not reconstruct or represent the famous Attitudes to delight our gaze. Vivien Leigh gives a wonderfully playful and entrancing performance in the title role but she is denied the opportunity to show Emma being artistic. She does not sing or perform attitudes for the viewer although she does mimic several members of the Neopolitan court and she speaks Italian to the manner born. Also, it could be argued that Leigh in the title role conveys all the grace, poise and allure that the original Emma must have possessed. It is all the more poignant that the film frames her as a worn and emotionally shut down woman looking for the next drink and frozen in time since Nelson's death and her own demise. Leigh's last lines are 'there is no "then," there is no "after".'

Looking Back

As we know from Orpheus, this can be a hazardous process. To reverse the cautionary tale, I have found myself in danger of losing sight of the perfect woman of my title while discussing the form and content of individual movies. I trust Ovid has not been pushed too far out of the frame. It is probably no bad thing that the films tended to take on a life of their own. This is something recommended by Joshua (2001) whether the work is cinematic or literary. She urged those of us working on the reception of classical texts not 'to appropriate the modern work to such a degree as to abrogate the cultural identity of the author' (2001, pxiii). Joshua challenged the assumption that mythical archetypes operate subliminally and that subsequent texts are essentially moulded into an ancient pattern. Since Joshua suggested a less iconic approach to classical mythical narratives as the cultural fount Czarniawska has written in the introduction to Gabriel's *Myths, Stories and Organisations* (2004, p. viii):

> For those, who like myself, believe in surface connections rather than deep archetypes, plots are strong because they have been institutionalized, repeated through the centuries, and well-rehearsed with different audiences. One should therefore speak of conventional rather than traditional plots, and of dominant rather than strong plots; they are 'strong' in a given time and place. Observe there are many mythologies and each of them contains many myths, many Greek dramas and a great many folk tales, of which certain are better remembered in certain times than others.

Czarniawska does, however, recommend reading the original texts where these strong plots first appear to appreciate their context and complexity since their apparent simplicity in popular culture is an 'epiphenomenon of their constant retrieval and reuse'. That should be a comfort for the classicist except that it is not my experience that popular culture is synonymous with simplicity. The term 'popular culture' can muddy the waters whether it is applied to modern or ancient times as Winkler ably demonstrated in his introduction to the 2001 edition of *Classical Myth and Culture in the Cinema*. Storey (2003, pp. 1–47) provides a broadly historical critique of popular culture starting from the premise that it is a category invented by intellectuals. He challenges the assumption that mass culture is invariably homogeneous, diluting revolutionary consciousness (the Left perspective) or polluting 'the sacred sphere of culture' (the fear of the Right). See especially pp. 24–31 for a discussion upon the role of film and of the cultural products of the modern media in 'fettering consciousness' and achieving 'dull conformity'.

Ovid's myth of Pygmalion has enabled me to compare and contrast disparate films across the decades and from different cinematic genres. Ovidian scholars and devoted fans of the poet would agree that certain of his mythic narratives work better than others but all are testament to his supreme poetic skill. There is bound to be considerable variation in the quality of modern visual texts with a Pygmalion timbre. I still wonder why

FIGURE 8.1 This image appeared in The Sketch and is from the short silent film (Ivy Close Films, 1912) produced by Elwin Neame and Ivy Close, a successful husband and wife team. Elwin died tragically at age 37 in an accident. Their son Ronald Neame went on to be a famous cinematographer working on Pascal's 1938 film Pygmalion among many other productions. His mother Ivy stars as the central figure in the picture and could be both the statue and Venus who vivifies her. The pose is reminiscent of nineteenth century classical paintings (in the style of Alfred Moore, Lord Lytton, Alma Tadema et al.) Walter Crane, the socialist artist, also used female figures in classical garb to depict abstract notions of Liberty and Justice in posters and banners for the more militant organised labour movement in the late Victorian period. But the seated women at the bottom also recall the 1875 painting The Babylonian Marriage Market by Edwin Long.

The photograph is fascinating in many ways – the women in repose prefigure a Busby Berkeley tableau – they also form a densely packed frieze and a decorative backdrop to the 'arising' statue.

Image reproduced with kind permission of Dr Amanda Wrigley.

I wasted 88 minutes of my and my brother's life watching the 1973 film, *Miss Leslie's Dolls* at the National Film Theatre in 2010! Conversely, there is always 'the one that got away' factor and the frustration of a serendipitous and belated discovery of a flawed but fascinating story with an Ovidian statue subtext. *The Cloning of Joanna May*, a Granada television series based on the Fay Weldon novel and aired in early 1992, only recently came to my attention with its plethora of Pygmalion *topoi*. Aspects of the late twentieth century from nuclear science to the narcissism of youth and youth culture receive Weldon's mischievously satirical treatment.

Carl (Brian Cox) clones the ex-wife who betrayed him (Joanna is played by Patricia Hodge) but the three youthful Joannas summoned to Carl's mansion so he can choose his new perfect woman are a disappointment. They are judged by Carl's sinister chauffeur / assassin as 'typical of the age, at best promiscuous and at worst lesbian'. The love / hate relationship between Carl and the original Joanna was doomed because he worshipped her as a goddess and then condemned her as a whore when he witnessed her infidelity. After a number of narrative twists and turns, a dying Carl asks Joanna to 'remake him' and in the last scenes we see all the Joannas lavishing love and laughter upon toddler, Carl. 'Pygmalion' has been reborn.

Joanna May is yet another modern narrative that can refresh the response to Ovid's *Metamorphoses*. All the screen texts under discussion in this book engage on various levels (superficial to profound) with the story of Pygmalion and the statue into which Ovid introduced new layers of sophistication. The films like the myth, brings to the surface issues such as the ethics and aesthetics of constructing and controlling a synthetic being, the mutual manipulation that may take place between the creator and the created, the fragility of human identity on a physical, psychological and artistic level, and the role of the reader / viewer as a witness to a miraculous metamorphosis.

Moving Forward

It is a challenge to create a consistent exchange of discourses in the interplay between the ancient text and the modern medium. Where possible I have written of Ovid's strongly visual poetry in cinematic terms and conversely pictured movie characters and events as if they had passed into his text and through the mythical filter of the *Metamorphoses*. This is a showing rather than a telling technique. There may well be room for a further book (not necessarily by me!) that lays bare and delves deeper into the dialectical process of blending the theoretical frameworks and critical approaches used by academics in ancient literature and in film and media studies. If a cinematic text and an ancient poem can be used as mutually interpretative tools we probably need to say more about how and why this is happening.[13]

Paradoxically Ovid's statue story by its very nature encourages the reader to imagine a static rather than a moving image. I have been more successful in importing scenes. motifs and subtexts from the *Metamorphoses* into the movies and less so in applying cinematic tropes to the Pygmalion narrative and its related myths. Films can bring various versions of the myth to life but sometimes, as we have seen, the sculptor and his ivory girl might have a stronger figurative than palpable presence on the screen. Thinking back to Bloom's designation of the cinema as a Pygmalionesque space where the dream of the inanimate becoming animate is promised, I began to wonder whether the myth had an endless capacity as a metaphor for the history of film.

When the Silent Era gave way to the Talkies, the artistic product suffered initially because positioning the microphones for dialogue restricted the actors' movement on screen There were also some disappointing voices. Not all the stars spoke as elegantly as they looked and not all made the transition even after elocution lessons! (Both these problems were parodied in the 1952 film, *Singin' in the Rain*, directed by Gene Kelly and Stanley Donen and itself a movie about constructing images for the stars.)

Although the statue is silent in Ovid's narrative Myrrha (the statue's great grand daughter) delivers a rhetorical monologue on the (ironically) unspeakable passion she feels for her father. Myrrha's declamation echoes Pygmalion's desire for his ivory creation and so, in the eyes of many classical scholars, compromises the integrity of Pygmalion's passion for his statue. A woman's voice critiques the patriarchal desires of a man. On the other hand, the descendants of the ivory girl in the Shavian mould are all given voice but we have to ask whether they have a better or a suitable song to sing. Can we argue that the progress of Pygmalion's statue from dumb show to fully articulate woman will always be equally chequered and that she may still, in her various incarnations, be struggling to speak or indeed to be heard.

A similar but more tenuous point might be made about the painting of the statue and the prevailing artistic traditions that kept her a tasteful white marble. The beautiful black and white of *One Touch of Venus* produced a far more convincing goddess in Ava Gardner than Vanna White's deity who should have benefitted from 1980s's colour cinematography. Once again a significant advance in the history of film which should have made its representations more real can do so at the cost of its aesthetic impact. As with ancient sculptures, the restoration of faded colour (witness *Vertigo*) requires painstaking work and some processes (Eastman Color for instance) were particularly vulnerable to deterioration. The computer colouring of films which were originally black and white is as controversial as tinting ancient marble was in the nineteenth century.

Last Words?

In short, Ovid's Pygmalion and his ivory girl have an endless capacity for reinvention both as narrative and as image or signifier on screen. Verdoodt and Rutten posed the questions 'What do popular movies teach us?' and 'How can we use (popular) movies to teach?' They do not neglect the learning curve this involves for teachers who will need, like their students, to become 'bi- or multi-Discoursal'. The classical community working on myth in mass culture is also taking academics out of their comfort zone. Doherty (2001, pp. 154–155) concurs with Rose (in Winkler, 2001) that in analysing recent films we can consciously use the same theoretical approaches we apply to myths.

When modern myth makers at the movies and on television transform seminal stories from the distant past they demonstrate their creativity but also reveal the commercial considerations that go with the entertainment territory. The role of the receivers (audience and viewers) is a complex one in which both passivity and pro-activity can influence the cinematic narrative and its processes. The challenge of defining this relationship has motivated me to revisit scholarship on Ovid such as Wheeler (1999, pp. 165–177) and Feldherr (2010, pp. 52–59) who discuss the diversity of reader responses and the different levels of credulity Ovid consciously created among contemporary receivers of his text. Drawing analogies between performances and audiences then and now might be methodologically insupportable (there were no fan sites forcing Ovid to redirect his narrative arc!) but the tension between producing great art and bowing to contemporary cultural norms and expectations might be a point of correspondence. External pressures whether these take the form of movie moguls, studio industries or emperors with an eye on image making is another possible area where Foucauldian theories of power structures and their discourses might be equally applied.

Students, teachers and researchers who are exploring and interpreting a very different civilization and putting into historical context the stories it tells about itself, could be more explicitly encouraged to do the same with their own culture. The contemporary media continues to refashion ancient narratives for a modern-day constituency. If we are genuinely interested in the impact of classical myth on current viewers we need to be aware of the social and ideological situatedness of audiences today and to acknowledge their global diversity. I am more and more convinced that those of us researching into and teaching myth in mass culture will be missing a trick if we do not endeavour to understand what happens to myth at the point of entry.

We are better at exploring the motives of the creators of mythical motifs and tropes on screen than we are in valuing the reactions of the consumers.[14] My PhD student's research is already yielding insights into what knowledge of the classical world viewers of the twenty-first century bring to the process and into the awareness (or not) of mythical referencing on screen. After all, in an age when visual imagery constantly washes over us, we have become a community of viewers whether or not we operate in the spheres of teaching, learning and researching. If by promoting powerful myths like Pygmalion we could persuade those just watching to start studying with us, then classical reception studies really will have taken a democratic turn.[15]

Appendix: Ovid's Pygmalion

Metamorphoses, Book Ten, Lines 238–297

Sunt tamen obscenae Venerem Propoetides ausae
esse negare deam; pro quo sua numinis ira
corpora cum fama primae vulgasse feruntur,
utque pudor cessit, sanguisque induruit oris,
in rigidum parvo silicem discrimine versae.
Quas quia Pygmalion aevum per crimen agentis
viderat, offensus vitiis, quae plurima menti
femineae natura dedit, sine coniuge caelebs
vivebat thalamique diu consorte carebat.
interea niveum mira feliciter arte
sculpsit ebur formamque dedit, qua femina nasci
nulla potest, operisque sui concepit amorem.
virginis est verae facies, quam vivere credas,
et, si non obstet reverentia, velle moveri:
ars adeo latet arte sua. miratur et haurit
pectore Pygmalion simulati corporis ignes.
saepe manus operi temptantes admovet, an sit
corpus an illud ebur, nec adhuc ebur esse fatetur.
oscula dat reddique putat loquiturque tenetque
et credit tactis digitos insidere membris
et metuit, pressos veniat ne livor in artus,
et modo blanditias adhibet, modo grata puellis
munera fert illi conchas teretesque lapillos
et parvas volucres et flores mille colorum
liliaque pictasque pilas et ab arbore lapsas
Heliadum lacrimas; ornat quoque vestibus artus,
dat digitis gemmas, dat longa monilia collo,
aure leves bacae, redimicula pectore pendent:
cuncta decent; nec nuda minus formosa videtur.

conlocat hanc stratis concha Sidonide tinctis
adpellatque tori sociam adclinataque colla
mollibus in plumis, tamquam sensura, reponit.
"Festa dies Veneris tota celeberrima Cypro
venerat, et pandis inductae cornibus aurum
conciderant ictae nivea cervice iuvencae,
turaque fumabant, cum munere functus ad aras
constitit et timide 'si, di, dare cuncta potestis,
sit coniunx, opto,' non ausus 'eburnea virgo'
dicere, Pygmalion 'similis mea' dixit 'eburnae.'
sensit, ut ipsa suis aderat Venus aurea festis,
vota quid illa velint et, amici numinis omen,
flamma ter accensa est apicemque per aera duxit.
ut rediit, simulacra suae petit ille puellae
incumbensque toro dedit oscula: visa tepere est;
admovet os iterum, manibus quoque pectora temptat:
temptatum mollescit ebur positoque rigore
subsidit digitis ceditque, ut Hymettia sole
cera remollescit tractataque pollice multas
flectitur in facies ipsoque fit utilis usu.
dum stupet et dubie gaudet fallique veretur,
rursus amans rursusque manu sua vota retractat.
corpus erat! saliunt temptatae pollice venae.
tum vero Paphius plenissima concipit heros
verba, quibus Veneri grates agat, oraque tandem
ore suo non falsa premit, dataque oscula virgo
sensit et erubuit timidumque ad lumina lumen
attollens pariter cum caelo vidit amantem.
coniugio, quod fecit, adest dea, iamque coactis
cornibus in plenum noviens lunaribus orbem
illa Paphon genuit, de qua tenet insula nomen.

Notes

Introduction

[1] In her chapter for Charles Martindale's collected essays, *Ovid Renewed* published in 1988, Jane Miller was an able to distil her discussion of Ovid's literary legacies in the Victorian period concentrating upon W.S. Gilbert's *Pygmalion and Galatea* and G.B. Shaw's *Pygmalion*.

[2] Hardwick (2003, p.4) writes: 'It used sometimes to be said that reception studies only yields insights into the receiving society. Of course they do this, but they also focus critical attention back towards the ancient source and sometimes frame new questions or retrieve aspects of the source which have now been marginalized or forgotten.'

[3] Laurie Taylor chaired a discussion on *Thinking Allowed* (Radio 4, 13 October 2010) in which Rachel Lara Cohen talked about her article 'When it pays to be friendly: employment relationships and emotional labour in hairstyling' (*Sociological Review* vol. 55, Issue 2, May 2010, 197–218.). Such skilled service workers might develop a sustained and close relationship with clients but their creativity in beautifying them is still at bottom a commodity. They still sell their labour power. It was interesting to hear that subtle forms of alienation occur when the emotional labour the hair stylist invests especially in long standing customers might not be valued or leads to exploitation of their energy and time.

[4] I was asked what I thought about the film *Stepford Wives* (see Chapter 5). On reflection and given the age of the girls, they may have been thinking about the uninspiring 2004 remake or the TV sequels rather than the 1975 movie.

[5] There are a number of persuasive interpretations of Ovid's poetry that argue for an anti-Augustan subtext or at least an ideological equivocation about the nature of imperial rule. Scholarly responses to Ovid's ethics as well as his aesthetics will figure at appropriate moments in this book. D. Feeney's introduction to the Penguin Classics, *Ovid Metamorphoses*, London 2004, (translated by David Raeburn), especially pp. xvi–xix, and pp. xxxi–xxxiii, gives a balanced and thoughtful view of Ovid's poetic programme and his relationship to the Augustan regime.

Chapter 1

[1] These are women of Cyprus or more specifically of the Amathus region of the island.

2   I have kept to the variety of tenses, past and present, in the original Latin. This might be a little awkward in English but it indicates where Ovid selects a vivid immediate 'as it happens' tense. I have not attempted to reproduce the poetic rhythms of the original, the six beat line that characterizes the epic metre of dactylic hexameter. There are a number of accomplished and elegant translations which give the English a poetic shape and sound. Raeburn and Melville appear in the bibliography.

3   See recently, P.J. Johnson (*Ovid Before Exile*, p. 96).

4   Ennius' source for this practice is Euhemerus of Messene who wrote an imaginary travelogue *The Sacred Scripture* in the fourth century BCE. Euhemerus makes Venus responsible for the founding of the art of the courtesan on the island so that she would have human companions in her shameless whoring. The existence of temple prostitution in Cyprus is disputed as is evidence of the practice in any of Venus' major cult centres, Corinth included, a city know for its many brothels. See Cyrino (2010, p. 42) and *The Oxford Classical Dictionary* (1996, p. 120). A similar consensus was reached in essays of 2009 (Scheer and Lindner, eds).

5   We know that the Propoetides are a kin group. The *ides* ending suggests they are the daughters of Propoetus but there are no existing references to this figure. Their family name also contains the words *pro* and *poeta* meaning on behalf of the poet, which might suggest that they are Ovid's invention. See Bauer (1962, pp. 13–14). The name Ovid gives them is similar to a group of girls called the Proetides. They were the daughters of Proetus, king of Tiryns. The Proetides insulted the goddess Hera's statue and were driven mad by her. Earlier in the poem the grieving figure of an Assyrian king, Cinyras, is woven into Minerva's (the Greek goddess, Athena) tapestry (*Met.* 6, 98–99). This king's daughters were turned into the stone steps of her temple. Cinyras is also the name of the descendant of Pygmalion and the statue. Ovid may be importing names and motifs from other myths with his introduction of the Propoetides in the Pygmalion cycle of stories.

6   In making this observation I am reminded of the riposte uttered to Marilyn Monroe in an early role as Miss Casswell (*All About Eve*, 1950, directed by Joseph L. Mankiewicz) when she does not want to call the waiter 'butler' in case someone's name is Butler. George Sanders (playing cynical theatre critic, Addison de Witt) admits half-amused, half-exasperated that she has a point, 'an idiotic one but a point.'

7   See James (2003, pp. 71–75).

8   Stoichita (2008, pp. 1–6).

9   F. Ahl (1985) raises the possibility of a pygmy size Pygmalion. Barolsky and D'Ambra (2009, 19–23) have recently written on the doll like nature of the statue and Pygmalion's playing with a girl's toy. Perhaps their view of Pygmalion as emotionally regressive could be further teased out. ('For he captures the innocence of a child deep in a world of make-believe, lost in an illusion', p. 21. Discuss!) A boyish Pygmalion gives his doll childish trinkets and then matures into a man ornamenting her with adult jewellery.

10 Sharrock (1991, p. 43) observes: 'It could be, however, that the *livor* Pygmalion fears is Envy as well as bruising. Consummate beauty and consummate artistic

creation always risk attracting the attention of *Livor*. The hint that Envy might be involved reinforces the point of the successfulness of Pygmalion's art.'

11 Onions (1980, p. 23) points out that the Romans had a fondness for unpainted marble statuary. By the second century CE marble in its natural state was increasingly being praised for its subtle shades and for the shapes and figures it possessed for the imaginative viewer. Onions' article is seminal in its observations upon abstraction and imagination in late antiquity and the increase in literary descriptions of art when artworks themselves were becoming less descriptive.

12 The properties of ivory are complex. See O. Krzyszkowska's study (1990). It is particularly prone to discolouration if exposed to moisture. Ovid's choice of ivory as a material is variously interpreted in J. Elsner's and A. Sharrock's two-part article of 1993, 'Reviewing Pygmalion'. See also Fantham (2004, p. 60) on ivory functioning as an overlay material.

13 The correspondence between statues and corpses has been explored by a number of scholars in relation to the Pygmalion myth. Orpheus' loss, retrieval and second loss of Eurydice should remind the reader that the narrator of Pygmalion has attempted to summon up an ideal woman from the dead. For a thorough exposition of the death like properties of sculpted bodies, see Gross (1992, pp. 7–30). See Wood (2002, pp. xvii–xviii) for a similar view of the 'robot' replicant in *Blade Runner*. An android is a manufactured being but also corresponds to 'a revenant, returning from the grave to mimic humanity; as if death were inherent in the *simulacrum*'.

14 Sharrock (1993, pp. 179–180) notes that the horns of the moon feature in Ovid's periphrastic description of the statue's pregnancy (lines 295–297). This is part of her discussion on the imagery of creation and procreation in the Pygmalion and the Myrrha stories.

15 There are several mythical stories in Ovid's poem which have a 'two in one' motif from the illusion of Narcissus to the union of Salmacis and Hermaphroditus in *Metamorphoses* Book Four. This might occur on a more literal or locational level, for instance the joining together of Pyramus and Thisbe as ashes in one urn, the pathetic coda to the story of the star-crossed lovers: *una requiescit in urna* (Book 4, line 166). For Salmacis, see Chapter 8.

16 Perhaps Ovid is marking the end of elegy by transferring the elegiac lover// poet to the mythical realm and then having Pygmalion make an honest woman of the statue/mistress – a sop to the wrathful Augustus? This is of course highly speculative and could be argued the other way!

17 As with Pygmalion, Ovid puts another pertinent myth in proximity to Narcissus by having the nymph Echo chase after him. Echo proves to another person even though she can only repeat the words of Narcissus. She is an auditory reflection with a body. P. James (2004, pp. 1–20) has also observed that Narcissus' parents are a river god and a water nymph so his mistaking of a lovely creature in the pool as a real inhabitant with a substance of its own is not quite as delusional as it first seems. See Bartsch (2006, pp. 84–94) for a similar point and also a discussion about the existence of a female twin for Narcissus in versions of the myth available to Ovid.

18 The beauty gene passes down through the generations, culminating in the physical perfection of Adonis, the male child of Myrrha and her father. Adonis is beloved by Venus and we are told that Envy itself praised his beauty (*Metamorphoses* Book Ten, line 515, *laudaret faciem Livor quoque*). However, Adonis dies young, savaged by the tusks of the boar he has wounded. See Viarre (1968, p. 240) for the prevalence of vegetation myths in Orpheus's Cypriot cycle of stories.

19 Miller (1988, p. 208) calls Ovid's narrative a remythologization of the legend narrated in Philostephanus' lost work *On Cyprus* (written in Alexandria, in the third century BCE) in which the king of Cyprus falls in love with a cult statue of Aphrodite. The Christian apologists Clement and Arnobius (from which we derive our knowledge of the pre-Ovidian version) turned the *hieros gamos* story into an episode demonstrating the obscene and perverse in pagan belief.

20 Keen (1982, p. 138) describes the statue pitching forward as if at the moment of her birth and so needing to be steadied.

21 The monstrous aspect of the living statue and its influence on Gothic horror is examined by Gross (1992, pp. 9–30), as is Medusa. Medusa the gorgon whose glance had the power of petrifaction lurks beneath the flesh turned to stone motif and its reverse process throughout Ovid's *Metamorphoses*. See Bauer's 1962 comprehensive article on the motif in general.

22 Myrrha is described by the narrator as not daring to ask for what she really wants. The Latin word *ausus* from the verb *audeo* 'I dare' is used for the audacity exhibited by the women of Cyprus in their denial that Venus is a goddess. Pygmalion 'not daring' to pray for his statue as a wife drew a positive contrast with the Propoetides. However, the same word links Myrrha to her great grandfather Pygmalion as she is equally hesitant about articulating her true feelings. She then nervously indicates that she would be willing to entertain a husband 'like her father', just as Pygmalion prayed for someone like his statue, his own creation. Myrrha's unfortunate desire goes unnoticed as she appears to be exhibiting appropriate affection and complimenting Cinyras by asking for a bedfellow in his image. See Viarre (1968, pp. 235–236), Leach (1974, p. 123) and McKinley (2001, pp. 33–42) for the re-reading and rehabilitation of Myrrha's character in medieval and Renaissance commentaries.

23 Elsner (1993, pp. 165–166) argues that Ovid excludes the reader at the point of transformation and ultimately cheats us of participating in Pygmalion's fantasy. In 2007, p.131, he wrote of the reader being metamorphosed into an excluded voyeur.

24 I appreciate the generosity of *The Classical Bulletin* editors, Shannon Byrne and Ed Cueva who have permitted my re-use in this book of some sections from my 2003 article.

25 O'Sullivan does not engage with the extended explorations of *Vertigo* for its Ovidian resonances and proximity to the Pygmalion myth which feature in James (2003) and Stoichita (2008).

26 For Ovid's sources and his manipulation of the myths see the now standard works of Bömer (the 1980 commentary) and Brewer (1941).

Chapter 2

1. Kord and Krimmer (2005, pp. 1–15) analyse the female role models that have populated Hollywood films since the 1990s but they also address the screen personas with which the mainstream 'star' actresses have become associated through the parts they have played.
2. Leslie in Waine (2005, p. 46) makes the interesting point that the demystification that has occurred with films, techniques and actors (through the culture industry and apparatus surrounding the process of film-making) prompted the Hollywood star system to 'reinstate the awe before the product, by glorifying certain individuals, creating hierarchies, making them superhuman, reinforcing what Benjamin saw as the rotten shimmer of commodified star personality by creating cults around them'.
3. The film was first made by Cukor as *What Price Hollywood* in 1932 from the novel of that name by Adela Rogers St Johns. William Wellman directed *A Star is Born* in 1937 with Janet Gaynor as the ingénue actress and Fredric March as her patron and lover. Frank Pierson directed a version with Barbra Streisand and Kris Kristofferson in 1976.
4. The director's debt to classicising art of the nineteenth century was featured in the 2001 Hitchcock et L'Art (Montreal and Paris.)
5. Hitchcock was in the habit of briefly appearing in his films. Viewers could play 'spot the director' and I imagine that this was Hitchcock's equivalent to the artist signing his work.
6. The director's leading ladies are often lumped together as Hitchcock's blondes. However, from the Silent Era to the early Talkies there was a counter-image to the fiery sexually forward redhead or brunette, that of the blonde bombshell (Jean Harlow was a case in point – she is rumoured to have had her pubic hair lightened!) Hitchcock made Miriam, a wife of easy virtue, fair-haired in his 1951 film *Strangers on a Train*. Laura Elliott played the part and Farley Granger took the role of the wronged husband Guy who is romantically involved with respectable high-class girl Anne (played by brunette Ruth Roman). Roman did not convey much suppressed passion, according to the director. (She was foisted on Hitchcock by Warner Brothers.)
7. The use of doorways as real and symbolic framing devices is discussed by Stoichita in relation to *Vertigo*. See also the analysis of Burne-Jones' Pygmalion paintings in Chapter 1 and the significance of thresholds for his creation of an otherworldliness for the myth.
8. The wobbly and wailing refrain for JB's strange interludes is reprised by Bernard Herrmann in his full orchestra score for *Marnie*. The musical homage is particularly noticeable in the hunting scene.
9. Peter Conrad (2001, p. 10) did not find it a profound image: 'with Ingrid Bergman (in footage junked by the producer, Selznick) calcifying into a columnar white goddess who sports a spiky dog collar'.
10. Lawrence (1991) discusses the control exercised over the voice of Alicia, taking the myth of Echo and Narcissus (pp. 1–7) as a metaphor for the suppression of the difficult speaking woman in films of this era.

11 In 1941 Bergman had taken the part of Ivy in the 1941 remake (effectively) of Rouben Mamoulian's 1932 *Dr Jekyll and Mr Hyde*. She was originally earmarked for the part of Jekyll's refined fiancée but Bergman and Lana Turner asked to have their roles swapped. So Bergman broke out of a pattern of parts in which she was wide eyed and innocent to play Ivy, a London East End girl of easy virtue whom Hyde controls, torments and finally murders. Turner, also against type, plays the doctor's loyal and loving wife to be, an ideal woman simultaneously warm and virginal. The 1941 film was directed by Victor Fleming and has a fascinating and risqué delusion scene in which Spencer Tracy in the title role(s) imagines he has the two women in his life harnessed like horses. He whips them along with a maniacal expression of arousal on his face. Mamoulian's earlier film had enhanced the eroticism of Robert Louis Stevenson's novel by introducing two women, angel and whore, to fulfil Jekyll's suppressed desires as well as Hyde's sadism.
12 In her last film *High Society* (a musical version of *The Philadelphia Story*) Kelly played Tracy Lord who undergoes a metamorphosis from ideal to real, unblemished to fallible. Kelly looks stunning but Katherine Hepburn in the original film was a very hard act to follow. In both films (the screenplay was only slightly altered) there are plenty of references to the heroine's stony heartedness, her inability to soften towards her errant father and her uncompromising rigidity towards her ex-husband. However, she remonstrates with her fiancé, George, when he calls her a goddess and praises her purity. The musical number 'Fair Miss Frigidaire' (sung to Tracy by the smitten journalist) could be a refrain for a modern-day Pygmalion serenading his statue, especially the line 'what you require/is the proper squire/to fire your heart'.
13 Hedren gives a heartfelt delivery of this line. At this stage in their director/actor relationship, Hitchcock and Tippi Hedren, the star, were barely talking. She was disturbed by his obsession with her (verging on infatuation) and resented his attempt to control her career. Hitchcock had groomed Hedren for stardom after seeing her in television commercials.
14 Lil, Mark's sister-in-law, asks 'Who's the dish?' when she first notices Marnie. Attractive brunette, Diane Baker, played Lil who clearly lusts after Mark and yet mirrors his ruthless pursuit of Marnie in her determination to find out the truth of the heroine's identity.
15 Hitchcock's cinematic tour de force was out of circulation for many years. The director jealously guarded this masterpiece of movie-making for his private consumption, which suggests it was as much a labour of love as an artwork, rather like Pygmalion's statue. The negatives suffered significant deterioration in storage but the film was restored by Robert A. Harris and James C. Katz and reissued in the 1990s. Particularly interesting (and with further shades of the statue) is their search for a pastiche of colours that would reproduce the effects of the original Technicolor process.
16 I have already alluded to Brown (2005), Stoichita (2005, 2008) and O'Sullivan (2008). 'Marías' May 2011 article (pp. 44–47) in *Sight and Sound* revisits Hitchcock's *Vertigo* as the apogee of the director's skilled artisanship and celebrates the 'structural audacity' of his mise en scènes. Particularly interesting

is Marías' recognition of Hitchcock's 'strange synthesis of various myths of Western culture, connected to the mystery of artistic creation' (p. 46) and 'of the way in which the Pygmalion, Prometheus and Orpheus narratives are evoked through the sieve of romanticism and German expressionism.'

17 Interestingly, the French gave *Vertigo* the title *Sueurs Froides*. This translates as Cold Sweat. Sueurs sounds like Soeurs – I am sure no Ovidian pun was intended but Cold Sisters would be a wonderful allusion to the Propoetides!

18 Rosati (1983, p. 67, n.33) observes the ambiguity in the Latin word *umbra* both image and ghost in the Narcissus and Pygmalion myths. Brill calls Judy as the *umbra* of Madeleine 'a failed Persephone unable to return to the kingdom of Pluto to give new life to the forlorn lover'.

19 See James (2003, p.81, n.56) on Modleski's analysis. O'Sullivan (2008, p. 139) also uses Modleski on the concept of femininity as a male construct and 'a matter of external trappings, of roles and masquerades, without essence'.

20 The swirl of Madeleine's bun in imitation of Carlotta's hair is one of many vertiginous visual images in the film.

21 O'Sullivan (2008, p. 139) links Pygmalion's timidity and fear of his own desire for a fetishized model of femininity with Scottie's naivety about women and his love–hate relationship with Madeleine/Judy.

22 Enterline (2000, pp. 137–139) gives a close analysis of Marston's levels of meaning in this stanza. The Elizabethan poet is playing a subtle linguistic game which culminates in his claim that sex with a statue is 'sayable' whereas intercourse with actual female substance is not fit reporting. As Kuchar (2002, p.3) concludes in his review, Enterline convincingly demonstrates that Ovid's rhetorical strategies as well as his narratives have been inspirational: 'Petrarch, Marston and Shakespeare emerge as sophisticated theorists of language as well as working within and against a tradition that closely aligns language and eroticism, rhetoric and subjectivity'.

23 Flavières has already decided that this imitation of Madeleine has bad taste in earrings and he detests her painted nails. He has the impression he is looking at a badly dubbed film with some nonentity speaking the part of a star. (See Stoichita, 2008, p .192 for part of this extract and James 2003, pp. 87–88 for relevant excerpts from the novel.) Unlike Scottie, he has tracked down this resemblance of Madeleine after seeing her in a newsreel shot at the cinema. Renee's first appearance *as Renee* is significantly as a fleeting shadow on the screen.

24 This is a refrain we find in Shaw' play *Pygmalion* about Eliza's predicament once she is removed from her social setting and made into a lady. See Chapter 3.

25 Gévigne does not pull off the brilliant crime in the novel because Flavières flees from the scene and is too bereaved and cowardly to give evidence at the hearing.

26 In the novel *The Living and the Dead*, Flavières strangles Madeleine when the whole truth is finally revealed.

27 I finally caught up with *Corridor of Mirrors* in August 2010 when I viewed it on video at the British Film Institute's archives in London. My thanks go to Steve Deahl who offered some helpful interpretations of the film and researched into the missing footage. There were clearly scenes set in the court room, as the

cast list includes a counsel for defence, a public prosecutor and a psychiatrist, none of whom appears in the archive print. At a rough calculation the film at the BFI was around ten minutes short. To date it is unavailable commercially.
28. Stoichita (2008, p. 185) observes the symbolic power of thresholds. He notes about the doorways and framing shots in general that 'the form of a frame conversing with a "living form" is one of the obsessive motifs of *Vertigo*'.

Chapter 3

1. I like to see Daphne as a prototype of Betty Grable whose highly praised legs were famously insured by the studios with Lloyds of London for a million dollars each. Thomson (2010, p. 390) notes her appeal to the GIs on Pacific atolls and characterizes her as 'brassy, energetic, and amused, but her body was too pert to be disturbing, too thoroughly healthy to be interesting'.
2. Hardie (2006, pp. 46–51) explores the satire and the subtleties in Ovid's portrayal of the god and the figurative layers of Daphne's metamorphosis. See also Feldherr (2001, pp. 172–173 and 2010, pp. 90–96) for the metamorphic dynamics of Daphne's fate and especially (p. 94) Apollo as artist and external focalizer wishing to freeze frame and prolong the visual erotics of his pursuit.
3. Daphne's transformation saves her from the proverbial fate worse than death but it also looks forward to the metamorphosis of Myrrha into the myrrh tree (*Metamorphoses*, Book Ten, lines 489–498). Myrrha prays for oblivion. She does not want to belong to the living or the dead so she sinks down into the bark and embraces anonymity. The troubled princess of Cyprus treats transformation as a voluntary suicide but she still has to give birth to Adonis. Her suffering and travail do not cease until the tree trunk splits apart and Myrrha's baby tumbles forth. The boy Adonis is so beautiful that Venus takes him as a mortal lover.
4. The bibliography on Shaw's *Pygmalion* and its relationship with the myth continues to expand. I have not consciously duplicated the interpretations of others but hope to have added additional nuances to the play which simultaneously highlight the multi-layering in Ovid's narrative.
5. Joshua (2001, pp. 97–133) and Miller (1988, pp. 209–211 but in greater detail in her 1982 thesis) helpfully place Shaw and nineteenth-century Pygmalion plays firmly within their historical and literary context.
6. Even though Hepburn needed to be dubbed by Marnie Nixon, she was the iconic star while Julie Andrews was at that point a relative unknown at the box office. The title of the musical version suggests a Cockney pronunciation of Mayfair Lady, which could be interpreted as a comical allusion to Eliza's duality at the outset.
7. No doubt the programme now includes *The King's Speech* (based on the true story of King George VI). This film was called a reverse Pygmalion film in the *Guardian* weekend short synopsis Reviews throughout January 2011. Based on historical fact, the film tells the story of an unorthodox but talented speech therapist who successfully teaches a member of the royal family to conquer a stammer and prepare for a key radio broadcast to the nation (hence the double entendre of the title). As a duke and then a king, the pupil stands in a

godlike relationship to the teacher but the arrangement develops into a friendship based on mutual respect (but then these are two men, after all!).

8. Shaw gave Pygmalion a futuristic and scientific spin in his play *As Far as the Eye Can See* (the fifth and last drama in the collection *Back to Methuselah*, 1918–1920). The scientist hero produces a synthetic man and woman but is killed by the female automaton when trying to intervene in their lovers' tiff. The creatures willingly 'commit suicide' aware that they are a failed experiment.

9. Joshua, (2001, pp. 97–100) summarizes conflicting views about the play which has been seen as a complete departure from the Ovidian myth and a stand alone in respect of other Pygmalion stories.

10. Martin's 2001 article is a mine of information on the gestation of both films of Shaw's play and also alludes to the German and Dutch cinematic versions of the 1930s. I have referenced her regularly in my critique of the screen Pygmalions and why they can be related back to Ovid. Martin describes (p. 51) how director Martin Scorsese saved *My Fair Lady* from oblivion by rescuing and organizing the restoration of its delicate 70 mm SuperPanavision negatives. It was re-launched in 1994 to great acclaim.

11. Martin (2001, p. 51) points out that black, white and grey predominate in these scenes.

12. The relevant passages are quoted in Miles (1999, 374–378) and the parallels noted in Kirchner (1952, pp. 409–417) and Myer (1981, pp. 430–431).

13. My father Alfred Deahl, born 1901, often chuckled about the hilarity Eliza's outburst continued to provoke in subsequent performances.

14. Holroyd (1989, p. 326) notes the similarity between Higgins and Mary Shelley's protagonist.

15. According to Liveley (1999, pp. 207–209) the statue may be playing her own game of deception, being a real but resisting girl all along. Liveley makes intriguing points about the role play of both sculptor and statue; the latter imitates the modest mistress who cannot be aroused and becomes a woman by acting like one. Pretence is the name of the game but so is art's potential to make illusion reality. I wonder if the accommodating girl is simply going through the motions and in this respect retaining the deceptive quality of ivory.

16. Martin (2001, pp. 53–56) assesses the songs and their opening up of the characters' intimate inner thoughts. She also notes (p. 50) the claim of the producers of *My Fair Lady* that they had used more of Shaw's screenplay written for the Pascal film than had survived in the 1938 version.

17. Martin does make the telling point (p. 56) that Classic Hollywood approved of and promoted the concept of crusty older men appealing to young girls. Witness films like *Funny Face*,(1957) and *Charade* (1963) also starring Audrey Hepburn and actors of more advanced years. Perhaps this helped to sell the Hepburn and Harrison happy ending?

18. Holroyd (1989, pp. 301–341) gives a detailed account of the play's gestation, tracing Shaw's infatuation with Mrs Patrick Campbell who played Eliza (at the age of 47!) Holroyd also offers an illuminating analysis of the relationship between Eliza and Higgins integrating the Ovidian timbres with the playwright's personal and literary agendas in the comedy's resolution.

[19] See Wood (2002, pp. 178–181) for a description of this 1898 short silent film (possibly the first of the moving image genre) and her conclusion about its significance on p.180: 'Méliès, a magician familiar with the uncanny wonder of mechanical automata, has constructed a perfect metaphor for the magic of moving film. Everything that was wrapped up in the medium's early days is there: the desires, the fears, the superstitions, the power and the hysterical zaniness of its first jagged steps.'

[20] Louise Brooks, a remarkably charismatic star of silent film, played the sexually irresistible and exploited Lulu in G.W. Pabst's iconic 1928 film, *Pandora's Box*. Casting Roberts in the part of a hooker in *Pretty Woman* was bound to invite comparison with actresses playing 'fallen women' in earlier and often darker movies.

[21] Vivian's attempt to keep her emotional distance recalls Jane Fonda's call girl in Alan J. Pakula's 1971 film, *Klute*. She 'never comes with a john' (i.e. a client) but by the end of the film she has become involved with the detective (Donald Sutherland) and weeps with remorse at her own words caught on tape – a practised speech for sexual arousal which fed into the delusions of a psychotic killer.

[22] In their excellent critique of the film, Kord and Kimmer (2005, p. 21) draw attention to Vivian's full name Vivian Ward as word (ward!) play. They interpret this as an indication of her subordinate position as ultimately Edward's ward. Vivian does exhibit a childlike demeanour and body language. She is in need of parenting and instruction. The pun could also indicate that she is doomed to be an adjunct and extension of her unconventional benefactor. 'Edward' is a name that will recur in Chapter 3 as Eddie and Ted are the heroes in films about statues of Venus coming to life.

[23] Rita's hairdressing job suggests that she is both a sympathetic listener (see my comments in the Preface about the profession) and has transformative skills on a surface level. In one short scene in the salon, we see a middle-aged somewhat plain working class woman slapping down a photograph of Princess Diana and demanding that Rita transforms her accordingly. 'I want to look like that!'

[24] I chose this as the title for my 2003 article as I was arguing that Ovid's statue was 'all that' in that her many cultural identities could be traced back to his complex reconstruction of the legend. I shall revisit this theory in the conclusion to the book.

[25] Gracie is an Annie Oakley or Calamity Jane for the twenty-first century. She can handle a gun as well as the detective she is attracted to just like Annie in the musical, *Annie Get Your Gun*. (directed by George Sidney, 1950). Betty Hutton in the title role has to misfire in the final competition so that Howard Keel does not lose face and Annie can get her man. Doris Day played the sharp shooting heroine opposite Howard Keel as Wild Bill Hickok in *Calamity Jane* (directed by David Butler, 1953.)

[26] For *The Philadelphia Story* see comments in Chapter Two. The newly awakened woman has to tread carefully. Her father warns heroine Tracy that it is quite a tumble down from the pedestal. Stoichita (2008, pp. 114–125) details the artistic traditions in the depiction of the 'nervous statue' making her way down from lofty plinths.

Chapter 4

1. For this story of a demonic Venus statue and an unintentional Pygmalion see Hersey (2010, pp. 121–123). He cites Prosper Mérimée's 1837 *La Vénus d'Ille* and has a passing reference to Anstey.
2. The inspector's name is Frodo and his interest in the missing ring might set devotees of J.R.R. Tolkien's epic trilogy *The Lord of the Rings* and fans of the Peter Jackson film versions wondering about the strange coincidence of names!
3. Arscott and Scott (2001, pp. 6–7) observe that an art object's 'irreducible material grounding in paint, stone and fabric' has 'repeatedly proved an embarrassment for those wishing to make elevated claims for art'. Venus being coterminous with art also has her ethereal and earthly aspects. Gronberg's chapter in Arscott and Scott analyses 'the ways in which fur stands on the border between painting and *art decoratif*, facing forwards as a sign of the (male) artist's mastery of his materials to the point of *trompe l'oeil*, and facing backwards as the feral stuff of female high fashion' (p. 7).
4. Venus appears to her son Aeneas in the guise of a young girl or nymph dressed for the hunt (Virgil, *Aeneid* Book One, lines 314–320). More pertinent however is her adopting of outdoor sports in order to be a constant companion of Adonis (the aftermath of the Myrrha story in Ovid's *Metamorphoses* Book 10). Venus cannot save her rash mortal lover from being savaged by a boar and dying young.
5. Walker was better cast in dramatic roles. He gave a subtle and sinister performance as deranged villain, Bruno, in *Strangers on a Train*. See Chapter 2. In real life he lost his actress wife, the lovely Jennifer Jones, to David O. Selznick, which devastated him. Studio bosses and owners were fully capable of playing god to get what they wanted. For Walker's obsession with Gardner and Gardner modelling bare breasted for the studio statue of Venus, see Server, 2006, 153–157.
6. I am reminded of Marx's comments on the disappearance of the gods at the advent of technology: 'What chance has Vulcan against Roberts and Co., Jupiter against the lightening-rod and Hermes against the Crédit Mobilier?' (*Grundrisse* 1857–58, Introduction, Section 4).
7. See March (1998, p. 56) on Aphrodite being given a taste of her own medicine after visiting inappropriate passions on the gods.
8. Maltin (2010, p. 871) gives it the lowest possible rating of BOMB with the blistering comment 'Attempts to recreate the feeling of old screwball comedies is absolute rock-bottom fare. Dispiriting to anyone who remembers what movie comedy ought to be'.
9. See Walker (2006, p. 223). Hayworth was referring to her famous role in the 1946 film of that name (directed by Charles Vidor and co-starring Glenn Ford). Her performance (in private and then in public) of the song 'Put the blame on Mame' has gone down in movie history.

Chapter 5

1. Medical science may turn us into hybrids of human and technological tissue (and use parts of other living species to keep us alive) but this is in response to

some of the cruellest and invasive diseases that transform our bodies and ossify or paralyse our organs and internal functions from within. The slow obliteration of body and mind is like the undeserved punishments visited upon mythical victims who sink down into suffocating tree bark or submit to a petrifying process that removes their original identity.

2 The Trojan horse seems to have been portrayed with robotic qualities in the *Iliupersis*. Ascribed to Arctinus, this is part of an early Greek epic cycle which survives only in fragments. According to the scholia on line 15, Book 2 of the *Aeneid* (the later Latin epic by Virgil) 'cuius cauda, genua, oculi moverentur', which translates as 'its tail, its knees and its eyes were in movement'.

3 Talos is more familiar from his appearance in *Jason and the Argonauts* (1963, directed by Don Chaffey) and as a triumph of special effects wizard, Ray Harryhausen, a modern-day Daedalus or Hephaistus. crafting miraculous representations for the screen.

4 Ancient automata could be included in the examples of Greek mythology's imaginative glimpses of a future given by Maxim Gorky at the 1934 Soviet Writers' Congress. Gorky sited self-generating feasts and speedy travel on seven league boots as early aspirations to technological miracles and material plenty. Such a society would only be achievable after the advances made under the ruthless driving forces of capitalism and only enjoyed by all with the humanizing socialization of production.

5 Haraway has been taken to task by Marxists feminists like Teresa Ebert who is sceptical about 'the products and tools of an advanced capitalist and patriarchal economy as useful to Marxists or to feminists seeking to dismantle the social, political and ideological structures of that economy' (Liveley 2006, p. 288).

6 The most advanced robots are being developed in Japan. On radio 4's *Thinking Allowed* (4 August 2010) Jennifer Robertson (University of Michigan) was interviewed about her forthcoming book *Body and Society: Gendering Human Robots:* It was a fascinating discussion around social and philosophical issues. It was suggested that the rapid development of robot helpers, household companions and sexualized Fembots in Japan was not simply driven by an economic imperative (creating a biddable workforce for the future). Shinto belief with its emphasis on animism and fluid boundaries between the organic and inorganic eases the acceptance of robot facilitators in a gadget-friendly culture.

7 See Cornea (in Seed, ed. 2008, pp. 275–288) for a further critique of Haraway and for a cautiously optimistic conclusion that the concept of the cyborg 'still presents the viewer/reader with opportunities to question and contest the premises of what it means to be human'. Cornea does point out that popular cultural texts (visual and written) tend to submit to a conservative containment of the hybrid, composite, cyborg configuration with its attendant transgressive implications (p. 287).

8 See the introduction for my rationale. However I have had the privilege of reading Gabriella Barbier's accomplished paper 'The Myth of Pygmalion revisited: from Mythology to Automata, Robots and Androids', presented at the Durham University Conference, 'Myths of Transformation' (September 2008). Barbier integrates the statue into ancient traditions of moving and mechanized humanoids and traces their historical and fictional path through the centuries. She

discusses the 'mostly unhappy' robots of the twentieth century including Marvin the Paranoid Android from Douglas Adams' 1979 *Hitchhiker's Guide to the Galaxy* and the dangerously disturbed sentient machines of dystopian science fiction but finishes with the realistic replicas of Japanese technology, ReplieeQ2 android produced to 'blink, gesture, speak, breathe and even show emotions. These are the 'real girls' of Osaka University and Kokoro Co Ltd, Japan.

9   In this 2004 novel by Chris Beckett Lucy is the robot sex worker with whom the hero runs away. He has stimulated her intellectually and she transforms herself into something much more human than her programming should allow. Up to this point, there are bizarre Shavian echoes in the narrative. When Lucy's humanoid body is destroyed by fire she reinvents herself as the holy machine, the robot Messiah. Her transition from automaton to human and then god evokes the various identities associated with Pygmalion's statue.

10   It is interesting that director's cuts of *Blade Runner*, the most recent being 2007, indicate that Scott kept on 'perfecting' his artistic product. Another film set in a futuristic cityscape beholden to *Metropolis* is the 1997 *Fifth Element* directed by Luc Besson. This features a beautiful and benign artificial body, a cosmic construction called Leeloo (Milla Jojovich). She saves the world with an air of spontaneity and innocence, reprising many a past Pygmalion-type heroine who is inclined to social inappropriateness. Bruce Willis plays Korben Dallas, her human helper and protector. Interestingly he has been waiting for the perfect woman to come along.

11   Kim Newman (2010, p. 20) discusses Thea von Harbou's Nazi sympathies. Von Harbou was married to Lang at the time but the director was later dismissive of her concept of reconciliation between heart and hand (employer and employee), which may have been inspired by one of Goebbels' speeches. See the 1966 Berg interview (2000, p. 69). I am grateful to Suman Gupta (Open University, Department of English) who sent me drafts of his excellent critique of *Metropolis*, which is a unit of study in a forthcoming OU Literature module.

12   Eve has like Myrrha in the *Metamorphoses* experienced carnal relations with a parent (but against her will; he has violated her). Her readiness to project her likeness onto a new and invulnerable body could be considered an equivalent to Myrrha's prayer to become something that belongs to neither the living nor the dead.

13   See Bloom's discussion (2003, pp. 139–152) of these films as part of a tradition of splitting Pygmalion into the dual-natured man (Jekyll and Hyde) and the strong vein of necrophilia that underlies remoulding and resurrecting the desired woman.

14   Both Annes Brown (2005) and O'Sullivan (2008) have alluded to this film as a modern Pygmalion story with a sinister edge.

15   Diane Keaton turned down the part of Joanna on the advice of her analyst who had 'bad vibes' from the script (*Forbes*, 1998, quoted on p. v of the 1972 edition of the novel).

16   Irene Handl reprises her distrust of artificial constructs in her role as the landlady in the 1960 British film *The Rebel* (directed by Robert Day), which starred Tony Hancock. Handl expresses exasperation and dismay at the large statue Hancock is sculpting in the privacy of his rented room.

17 My thanks go to Deborah Thomas who pointed this out to me at the 2005 Huddersfield conference on 'The Genius of Joss Whedon'.
18 Newmar who received a television award nomination for her performance enjoyed the challenge of playing the robot woman and is quoted as saying 'she felt like she was giving birth to something new'.

Chapter 6

1 See Tonkin (2004, pp. 37–53) for the entropic landscape of the St Andreas fault and Siemann (2002, p.127) on Whedon's intentional portrayal of the high school as the Hellmouth with humiliation, alienation and confusion taken to demonic proportions.
2 For classically heroic Buffy and parallels with Virgil's Aeneas, see James (2009, pp. 237–260), and Haynes (2010). Bowman (2002, p. 9) makes the telling point that Whedon has based Buffy's story more on a theory of Greek heroic myth than on any specific mythic narrative or figure. In this he follows in the footsteps of previous mediators of mythical types who work in film and television. Joseph Campbell's *Hero with a Thousand Faces* (1949) has been very influential upon re-creators of heroes and the heroic quest on screen.
3 Julia Courtney's paper on Xander as Holy Fool was delivered at the 2004 conference in Milton Keynes, UK. This was a day on Greco-Roman strands in the Buffyverse and was organized jointly by Paula James of the Open University Classical Studies Department and David Scourfield (Professor of Classics) at Maynooth, National University of Ireland.
4 April is just one example of classical resonances in the Whedon universe. See Art Pomeroy's 2008 book *Then It Was Destroyed By The Volcano* in which chapter two is entitled 'Hymns to the Ancient World in the Buffyverse' and also James (2009).
5 This moment is also a homage to Stanley Kubrick's *2001: A Space Odyssey* (1968) as it evokes the scene in which HAL the computer starts to revert to a mechanical voice and loses his soothing and modulated human tones.
6 I am grateful to Amanda Potter's viewing group (see Introduction) as this was a comment at least one participant made after reading the myth and being asked to look for parallels. Although most of the viewers were initially unaware of Ovid's version of Pygmalion they suggested a number of Pygmalion-related film texts that fed into the episode. April's fixed smile as she looked out from the swing was identified as the reason for Warren's frustration with her. She reflected rather than returned her creator's gaze, just as the statue would have been created with ever open eyes and yet she does not truly see Pygmalion until she is vivified. Liveley (1999, p. 207) interprets the awakening in the Ovid narrative with additional nuances.
7 This scene is closely analysed by Thomas (2006, pp. 188–191). Thomas sees distinct similarities between April's 'death' on the swings and Judith's demise in Goulding's 1939 melodrama, *Dark Victory* (p. 190). She also notes the reference to *Stepford Wives* (Joanna and Bobby talk about the enigmatic spouses while sitting on swings in the playground.) Thomas' chapter in *Close Up* is a superb

interpretation of the series especially her approach to the cinematic cultural layering in key episodes and seasons of *Buffy*.

8 See Alderman (2006, pp. 2–6) on the classical feel to the god, Glory, with her Dionysiac and psychotic aspects. James (2009, p. 251, n.20) celebrates the power of even the small screen to convey the menace of the god. There is a terrifying metamorphic moment when Glory appears before Dawn in Season Five. The scene is a divine encounter worthy of Ovid's visualizations of Olympian epiphanies in the *Metamorphoses*.

9 Spike has already forced blonde and dim vampire, Harmony, to impersonate Buffy so he can fight and then have sex with a Slayer substitute. For Spike's obsession and his search for the *simulacrum* that will ultimately disappoint him, see Pateman (2006, pp. 193–195).

10 Thomas (2006, p.194) observes 'the thingness' of Joyce's body (a point we agreed upon in the Huddersfield 2005 conference.) In the acclaimed episode 'The Body' (Season Five, episode 16) Buffy fantasizes briefly that she has resuscitated her mother and brought her back from the dead. This Orpheus moment is one of many poignant and well observed sequences in 'The Body' which is almost a sociological study in grief and bereavement. In the next episode Dawn attempts to recall Joyce from the grave by means of magic, only to realize just in time that this is dangerous, that the dead can come back wrong. This prefigures Buffy coming back wrong from the grave in Season Six. Whedon may have had in mind the W.W. Jacobs' 1902 short story *The Monkey's Paw* in which an embalmed corpse is revivified but wished away once his parents realize what they have summoned up.

11 I can only note without comment that the name Edward has once again been chosen for a male Pygmalion figure.

12 Dawn (actress Michelle Trachtenberg) did not actually feature in this past episode because as a constructed sister she was, of course, never there for the cast or the viewer (but she and the other characters had memories encoded that imprinted her presence on the events of the past four seasons).

13 Calvert (2006, pp. 1–10) applies Baudrillard's five phases of the image or *simulacrum* to the Buffybot demonstrating that the robot double of the Slayer is more complex and significant to the narrative than April. The Buffybot is a reflection of basic reality; it masks and perverts a basic reality. It also masks the absence of basic reality and finally it is pure *simulacrum*, bearing no relation to reality. Jowett (2005, pp. 47–49) gives an excellent analysis of April from the perspective of gender stereotypes in Season Five. For the splitting of Buffy and her narcissistic personality disorder, see Poole (2007, pp. 24–28).

14 In fact there seems to be some crossover between the role of the Buffybot and Gellar's performance as daffy Daphne in the Scooby-Doo movies. As all the Scooby characters started out on television as cartoon creatures, Gellar is bringing an animated drawing to life in these films.

15 Willow's spell involves a prayer to Osiris ('Here lies a warrior of the people; let her cross over!') along with an animal sacrifice. Ironically the Buffybot's dismemberment by the biker demons functions as a modern replay of the death of Osiris in Egyptian mythical traditions. The *simulacrum* of Buffy is sacrificed as the real (but dead and therefore ghostly) Buffy wakes to a suffocating prison

below ground. Amanda Potter has, in past presentations, pointed to parallels between Buffy and Alcestis, speculating on whether Alcestis wished to return from the Underworld.

Chapter 7

1. I have drawn upon the Viewing Notes by Andrew Pixley which accompany the BBC produced DVD of 2006 entitled *The Andromeda Anthology*. Pixley gives a detailed account of the series' gestation and a synopsis of the episodes of both *A for Andromeda* and *The Andromeda Breakthrough*.
2. See the assessment of its significance in the history of science fiction on television and as a vehicle for political comment by Wright in Seed, ed. (2008, pp. 292–293).
3. Rizov finds this scene risible and a rather heavy-handed way of demonstrating Dren being a double of Elsa. See *Sight and Sound* (August 2010, p. 75).
4. Rizov notes the names Clive and Elsa are a movie homage to the actors Colin Clive and Elsa Lanchester who starred in Whale's 1935 *Bride of Frankenstein*.
5. See Chapter 8 on Salmacis and Hermaphroditus and their link with Pygmalion and Narcissus. Rizov suggests that Dren's rape of Elsa is an excessive underlining of the point already driven home about 'the arbitrary nature of gender coding (Judith Butler style)'. Haraway would no doubt find a place for the creature's hybridity in her Cyborg Manifesto. See the introduction to Chapter 5.
6. The automata of Karel Čapek's play *Rossum's Universal Robots* (which premiered in Prague in 1921) are the product of genetic engineering and are earmarked for drudgery and slavery. 'Robotnik' is the Czech for serf or peasant. Many have mulled over the reasons why robots became so closely associated with mechanical creatures. See the recent discussion in Koontz (2010, p. 2) who regards the human inhabitants of Whedon's *Dollhouse* as true descendants of *R.U.R.*
7. Hank Aleno can be condensed into Hal, which is a nod towards the computer in Kubrick's *2001: A Space Odyssey*.
8. It is possible that Lainey (mature for her years and very much a youthful copy of her mother Elaine) is supposed to remind us of the Laney in Iscove's 1999 film, *She's All That*.
9. There is some similarity between the names Taransky and Tarkovsky, the acclaimed Russian director. Andre Tarkovsky's 1973 tour de force *Solaris* lingered melancholically over the delusions of a psychologist sent to a space station to investigate supernatural phenomena. He succumbs to deceptive images of his ideal woman, the wife he has lost.
10. See Doherty (2001, pp. 127–140) for a succinct summary of structuralist approaches to myth that tie into Jungian psychologising on mythic narratives.
11. The hair is as ever a centrepiece to the transformation that brings perfection.
12. Isaac Asimov apologized to the readers of his 1955 short story, *The Talking Stone* in which he allows a small sentient asteroid to die without comment from the space crew: 'After this story appeared, I received quite a bit of mail expressing

interest in the silicony and, in some cases, finding fault with me for letting it die in so cold-blooded a fashion. As I reread the story now, I must admit the readers are right. I showed a lack of sensitivity to the poor creature's death . . . '

Chapter 8

[1] The correspondences with Narcissus and Pygmalion have been thoroughly explored by classical scholars. See James (2004) and references therein to Hardie (2002) and Rosati (1983).

[2] Possibly the bleakest and most macabre story of a woman worshipping a statue is Thomas Hardy's *Barbara of the House of Grebe* (unfilmed and probably unfilmable!) Barbara's beautiful young husband Edmond is horribly disfigured in a fire. Realizing her repulsion he leaves her and after many years she marries the local lord (who declares he can cope with her coldness and lack of love for him). But Barbara becomes passionately obsessed with the sculpture of Edmond completed before his accident. Her second husband takes a cruel revenge, commissioning a poor but ingenious mechanic and painter to work upon the statue's godlike countenance and disfigure it so it resembles the deformed Edmond.

[3] Burne-Jones had expressed a desire to leap into one of his paintings and live in its idyllic landscape. See Keen (1983, p. 129).

[4] There is a short story by Isaac Asimov, *Satisfaction Guaranteed*, which was televised on BBC as part of the 1960s' *Out of the Unknown* series. Wendy Craig played Claire, a downtrodden wife in serious need of a make-over. Her uncaring husband volunteers Claire for a trial run with a robot, Tony (TN3), a kind of au pair in a male guise. Tony realizes that Claire needs empowering to be happy. (He is obeying the first law of robotics and being proactive in keeping her from (self) harm.) Tony starts by improving her appearance and self-image and then simulates desire for her. Claire's female neighbours are fooled but so is she. Along with her new-found confidence she is also disturbed by Tony's 'feelings'. The TN3 is returned to the laboratory as 'faulty'.

[5] On the subject of females creating perfect males, the writer Stella Duffy came up with the idea of an ice sculptress vivifying her beautiful frozen man with a kiss. This formed the basis of a novel she wrote for publishers Mills and Boon as a challenge. The gestation of the project was the subject of BBC2's *Time Shift* (produced by Claire Martin in 2008). Avid readers of this 'female fiction' genre advised Duffy on her characterization and plot, suggesting that the heroine has made the ice man in the image of the flesh and blood hero who will eventually sweep her off her feet and into bed. In spite of Mills and Boon branching out into several sub-genres (from modern to magic realism) and allowing raunchy sex scenes it was impressed upon the author that male and female bodies must be beautiful at all times. Physical perfection remains the norm for the heroes and heroines of Mills and Boon.

[6] In April 1999 *The Guardian* publicized a forthcoming film called *The Man on Platform 5*. The rights were bought by New Line Cinema. The novel was by

Robert Llewellyn (who came to fame playing a robot, the admirable Kryten, in the 1990s' comedy SF series, *Red Dwarf*) and the setting of the movie was Milton Keynes. It was a reversal of Shaw's Pygmalion with a girl artist improving a nerdy computer guy for a project (from dud to dude in six weeks). I have not managed to view this film but it seems to have predated the La Bute play. Gwyneth Paltrow and Winona Ryder were tipped to play the equivalent of Higgins and Pickering.

7   She is drawing upon Dörrie's influential 1974 treatise.
8   I had the privilege of hearing Dr Sue Blundell (Open University) presenting her splendid paper on Emma Hamilton at the Classical Association in Liverpool (April, 2008) and at the University of Michigan conference on Feminism and the Classics (May, 2008). I look forward to its publication.
9   The 1945 film *Kitty* (directed by Mitchell Leisen and starring Paulette Goddard and Ray Milland) told a fictional story of a guttersnipe passed off as a duchess. Set in the eighteenth century it could have been inspired by the episode in *Peregrine Pickle* but it echoes scenes in Shaw's *Pygmalion* and possibly borrows from Korda's film as well. *Kitty* was also lavish in costumes and sets. The 'educator' Milland is an impoverished rake whose motivation is mercenary but, of course, he starts to have feelings for Kitty.
10 This parallel was drawn very clearly in the Radio 4 programme *Emma Hamilton's i pod* (11 December 2010) in which Emma's musical abilities and cosmopolitan tastes in song were celebrated.
11 The film (Winston Churchill's favourite) was supposed to spur on America's commitment to fighting with the allies in World War II. Napoleon is described as a prototypical Hitler threatening the Commonwealth and the world. The American censors insisted on additional dialogue reflecting Nelson's and Emma's remorse and pain at committing adultery. In the UK the film was entitled *Lady Hamilton*.
12 Arscott and Scott (2005, pp. 3–4) discuss the finding and restoring a *Venus de Milo* as the story of a statue ravaged by conflict. There may have been a pitched battle over her possession between the French and the Turks on the beach of Melos. The comte de Marcellus (*Souvenirs de L'Orient*, 1839) seemed to be besotted by a beauty that violent conflict eroticized. Arscott and Scott comment on the sculpture, that 'she offered pleasure that was provisional; a dalliance that was prone to violent interruptions and violent reversals'.
13 Using ancient texts and genres to inform and enrich interpretations of film and visual media and interrogate the nature of cultural communications is becoming a significant stream in the reception of cultural studies. See Winkler (2001) and Lowe and Shahabudin (2009) for collections of stimulating scholarly essays which put Greek and Roman motifs in conversation with modern films, TV series and graphic novels.
14 Amanda Potter's focus group on the *Buffy* episode fed into my discussion in Chapter 6. This kind of approach to the reception of the ancient world is breaking new ground as it is looking beyond the responses of those viewing myths on screen in an educational environment. Of course, the focus group method is distinct from broader sociological surveys. For the challenges of research into audience response and behaviour see Stafford (2007) and Williamson (2005).

[15] There is a lively debate ongoing in Classical Studies Reception Studies about the meaning of the Democratic Turn and how it might be achieved. The debate has a wide remit addressing the more radical use of classical material to question perceptions of the past and the present, responding to contested appropriations of the classical world, and monitoring the transmission of Greek and Roman culture in all its manifestations. See the proceedings of the international conference hosted by the Open University in June 2010 (Milton Keynes) on the Classical Reception Studies Network website. Chapters by Joanna Paul, Hanna Roisman and Marianne McDonald in Hardwick and Stray's stimulating *Companion to Classical Receptions* of 2008 expertly illustrate key issues and conundrums surrounding the presence of classical myths, motifs and narrative structures in modern art forms and what theories and methodologies are being developed to exploit these correspondences in research and teaching.

Coda to Paperback

(Paula James, November 1st 2012)

An Ur or Uber myth like Ovid's Pygmalion is a never-ending story. In the eighteen months since the publication of this book there have been further editions and literary commentaries on Ovid, panels on Pygmalion at classical conferences, new moves in myth and its contemporary cultural currency and cinematic 'events' well worth noting. I very much welcome the opportunity afforded me by Bloomsbury (thanks to Charlotte Loveridge) to mention recent developments in the study and afterlife of the Perfect Woman and also to engage briefly with scholarship in the field that slipped out of my sights the first time around. Thanks are due to Giles Herman for incorporating corrections and updates. I am grateful (again) to my brothers Steve and Ray Deahl for a few factual corrections and suggestions about clarifying my reading of the myth and the movies.

In writing a coda I discover that there is already almost enough material for a sequel, which could be entitled The Statue Strikes Back in deference to film franchises everywhere. Just after the submission of my manuscript, Virago published a collection of rediscovered short stories by Daphne Du Maurier. *The Doll* functions as the central story and is a disturbing tale dealing in the desire of a man for a bewitching and capricious woman. She is in turn obsessed with or possessed by a dummy. Dressed as a sixteen year old boy, the doll, Julio, has the face of a grinning and evil satyr. The story was written when Du Maurier was only twenty and it deserves a new chapter in the Pygmalion chronicles. It is part parable of a distorted and contorted sexuality in a Gothic horror framework and part experimentation in fractured narrative. Perhaps Mark Gatiss could convert both this tale and Hardy's *Barbara of the House of Grebe* to the small screen in a double bill of psychological scare stories.

Equally spooky but for different reasons was the 2012 documentary film *The Mechanical Bride* directed by Alison de Fren and narrated by Julie Newmar of My Living Doll fame. It was shown at BFI Southbank in May as part of the Sci-Fi London season and proved to be a compelling treatment of issues I raised in Chapters 5 and 6. The realm of the customised sex bots is both distasteful and poignant not least because the use and abuse of the mechanical 'brides' ranged from a hormonally charged teenage boy fucking a doll to destruction to a bereaved widower finding solace and safe intimacy in his pleasure model (once again the wife a lost lurks behind the plastic partner.) The film was a dispassionate deconstruction of the silicon simulacrum and the interviews (with professionals, academics and also doll users) were simply full of verbal and visual images from Ovid's poetic narrative.

The latest film fiction on a Pygmalion theme has had a limited general release. *Ruby Sparks* is being enjoyed by critics and audience for an eccentric charm (though Vadim Rizov in the November *Sight and Sound* found the hero 'a truly horrible person' and his creation 'equally empty, a metaphorical premise executed with flat liberalism.') Its central premise of 'write your own girlfriend' has intriguing parallels with Ovid's statue as a literary construction, an elegiac mistress who is designed never to behave badly. Cinematic derivations abound in this refreshed (discuss!) Rom Com but the problems of power (the patriarchal kind) and the angst surrounding creator and creature as they both come to life are clearly part of a moralising core.

In a reversal of the Pygmalion myth, the worst violation of Ruby occurs when she realises she is *not* real and flails about like an orgasmic puppet as Calvin (the author) noisily and manically types her speech and voice on an old fashioned machine (possibly a metaphor for the retro feel of the movie.) Although he finally frees Ruby to find her own way, Calvin goes through several stages of sculpting her, unable to harmonise her free will with his desires. At one point, after he rewrites her as biddable and needy, she freezes like an automaton in the crowd because he has let go of her hand.

The movie has a legion of post Pygmalion perfect woman motifs from the fear of incest (or mindcest as Calvin's brother dubs it) when the writer sleeps with his vivified creation to the fact that Ruby is written as parentless, an orphan with an air of innocence. She is, however, a twenty first century ideal, a composite of cookie Rom Com heroines, allowed artistic talent and artless spontaneity, human warmth and fallibility, along with a few of the hardy old perennials like cooking and caring skills. It is interesting that her Bohemian past with a smidgeon of tarnished virtue is easily eradicated or discounted for, on meeting Calvin, he puts words into her mouth about finding true love and starting life over.

Once again the sculptor and the statue demonstrate the malleability of their myth as a cultural barometer. I would warmly recommend that students of Pygmalion track down *Ruby Sparks* and see what cinematic mind games could emerge. A recent Jeff Goldsmith podcast interview with its directors Jonathan Dayton, Valerie Faris and actors Paul Dano and Zoe Kazan (who wrote the story and then starred as the fictional conception) was revealing. Kazan had called her writing folder Galatea and she cited the Pygmalion myth but not Ovid. Simon Goldhill wrote in 2007 about the challenges of reception studies when the creators of the cinematic text fail to mention the ancient narrative which seems so closely referenced for the classical viewer. Joanna Paul in her very useful 2010 article on 'Cinematic receptions of antiquity: the current state of play' engaged with Goldhill and his observations upon indirect allusivity and the need for new strategies to comprehend how 'classical paradigms enter a modern discursive place.'

Perhaps the answer is 'to boldly go'. Martin Winkler in *Apollo's New Light* (2009) produced scholarly and stimulating studies of classical myth on the big screen. He is particularly adept at reconfiguring the language of film criticism in terms of theoretical frameworks developed for Greek and Roman texts. In Ovid's *Myth of Pygmalion on Screen* I hoped to start a trend which would adapt the visual language of the movies to serve as an interpretative tool for ancient poetic narratives. There is much to be done in developing a methodology that will enrich our appreciation of classical texts and modern movies.

I continue to conjure with *Vertigo* which started me on the path of cross cultural dialogues. The recent elevation of *Vertigo* as greatest film (knocking *Citizen Kane* off top spot after many years but such a hierarchy while culturally telling is always aesthetically suspect) has re-opened debates on Hitchcock and his works. In *Sight and Sound* (September 2012) Peter Matthews commented that: 'the effort to model a real woman into an ideal, is nowadays commonly diagnosed as another reflexive text: the ultimate demystification of stardom and its origins in male fantasy.' Singer's chapter on 'Pygmalion Variations' in *Cinematic Mythmaking* (2008) brings more insights into the *Vertigo* phenomenon and introduces Preston Sturges's *The Lady Eve* into the equation.

As for the general theme of making over, there is an embarrassment of riches, not least an excellent thesis by Kendra Marston in 2010, *Representations of the Female Adolescence in the Teen Makeover Film*. In the introduction Marston reveals how her research radiated out from the Pygmalion premise. The artist / lover in such movies uncovers the 'feminine' core of the Galatea girl but has to avoid transforming his model into an empowered female consumer where social success and money may replace the modern Pygmalion. In the post-feminist age, the (in the main) male marketers have captured and packaged up girl power, persuading many women to change themselves with cosmetics, clothes and even surgery.

The self made woman seems to have been infected with Pygmalion's narcissism and these modern 'statues' touching themselves up (!) may have morphed into a Salmacis creature, the nymph who preens herself by her pool in Ovid, *Metamorphoses* Book Four. Marston draws upon Dana Heller's 2007 edited essays on *Makeover Television: Realities Remodelled.* Chapter Eight by Elizabeth Atwood Gailey on 'Self Made Women' exposes the 'hegemonic alliance of patriarchy and global capitalism' that manipulates women into carrying out their own objectification as 'emerging from their own ritualized ordeal of surgery, they are, paradoxically, both liberated from and reinscribed with their own subordination.'

In chapter Thirteen of the volume, Kathryn Fraser takes the first lines of Ovid's *Metamorphoses* 'Now I am ready to tell how bodies are changed into different bodies.' She examines the self commodification through consumption which convinces us that the female body is endlessly self malleable and plastic. Her analysis of the perpetual Pygmalion metaphor from Ovid to Shaw helps to unmask the pleasures of self creation (the statue without the sculptor). In her conclusion (p.192) she reminds us of 'the makeover's ideological participation in sustaining a world of middle class, not to mention masculine, privilege.' In that case my idea for a sequel entitled The Statue Strikes Back seems slightly wrong-headed. The passivity of Ovid's ivory girl tends to reassert itself. With this ironical perception in view I recommend that future scholars of the myth take a long, hard and critical look at the statue's modern counterparts and identify the dead hand of a patriarchal Pygmalion still at work.

Bibliographical Additions

Du Maurier, D. 'The Doll' (1927) in *The Doll: Short Stories.* (2011) London: Virago Modern Classics.

Goldhill, S. (2007) '*Naked* and *O Brother, Where Art Thou?* The politics and poetics of epic cinema,' in *Homer in the 20th Century: Between World Literature and the Western Canon (Classical Presences Series)*, B.Graziosi, E. Greenwood, eds, Oxford: OUP, 245–267.

Heller, Dana (2007) ed. *Makeover Television: Realities Remodelled.* London, New York: I.B.Tauris

Marston, K. (2010) *Representations of Female Adolescence in the Teen Makeover Film.* Doctoral thesis submitted to the Victoria University of Wellington.

Paul, J. (2010) 'Cinematic Representations of antiquity: the current state of play', *The Classical Receptions Journal* 2.1, 136–155.

Singer, I. (2008) *Cinematic Mythmaking: philosophy in film.* Cambridge, Massachussetts, London: The MIT Press

Bibliography

Ahl, F. (1985), *Metaformations: Soundplay and Wordplay in Ovid and other Classical Poets*. Ithaca, London: Cornell University Press.

Alderman, N (2009), 'Those whom the powers wish to destroy, they first make mad: the classical roots of madness in *Buffy the Vampire Slayer*' pp. 1–13 in slayageonline.com ISCBtVS _ Archive/SCBNS_Archive Left htm, accessed July 16th 2009.

Anderson, W.S. (1972), *Ovid's Metamorphoses Books 6–10*. Oklahoma: University of Oklahoma Press.

Anstey, F. (2010 edn of 1898 edn.), *The Tinted Venus: a Farcical Romance*. Milton Keynes: Lightening Source UK Ltd.

Anthony, A. (2004), 'Menacing Technologies: counterfeit women and the mutability of nature in science fiction cinema', *Fem Spec*, 5(1), 1–17.

Arscott, C. (2000), 'Venus as dominatrix: nineteenth century artists and their creations', in C.Arscott and K. Scott (eds), *Manifestations of Venus*, Manchester, New York: Manchester University Press, pp. 109–125.

Arscott, C. and Scott, K. (2000), *Manifestations of Venus: Essays on Art and Sexuality*. Manchester, New York: Manchester University Press.

Asimov, Isaac (1950), 'Satisfaction guaranteed', in *The Rest of the Robots* (1968), St Albans: Panther Books.

Asimov, Isaac (1955), 'The talking stone', in *Asimov's Mysteries* (1969), St Albans: Panther Books.

Auiler, D. (1998), *Vertigo: the Making of a Hitchcock Classic*. St Martin's Griffin & New York: St Martins Press.

Baccolini, R. (2000), 'In between subjects: C.L. Moore's *No Woman Born*', in K. Sayer and J. Moore (eds), *Science Fiction, Critical Frontiers*. London: Macmillan Press, pp. 140–153.

Barbier, G. (2008), 'The Myth of Pygmalion Revisited: from Mythology to Automata, Robots and Androids', paper presented at *Myths of Transformation*, University of Durham, September 2008.

Barkan, L. (1986), *The Gods made Flesh: Metamorphosis and the Pursuit of Paganism*. New Haven, CT and London: Princeton University Press.

Barolsky, P. (2007), 'Ovid's protean epic of art', *Arion*, 14 (3), 111–123.

Barolsky, P. and D'Ambra, E. (2009), 'Pygmalion's doll', *Arion*, 17 (1), 19–23.

Barr, C. (2002), *Vertigo*. London: BFI Publishing.

Bartsch. S. (2006), *The Mirror of the Self: Sex, Self Knowledge and the Gaze in the Early Roman Empire*. Chicago, IL: Chicago Press.

Baudrillard, J. (1998), 'Simulacra and simulations', in M. Poster (ed.), *Selected Writings*. Cambridge: Polity Press, pp. 166–184.

Bauer, D. (1962), 'The function of Pygmalion in the *Metamorphoses* of Ovid', *Transactions of the American Philological Association*, 93, 1–21.
Bazzoli, M. (2009), 'The metamorphoses of the Pygmalion myth: a narrative critique of *Lars and the Real Girl*', available at http://www.allacademic.com/meta/p368186 (accessed 5 January 2011).
Beckett, C. (2004), *The Holy Machine*, Holicong, PA: Wildside Press.
Bloom, M.E. (2000), 'Pygmalionesque delusions and illusions of movement: animation from Hoffmann to Truffaut', *Comparative Literature*, 52 (4), 291–320.
Bloom, M.E. (2003), *Waxworks: a Cultural Obsession*. Minneapolis and London: University of Minnesota Press.
Boileau, P. and Narcejac, T. (1956), *D'Entre les Morts*, translated by G. Sainsbury as *The Living and the Dead*. London: Bloomsbury Publishing plc.
Bömer, F. (1980), *P. Ovidius Naso, Metamorphosen, Kommentar. Buch X–XI*. Heidelberg: Carl Winter.
Bould, M. (2004), 'Taking the dream girls apart: Molly, Eve VIII, Barb Wire,' *Fem Spec*, 5 (1), 18–33.
Bowman, L. (2002), '*Buffy the Vampire Slayer:* The Greek hero revisited', available at http://web.uvic.ca/~lbowman/buffy/buffythehero.html (accessed 28 September 2007).
Brewer, W. (1941), *Ovid's Metamorphoses in European Culture* (3 vols), Boston: Marshall Jones.
Brill, L. (1988), *The Hitchcock Romance: Love and Irony in Hitchcock's Films*. Princeton: Princeton University Press.
Brown, S. Annes (2005), *Ovid: Myth and Metamorphosis; Ancients in Action*. Bristol: Bristol Classical Press.
Bullen, J.B. (1988), *The PreRaphaelite Body: Fear and Desire in Painting, Poetry and Criticism*. Oxford: Oxford University Press.
Calvert, B. (2004), 'Going through the motions: reading simulacra in *Buffy the Vampire Slayer*', in R. Wilcox and D. Lavery (eds), *Slayage Online: the International Journal of Buffy Studies* 15 (accessed 21 September 2010).
Campbell, J. (1949/1968), *The Hero with a Thousand Faces*. Princeton: Princeton University Press.
Čapek, K. (1923), *Rossum's Universal Robots*. London.
Cast, D. (2009) 'Review of Stoichita's *The Pygmalion Effect*', *Bryn Mawr Classical Review*, 20 April 2009, 1–3.
Conrad, P. (2001), 'The tainted saint: Review of Hitchcock and Art Exhibition', *The Observer* (April 22).
Cornea, C. (2008), 'Figurations of the cyborg in contemporary science fiction novels and films', in D. Seed (ed.), *A Companion to Science Fiction*. Oxford: Blackwell Publishing, pp. 275–288.
Cyrino, M.S. (2010), *Aphrodite*. London & New York: Routledge.
Czarniawska, B. (2004), 'Foreword: a semiotic reading of strong plots', in Gabriel (ed.).
de L'Isle Adam, V. (1982 edn), *Tomorrow's Eve*. Champaign: University of Illinois Press.
Dick, P.K. (1968), *Do Androids Dream of Electric Sheep?* London: Orion Books (2004 edn).

Doherty, L.E. (2001), *Gender and the Interpretation of Classical Myth*. London: Duckworth.
Doniger, W. (1999), *Splitting the Difference: Gender and Myth in Ancient Greece and India*. Chicago, IL: Chigago University Press.
Dorfman, E. (2001), 'Still lovers: artist's statement', in S. Plumb and J.Lewis (eds), *Guys 'n' Dolls: Art, Science, Fashion and Relationships*. Brighton and Hove: Royal Pavilion, Libraries and Museums, pp. 60–61.
Dörrie, H. (1974), *Pygmalion: ein Impuls Ovids und seine Wirkungen bis in die Gegenwart*. Opladen: Westdeutscher Verlag.
Due, O.S. (1974), *Changing Forms: Studies in the Metamorphoses of Ovid*. Copenhagen: Museum Tusculanum Press.
Durgnat, R. (1974), *The Strange Case of Alfred Hitchcock*. London: Faber and Faber.
Ebert, T. (1996), *Ludic Feminism and After: Postmodernism, Desire and Labor in Late Capitalism*. Ann Arbor: University of Michigan Press.
Elsaesser, T. (2000) *Metropolis*. London: British Film Institute.
Elsner, J. and Sharrock, A. (1993), 'Reviewing Pygmalion', *Ramus* 20, 149–181.
Elsner, J. and Sharrock, A. (2007), *Roman Eyes: Visuality & Subjectivity in Art & Text*. Princeton and Oxford: Princeton University Press.
Enterline, L. (2000), *The Rhetoric of the Body from Ovid to Shakespeare*. Cambridge: Cambridge University Press.
Fantham, E. (2004), *Ovid's Metamorphoses*. Oxford: Oxford University Press.
Feeney, D. (2004), 'Introduction to Ovid's *Metamorphoses*.' in David Raeburn's *Metamorphoses: A New Verse Translation*. London: Penguin Books, pp. xiii–xxxiv.
Feldherr, A. (2002), 'Metamorphosis in the *Metamorphoses*', in P. Hardie (ed.), *The Cambridge Companion to Ovid*, Cambridge: Cambridge University Press, pp. 163–179.
Feldherr, A. (2010), *Playing Gods: Ovid's Metamorphoses and the Politics of Fiction*, Princeton and Oxford: Princeton University Press.
Flynn, T. (1998), *The Body in Sculpture*. London: The Orion Publishing Group.
Gabriel, Y. (ed.) (2004), *Myths, Stories and Organisations: Premodern Narratives for Our Time*, Oxford: Oxford University Press.
Garrett, G. (1999), 'Hitchock's Women on Hitchcock: A Panel Discussion', *Literature Film Quarterly*. 27 (2).
Gilbert, W.S (1872), *Pygmalion and Galatea. Original Plays, First Series*, London.
Gorky, M. (1934), 'Soviet literature', in *Soviet Writers' Congress 1934: The Debate on a Socialist Realism and Modernism*, in M. Gorky, K. Radek, et al. (eds), London: Lawrence and Wishart (1977), pp. 27–72.
Grant, M.N. (2010), '*One Touch of Venus:* an appreciation', *Kurt Weill Newsletter*, 28 (1), 4–8.
Gronberg, T. (2000), 'Deco Venus' in Arscott and Scott (eds), 2000, pp. 142–155.
Gross, K. (1992), *The Dream of the Moving Statue*. Ithaca, NY: Cornell University Press.
Gunning, T. (2005), 'The desire and pursuit of the hole: cinema's obscure object of desire', in S.Bartsch and T. Barscherer (eds), *Erotikon: Essays on Eros Ancient and Modern*. Chicago, IL: University of Chicago Press, pp. 261–277.
Haraway, D.J. (1991), *Simians, Cyborgs and Women: The Reinvention of Nature*. London and New York: Routledge.

Hardie, P. (2002a), *Ovid's Poetics of Illusion*. Cambridge: Cambridge University Press.
Hardie, P. (ed.) (2002b), *The Cambridge Companion to Ovid*. Cambridge: Cambridge University Press.
Hardwick, L.P. (2003), *Reception Studies: New Surveys in the Classics, Greece and Rome* 33. Oxford: Oxford University Press.
Hardwick, L.P. and Christopher S. (eds) (2008), *A Companion to Classical Receptions*, Malden, Oxford, Chichester: Blackwell Publishing.
Hardy, T. (1986), *The Short Stories of Thomas Hardy*. Poole, Dorset: New Orchard Editions Ltd.
Harris, R.A. and Katz, J.C. (1996), *Vertigo: Production Notes*. DVD distributed by Columbia Tristar Home Video, UK.
Haynes, N. (2010), *The Ancient Guide to Modern Life*. London: Profile Books.
Hearn, M. and Rigby J. (2005) '*Four Sided Triangle* Viewing Notes', DVD distributed by DD Home Entertainment, 1–19.
Hearn, M. and Rigby J. (2005), '*Stolen Face* Viewing Notes', DVD distributed by DD Home Entertainment, 1–21.
Hersey, G.L. (2009), *Falling in Love with Statues: Artificial Humans from Pygmalion to the Present*. Chicago: University of Chicago Press.
Hoffman, E.T.A. (1816), 'Der Sandman', in *Die Nachstücke* translated by J.T. Bealby in *Weird Tales* (1885) New York: Charles Scribners' Sons.
Holroyd, M. (1989), *Bernard Shaw: The Pursuit of Power* (vol. II, 1898–1918), London: Chatto and Windus.
Holtsmark, E.B. (2001), 'The katabasis theme in modern cinema', in M. Winkler (ed., revd edn), *Classical Myth and Culture in the Cinema*. Oxford: Oxford University Press, pp. 23–50.
Hoyle, F. and Elliot, J.(1962), *A for Andromeda*. London: Souvenir Press.
Huyssen, A. (1981/1982), 'The vamp and the machine: technology and sexuality in Fritz Lang's *Metropolis*', *New German Critique* 24/25 (Autumn–Winter), 221–237.
Huyssen, A. (1986), *After the Great Divide: Modernism, Mass Culture, Post Modernism*. Bloomington: Indiana University Press.
Izod, J. (2006), *Screen, Culture, Psyche: a Post-Jungian Approach to Working with the Audience*. London and New York: Routledge.
James, P. (2003), 'She's all that: Ovid's ivory statue and the myth of Pygmalion on Film', *Classical Bulletin*, 79 (1), 63–92.
James, P. (2004), 'What lies beneath: fluid subtexts in Ovid's *Metamorphoses*', in M. Zimmerman and R. Van der Paardt (eds), *Metamorphic Reflections: Essays presented to Ben Hijmans on his 75th birthday*. Leuwen: Peeters, pp. 1–20.
James, P. (2009), 'Crossing classical thresholds: gods, monsters and hell dimensions in the Whedon universe', in D. Lowe and K. Shahabudin (eds), Cambridge: Cambridge Scholars' Publishing, pp. 237–260.
Johnson, P.J. (2008), *Ovid before Exile*. Madison: Wisconsin Press.
Joshua, E. (2001), *Pygmalion and Galatea: The History of a Narrative in English Literature*. Aldershot: Ashgate Publishing.
Jowett, L. (2005), *Sex and the Slayer: a Gender Studies Primer for the Buffy Fan*. Middletown, CT: Wesleyan University Press.

Kaveney, R. (2004), *Reading the Vampire Slayer: the New Updated Unofficial Guide to Buffy and Angel*. London: Tauris Parke.
Keen, J.M. (1983), *The Perseus and Pygmalion Legends in later nineteenth century Literature and Art, with special reference to the influence of Ovid's Metamorphoses* (unpublished doctoral thesis), University of Southampton.
Kehr, D. (1984), 'Hitch's riddle', *Film Comment* (May/June).
Kirchner, G. (1952), 'Shaw's *Pygmalion* and Smollett's *Peregrine Pickle*', *Neueren Sprachen* 10, 409–417.
Konigsberg, I. (1988), *The Complete Film Dictionary*. London: Bloomsbury.
Koontz, K.D. (2010), 'Czech mate: Whedon, Čapek and the foundations of *Dollhouse*', in R. Wilcox and D. Lavery (eds), *Slayage Online: the International Journal of Buffy Studies* (slayageonline.com/essays/slayage 30–31, accessed 5 November 2010).
Kord, S. and Krimmer, E. (2005), *Hollywood Divas, Indie Queens, and TV Heroines: Contemporary Screen Images of Women*. Oxford: Roman and Littlefield.
Kracauer, S. (1947), *From Caligari to Hitler: A Psychological Study of the German Film*. Princeton: Princeton University Press.
Kris, E. and Kurz, O. (1979), *Legend, Myth and Magic in the Image of the Artists: A Historical Experiment*. New Haven, CT: Yale University Press.
Krzyszkowska, O. (1990), *Ivory and Related Materials: an Illustrated Guide (Bulletin Supplement)*. London: Institute of Classical Studies.
Kuchar, G. (2002), 'Review of Lynn Enterline, *The Rhetoric of the Body: from Ovid to Shakespeare*,' Early Modern Literary Studies, January, 9, 1–5.
Lawrence, A. (1991), *Echo and Narcissus: Women's Voices in Classical Hollywood Cinema*. Berkeley/Los Angeles/Oxford: University of California Press.
Leach, E.W. (1974), 'Ekphrasis and the theme of artistic failure in Ovid's *Metamorphoses*', *Ramus*, 3, 102–142.
Leff, L. (1987), *Hitchcock and Selznick*. New York: University of California Press.
Leslie, E. (2005), 'Adorno, Benjamin, Brecht and Film', in M. Waine (ed.), *Understanding Film: Marxist Perspectives*. London: Pluto Press, pp. 34–57.
Levin, I. (1972), *The Stepford Wives*. 1998 edition, London: Bloomsbury Publishing.
Lively, G. (1999), 'Reading resistance in Ovid's *Metamorphoses*', in P. Hardie, A. Barchiesi, and S. Hinds (eds), *Ovidian Transformations: Essays on the Metamorphoses and its Reception*. Cambridge: Cambridge Philological Society Supplement 23, pp. 197–213.
Lively, G. (2006), 'Science Fiction and cyber myths: or, do cyborgs dream of dolly the sheep?' in V. Zajkon and M. Leonard (eds), *Laughing with Medusa: Classical Myth and Feminist Thought*. Oxford: Oxford University Press, pp. 275–294.
Llewellyn, R. (1999), *The Man on Platform 5*. Coronet Books.
Longley, M. (1994), 'Ivory and water', in M. Hofmann and J. Lasden (eds), *After Ovid: New Metamorphoses*. London: Faber and Faber.
Maltin, L. (2010), *Leonard Maltin's 2010 Movie Guide*. New York: Plume (Penguin Group, USA).
March, J.R. (1998), *Cassell Dictionary of Classical Mythology*. London: Cassell.
Marías, M. (2011) 'Forever falling', in *Sight and Sound* May, vol. 21, issue 5.44–47 (translated by Mar Diestro-Dópido).

Martin, S. (2001), 'Resistance and persistence: *Pygmalion* and *My Fair Lady*, two film versions of G.B.Shaw's *Pygmalion*', *Enter Text: An Interactive Interdisciplinary E-Journal for Cultural and Historical Studies and Creative Work*, 1 (ii), 37–60.

Marx, K. (1857–1858), *Grundrisse. (Foundations of the Critique of Political Economy.)* translated by M. Nicolaus, published 1973, Harmondsworth: Penguin Books.

McKinley, K.L. (2001), *Reading the Ovidian Heroine: Metamorphoses' Commentaries 1100–1618*. Leiden: Brill.

Melville, A.D. (1985), *Ovid's Metamorphoses*. Oxford: Oxford University Press.

Merimée, P. (1837), *La Vénus d'Ille*. Paris.

Milavec, M.M. and Kaye, S.M. (2003), 'Buffy in the buff: A Slayer's solution to Aristotle's love paradox', in J. B. South (ed.), *Buffy the Vampire Slayer and Philosophy*. Chicago and La Salle, IL: Carus Publishing, pp. 173–184.

Miles, G. (1999), *Classical Mythology in English Literature*. London and New York: Routledge.

Miller. J.M. (1988), 'Some versions of Pygmalion', in C. Martindale (ed.) *Ovid Renewed*. Cambridge: Cambridge University Press, pp. 205–214.

Modleski, T. (1988), *The Women Who Knew Too Much: Hitchcock and Feminist Theory*. New York: Methuen.

Moore, C.L. (1944), *No Woman Born*. in J.W. Campbell (ed.), *Outstanding Science Fiction* (December 1944 issue).

Mulvey, L. (1975), 'Visual pleasure and narrative cinema' inother pleasures', in *Visual and Other Pleasures*. Laura Mulvey (1989), Basingstoke: Macmillan, pp. 14–26.

Mulvey, L. (1995), 'The myth of Pandora: a psychoanalytical approach', in L. Pietropaolo and A. Testaferri (eds), Bloomington: Indiana University Press, pp.5–6.

Myer, V.G. (1981), '*Peregrine Pickle* and *Pygmalion*', *Notes and Queries*, 28, 430–431.

Newlands, C. (2009), 'Select Ovid', *Classical World*, 102 (2), 173–177.

Newman, K. (2010), 'Remake, remodel', *Sight and Sound*, 20 (10), 16–18.

Nugent, G. 1989 'The Sex Which is Not One: Deconstructing Ovid's Hermaphrodite', *Differences*, 2.1, 160–185.

Onions, J. B. (1980), 'Abstraction and imagination in late antiquity,' *Art History*, 3, 1–23.

O'Sullivan, J. (2008), 'Virtual metamorphoses: cosmetic and cybernetic revisions of Pygmalion's "living doll"', *Arethusa*,41, 133–156.

Païni, D. and Cogeval, G. (2001), *Hitchcock et L'Art: coincidences fatales*. Centre Pompidou: Mazzota.

Pateman, M. (2006), *The Aesthetics of Culture in Buffy the Vampire Slayer*. Jefferson, North Carolina and London: McFarland & Company, Inc., Publishers.

Peers, J. (2005), 'Doll History and Fashion Theory', in Plumb and Lewis (eds), pp. 22–35.

Pixley, A. (2006), '*A for Andromeda* viewing notes', DVD distributed by BBC Worldwide Ltd, pp. 1–32.

Plumb, S. and Lewis, J. (2005), *Guys 'n' Dolls: Art, Science, Fashion and Relationships*. Brighton and Hove: Royal Pavilion, Libraries and Musuems.

Pomeroy, A.J. (2008), *Then It Was Destroyed By The Volcano: The Ancient World In Film And On Television*. London: Duckworth.

Poole, C. (2007), 'Darn your sinister attraction!', in J. Davidson (ed.), *The Psychology of Joss Whedon: An Unauthorised Exploration of Buffy, Angel and Firefly*. Dallas, TX: Benbella Books, Inc., pp. 21–34.

Power, T. (2010), 'Review of Hersey's *Falling in Love with Statues.*', *Bryn Mawr Classical Review*, 2010. 02. 35, 1–4.

Raeburn, D. (2004), *Ovid Metamorphoses: A New Verse Translation*. London: Penguin.

Rizov, V. (2010), 'Review of *Splice*,' *Sight and Sound*, 20 (8), 75.

Rosati, G. (1983), *Narciso e Pigmalione: illusione e spettacolo nelle Metamorfosi di Ovidio*. Florence.

Salzmann-Mitchell, P.B. (2005), *A Web of Fantasies: Gaze, Image and Gender in Ovid's Metamorphoses*. Ohio: Ohio State University Press.

Scheer, T.S. and Lindner, M. (eds) (2009), *Tempelprostitution im Altertum: Fakten und Fiktionen, Oikumene. Studien zur antiken Weltgeschichte* 16, Berlin: Verlage Antike.

Seed, D. (2008), *A Companion to Science Fiction*. Oxford: Blackwell Publishing.

Segal, C.P. (1988), 'Ovid's metamorphic bodies: art, gender and violence in the *Metamorphoses*', *Arion*, 5, 9–41.

Server, L. (2006), *Ava Gardner – Love is Nothing*. London: Bloomsbury Publishing.

Sharrock, A. (1991), 'Womanufacture', *Journal of Roman Studies*, 81, 36–49.

Shelley, M. (1985), *Frankenstein; or the Modern Prometheus* (1831 edn), London: Penguin.

Siemann, C. (2002), 'Darkness Falls on the Endless Summer: Buffy as Gidget for the Fin de Siècle' in Wilcox and Lavery, pp. 120–132.

Solodow, J.B. (1988), *The World of Ovid's Metamorphoses*. Chapel Hill and London: University of Carolina Press.

Spoto, D. (1992), *The Art of Alfred Hitchcock*. New York: First Anchor Books Edition.

Stables. K. (2002) 'Review of SIMØNE', *Sight and Sound*, 12 (11), 55–57.

Stables. K. (2008), 'Review of *Lars and the Real Girl*', *Sight and Sound*, 18 (4), 66.

Stafford, N. (2002), *Bite Me! An Unofficial Guide to the World of Buffy the Vampire Slayer*. Toronto, Ontario: ECW Press.

Stafford, R. (2007), *Understanding Audiences and the Film Industry*. London: British Film Institute.

Steiner, D.T. (2001), *Images in Mind: Statues in Archaic and Classical Greek Literature and Thought*. Princeton and Oxford: Princeton University Press.

Stoichita, V. (2008) *The Pygmalion Effect: From Ovid to Hitchcock* (translated by A. Andrews), Chicago: Chicago University Press.

Storey, J. (2003), *Inventing Popular Culture*, Oxford: Blackwell Publishing.

Tonkin, B. (2004), 'Entropy as demon: *Buffy* in Southern California', in Kaveney (ed.), pp. 83–99.

Thomas, D. (2006), 'Reading Buffy', *Close Up*, 1, 170–241.

Thomson, D. (2010), *The New Biographical Dictionary of Film*, 5th edn. London: Little, Brown.

Verdoodt, I. and Rutten, K. (2009), 'Film choices for screening literacy: the "Pygmalion template" in the curriculum as contact zone', *Journal of Curriculum Studies*, 42 (4), 519–538.

Viarre, S. (1964), *L'image et la pensée dans les Métamorphoses d'Ovide*. Paris.

Viarre, S. (1968), 'Pygmalion et Orphée chez Ovide (*Met*.X 243–297)', *Revue des Etudes Latines*, 235–237.

Waine, M. (2005), *Understanding Film: Marxist Perspectives*. London/Ann Arbor: Pluto Press.

Walker, J. (2006), *Halliwell's Who's Who in the Movies*. London: HarperCollins Publishing.

Walker, J. (2007), *Halliwell's Film, DVD and Video Guide*. London: HarperCollins Publishing.

Wheeler, S.M. (1999), *A Discourse of Wonders: Audience and Performance in Ovid's Metamorphoses*. Philadelphia, PA: University of Pennsylvania Press.

Wollen, P. *Sight & Sound*, April 1997.

Wilcox, R.V. and Lavery, D. (eds) (2002), *Fighting the Forces: What's at Stake in Buffy the Vampire Slayer*. Lanham, Boulder, New York, Oxford: Rowman and Littlefield Publishers, Inc.

Wilcox. R.V. (2006), *Why Buffy Matters: The Art of Buffy the Vampire Slayer*. London, New York: I.B. Tauris.

Wildman, S. (1995), *Visions of Love and Life: Pre-Raphaelite Art from the Birmingham Collection, England*. Alexandria, Virginia.

Williams, L. (1989), *Hard Core: Power, Pleasure and the Frenzy of the Visible*, California: California University Press, expanded edition.

Williamson, M. (2005), *The Lure of the Vampire: Gender, Fiction and Fandom from Bram Stoker to Buffy*, London and New York: Wallflower Press.

Winkler, M.M. (ed.) (2001), *Classical Myth and Culture in the Cinema*, 2nd edition. Oxford: Oxford University Press.

Winkler, M.M. (2009), *Cinema and Classical Texts: Apollo's New Light*. Cambridge: Cambridge University Press.

Wood, G. (2002), *Living Dolls: A Magical History of the Quest for Mechanical Life*. London: Faber and Faber.

Wright, P. (2008), 'British Television Science Fiction', in Seed (ed.), 289–306.

Filmography

A for Andromeda. Dir. John Elliot, John Knight. BBC Television. 1961.
All about Eve. Dir. Joseph. L. Mankiewisz. TCF (Darryl F. Zanuck). 1950.
The Andromeda Breakthrough. Dir.John Elliot and John Knight. BBC Television. 1962.
Annie Get Your Gun. Dir. George Sidney. MGM. 1950.
The Birds. Dir. Alfred Hitchcock. Universal. 1963.
Blade Runner. Dir. Ridley Scott. Warner/Ladd//Blade Runner Partnerships. 1982.
The Bride of Frankenstein. Dir. James Whale. Universal. 1935.
Buffy the Vampire Slayer. Dir. Joss Whedon. Twentieth Century Fox Television. 1997–2003.
Calamity Jane. Dir. David Butler. Warner. 1953.
Charade. Dir. Stanley Donen. Universal. 1963.
Cherry 2000. Dir. Steve de Jarnatt. Orion. 1988.
Citizen Kane Dir. Orson Welles. RKO. 1941.
The Cloning of Joanna May. Dir. Philip Saville. Granada Television. 1992.
A Connecticut Yankee in King Arthur's Court. Dir. Tay Garnett. Paramount (Robert Fellows). 1949.
Corridor of Mirrors. Dir. Terence Young. Cartier-Romney-Apollo. 1948.
Dark Victory. Dir. Edmund Goulding. Warner (David Lewis). 1939.
Devil Doll. Dir. Lindsay Shonteff. Galaworld/Gordon. 1963.
The Devil-Doll Dir. Todd Browning. MGM. 1936.
Dollhouse. (Seasons One and Two) Dir. Joss Whedon. Twentieth Century Fox Television. 2009–2010.
Down To Earth. Dir. Alexander Hall. Columbia. 1946.
Dr Jekyll and Mr Hyde. Dir. Rouben Mamoulian. Paramount. 1932.
Dr Jekyll and Mr Hyde. Dir. Victor Fleming. MGM. 1941.
Educating Rita. Dir. Lewis Gilbert. Rank/Acorn. 1983.
Eve of Destruction. Dir. Duncan Gibbins. MGM. 1991.
The Fifth Element. Dir. Luc Besson. Columbia/Gaumont. 1997.
Four Sided Triangle. Dir. Terence Fisher. Exclusive/Hammer (Michael Carreras, Alexander Paal). 1953.
Funny Face. Dir. Stanley Donen. Paramount (Roger Edens). 1956.
Gilda. Dir. Charles Vidor. Columbia. 1946.
Goddess of Love. Dir. James R. Drake. Phoenix Entertainment Group. 1988.
High Society. Dir. Charles Walters. MGM. 1956
Jason and the Argonauts. Dir. Don Chaffey. Columbia / Charles H. Schneer. 1963.
The King's Speech. Dir. Tom Hooper. U.K. Film Council, See-Saw Films, Bedlam Productions. 2010.
Kitty. Dir. Mitchell Leisen. Paramount. 1945.

Klute. Dir. Alan J. Pakula. Warner. 1971.
La Belle et La Bête. Dir. Jean Cocteau. Discina. 1946.
Lars and the Real Girl. Dir. Craig Gillespie. MGM and Sidney Kimmel Entertainment. 2007.
Mad Love. Dir. Karl Freund. MGM. 1935.
Mannequin. Dir. Michael Gottlieb. TCF/Gladden. 1987.
Marnie. Dir Alfred Hitchcock. Universal. 1964.
Metropolis Dir. Fritz Lang. Universum Film AG (U.F.A Erich Pommer.) 1927.
Mighty Aphrodite. Dir. Woody Allen. Miramax. 1995.
Miss Congeniality. Dir. Donald Petrie. Warner/Castle Rock /Village Roadshow/MPU/Fortis/S. Bullock. 2000.
Miss Congeniality 2: Armed and Fabulous. Dir. John Pasquin. US/Australia. 2005.
Miss Leslie's Dolls Dir. Joseph G Prieto. World Wide Productions. 1973.
The Muse. Dir. Albert Brooks. Entertainment/October. 1999.
My Fair Lady. Dir. George Cukor. CBS/Warner. 1964.
My Living Doll. Dir. Lawrence Dobkin, Ezra Stone. Jack Chertok Television Productions, CBS Television Network. 1964–1965.
North By Northwest. Dir. Alfred Hitchcock. MGM. 1959.
Notorious. Dir. Alfred Hitchcock. RKO. 1946.
Notting Hill Dir. Roger Michell. Polygram – UK Title Entertainment. 1999.
Obsession. Dir. Brian de Palma. Columbia. 1976.
One Touch of Venus. Dir. William A. Seiter. Universal. 1948.
The Opening of Misty Beethoven. Dir.Radley Metzger. VCA Pictures. 1976.
Orlacs Hände. Dir. Robert Wiene. Pan Film, Austria. 1924.
Pandora and the Flying Dutchman. Dir. Albert Lewin. Romulus (Albert Lewin). 1950.
Pandora's Box (Die Büchse der Pandora). Dir. G.W. Pabst. Nero Film. 1929.
The Perfect Woman. Dir. Bernard Knowles. GFD/Two Cities. 1949.
The Philadelphia Story. Dir. George Cukor. MGM. 1940.
Pimpernel Smith. Dir. Leslie Howard. British National. 1941.
The Prestige. Dir. Christopher Nolan. 2006.
Pretty Woman. Dir. Garry Marshall. Buena Vista/Touchstone. 1990.
The Purple Rose of Cairo. Dir. Woody Allen. Orion. 1985.
Pygmalion. Dir. Anthony Asquith. Gabriel Pascal. 1938.
Radio Days. Dir. Woody Allen. Orion Pictures. 1987.
Rear Window. Dir. Alfred Hitchcock. Paramount. 1954.
The Rebel. Dir. Robert Day. Associated British (W.A.Whitaker). 1960.
The Shape of Things. Dir. Neil La Bute. UIP/FocusStudio/Canal/Working Title/Pretty Pictures. 2003.
She's All That. Dir. Robert Iscove. Miramax/Tapestry/Film Colony. 1999.
SIMØNE. Dir. Andrew Niccol. New Line Cinema. 2002.
Solaris. Dir. Andrei Tarkovsky. Visual Programme Systems (UK). 1973.
Some Like it Hot. Dir. Billy Wilder. UA/Mirisch. 1959.
Spellbound. Dir. Alfred Hitchcock. David O. Selznick. 1945.
Splice. Dir. Vincenzo Natali. Warner Bros Pictures with Dark Castle Entertainment. 2010.
A Star Is Born. Dir. William A. Wellman. David O. Selznick. 1937.
A Star Is Born. Dir. George Cukor. Warner/Transcoa (Sidney Luft). 1954.

A Star Is Born. Dir. Frank Pierson. Warner/Barwood/First artists. 1976.
The Stepford Wives. Dir. Bryan Forbes. Fadsin/Palmer/Bryan Forbes. 1974.
Stolen Face. Dir. Terence Fisher. Exclusive Hammer. 1952.
Strangers On A Train. Dir Alfred Hitchcock. Warner. 1951.
That Hamilton Woman. Dir. Alexander Korda. Alexander Korda Films. 1941.
The Truman Show. Dir. Peter Weir. Paramount. 1998.
2001: A Space Odyssey. Dir Stanley Kubrick. MGM. 1968.
Vertigo. Dir Alfred Hitchcock. Paramount. 1958.
Virtual Sexuality. Dir. Nick Hurran. Columbia TriStar/The Bridge/Noel Gay (Christopher Figg). 1999.
Weird Science. Dir. John Hughes. Universal. 1985.
What Price Hollywood. Dir. George Cukor. RKO. (Pandro S. Berman). 1932.
Xanadu. Dir. Robert Greenwald. Universal. 1980.

Index

Glosses

automata self propelling non human figures – a term that can cover moving statues, Vulcan's golden slaves, mechanical beings of science fiction or the electronic figures of modern robotics. The first occurrence of the word android to describe an articulated, mobile but synthetic creature is found in Villiers de L'Isle Adam's *The Future Eve*.

cyborg a combination of human and mechanical parts ('biomorphic'), first and memorably realised in fiction as Frankenstein's monster but similar creatures (factory produced) were designated as robots (derived from Czech for peasant, Slavic for slave,) by Karl Čapek in *Rossum's Universal Robots*.

ecphrasis elaborate description in Greek and Latin literature (especially applied to artefact and its making) emphasizing visuality of the scene and positioning reader / listener as viewer. Like an extended epic simile an ecphrasis can restate or subvert the theme or content of the overall work.

liminality an in between state but also a condition that straddles thresholds both real and figurative, especially applied to those neither living nor dead or those undergoing a psychological struggle to find a stable identity.

The abbreviation 'dir.' stands for 'directed by'.
***Met* stands for Ovid's *Metamorphoses*.**
***passim* indicates the author, figure or concept appears throughout.**

* marks to indicate the terms discussed in glosses

A for Andromeda (1961 British TV series) 35, 150–3, 203n. 1
Actaeon (*Met*. Book Three) 7
Admetus 6, 25 *see* Euripides
Adonis (*Met* Book Ten) 100, 157, 165, 191, 196, 198
Aeneas 198, 201 *see* Virgil and *Aeneid*
Aeneid (epic by Virgil) 198–9

Ahl, Friedrich 19, 21
Alcestis 6, 25 *see* Euripides
Alderman, Naomi 202n. 8
All about Eve (1950 film dir. Joseph L. Mankiewicz) 189n. 6
Allen, Woody 69, 175–6 *see Mighty Aphrodite, Purple Rose of Cairo, Radio Days*

'All is Full of Love' (song by Bjork) 116
Anchises 27, 101, 109 *see Homeric Hymn to Aphrodite*
Anderson, William S. 12, 69
Andrews, David 134
Andrews, Julie 67, 195n. 6
android* 118, 190n. 13, 199n. 8, 200n. 8 *see also* artificial life, automata, gynoid, cyborg, robot
Andromeda (*Met* Books Four and Five) 152–3 *see* Perseus
The Andromeda Breakthrough (1961 British TV series) 153, 203n. 1
anima (life breath, soul) 162, 164–5, 170 *see* Izod
Annie Get Your Gun (1950 film dir. George Sidney) 136, 197n. 25
Anstey, F. (Thomas Anstey Guthrie, 1856–1934) 97, 102, 105–11, 132, 198n. 1 *see The Tinted Venus*
Anthony, Albert 119–22
Aphrodite 1–2, 23, 27, 51, 69, 93–5, 100–5, 174, 189, 191n. 19, 198n. 7 *see* (Roman) Venus
Apollo 24, 65–6, 108, 195n. 2
Apollonius of Rhodes (poet, 3rd century BCE Alexandria) 116 *see Argonautica*
Arachne (*Met* Book Six) 12, 24
Arctinus (early poet of Miletus, dates unknown) 199n. 2 *see Iliupersis*
Arden, Eve 105, 107
Argonautica 116 *see* Apollonius of Rhodes
Aristophanes (Greek comic playwright, 5th century BCE) 57 *see Symposium*
Arscott, Caroline 17, 92–3, 198n. 3, 205n. 12
Artemis *see* (Roman) Diana
artificial life 4 *see also* androids, automata, cyborgs, dolls, gynoids, robots
As Far as the Eye Can See 196n. 8 *see Back to Methuselah* by George Bernard Shaw

Asimov, Isaac 203n. 12, 204n. 4 *see Satisfaction Guaranteed, The Talking Stone*
Asquith, Antony 70, 72 *see Pygmalion*
Athena 150, 189n. 5 *see* (Roman) Minerva
Athenian tragedy 8
auctoritas 8
Augustus (Roman emperor 63 BCE–14 CE) 1, 7–8, 66, 190n. 16
Auiler, Dan 47, 50, 54–5
automata* 21, 33, 115–16, 127, 197n. 2, 199n. 4 & n. 8, 203n. 6 *see also* androids, cyborgs, gynoids, robots, statues

Baccolini, Rafaella 118
Back to Methuselah (1918–1920 'pentateuch' by George Bernard Shaw) 196n. 8 *see As Far As The Eye Can See*
Battle, Hinton 148
Baker, Diane 193n. 14
Barbara of the House of Grebe (in collection, *A Group of Noble Dames*) 204n. 2
Barbier, Gabriella 199n. 8
Barkan, Leonard 170
Barolsky, Paul 167, 189n. 9 *see* D'Ambra
Barr, Charles 53
Barthes, Roland 33
Bartsch, Shadi 190n. 17
Baudrillard, Jean 202n. 13
Bauer, Douglas 189n. 5, 191n. 21
Bazzoli, Meredith 170–3
Beckett, Chris 200n. 9 *see The Holy Machine*
Beckman, Henry 133
Beerbohm Tree, Herbert 78
Bel Geddes, Barbara 48
Bergman, Ingrid 41, 42–5, 192n. 9, 193n. 11
Besson, Luc 200n. 10 see *The Fifth Element*
The Birds (1963 film dir. Alfred Hitchcock) 45
Black, Karen 39

Blade Runner (1982 film dir. Ridley Scott) 116, 118, 123, 157, 190n. 13, 200n. 10
Bloom, Michelle E. 19, 33, 36, 61, 98–9, 183, 200n. 13
Blundell, Sue 178, 205n. 8
Boileau, Pierrre 47, 62 *see also* Narcejak *D'Entre Les Morts*
Bömer, Franz 191n. 26
Bonanza (US 1960s TV series) 133
Bonham Carter, Helena 69
Bortolin, Diego 166, 171
Bould, Mark 122–3
Bowman, Laurel 201n. 2
Brett, Jeremy 76, 78
Brewer, Wilmon 191n. 26
Brian, Dora 128
Bride of Frankenstein (1935 film dir. James Whale) 125, 168, 203n. 4
Brill, Lesley 47, 52, 58, 194n. 18
Brody, Adrien 154
Brooks, Albert 96 *see The Muse*
Brooks, Louise 197n. 20
Brown, Sarah Annes 39, 118, 193n. 16, 200n. 14
Browning, Robert 61 *see My Last Duchess*
Browning, Todd 168 *see The Devil-Doll*
Bryant, Antoinette Terry 156 *see Splice*
Buffy the Vampire Slayer (US TV series, 1997–2003) 4, 34, 132–49
Bujold, Genevieve 63–4
Bullock, Sandra 88–90
Burne-Jones, Edward Coley 3, 10, 14–17, 26, 53, 77, 89, 162, 192n. 7, 204n. 3
Busch, Adam 140
Butler, David 197n. 25 *see Calamity Jane*
Byrne, Shannon 191n. 24

Caine, Michael 85–6, 88–9
Cairns, David 61–2 *see* Shadowplay Blog
Calamity Jane (1953 film dir. David Butler) 136, 197n. 25
Callisto (*Met* Book Two) 37

Calvert, Bronwen 147, 202n. 13
Campbell, Joseph 201n. 2
Campbell, (Mrs) Patrick 78, 196n. 18
Čapek, Karl 203n. 6
Carroll, Leo G. 43
Cast, David 20
Cattrall, Kim 112, 159
Cerastae (*Met* Book Ten) 12, 18
Chaffey, Don 199n. 3 *see Jason and the Argonauts*
Chanéac, Delphine 156
Charade (1963 film dir. Stanley Donen) 196n. 17
Chekhov, Michael 43–4
Cherry 2000 (1988 film dir. Steve de Jarnett) 118, 134–6
Christie, Julie 151–2
Churchill (Sir) W.S (1892–1965) 205n. 11
Cinderella 70–1, 80, 82, 107
Cinyras
  Met Book Six (Assyrian king) 187
  Met Book Ten (king of Cyprus) 65, 189
Citizen Kane (1941 film dir. Orson Welles) 1
Clive, Colin 203n. 5
cloning 123–5 *see also* genetic engineering
The Cloning of Joanna May
  1989 novel by Fay Weldon 182
  British 1992 TV series 182
Cocteau, Jean 61 *see La Belle et La Bête*
Cohen, Rachel Lara 188n. 3
A Connecticut Yankee in King Arthur's Court (1889 novel by Mark Twain) 107
A Connecticut Yankee in King Arthur's Court (1949 film dir. Tay Garnett) 107–8
Connery, Sean 46
Conrad, Peter 192n. 9
Conway, Tom 105, 107
Cook, Rachel Leigh 86–8
Cornea, Christine 197n. 7
corpses 17, 33, 125, 190n. 13
Corinna 6 *see* Ovid *Amores*

Corridor of Mirrors (1948 film dir. Terence Young) 35–6, 58–62, 168, 194n. 27
Courtney, Julia 201n. 3
Cox, Brian 182
Craig, Wendy 204n. 4
Crosby, Bing 107
Cueva, Ed 191n. 24
Cukor, George 37–8, 70, 73, 192n. 3 *see My Fair Lady, A Star is Born, What Price Hollywood, The Philadelphia Story*
Cummings, Robert (Bob) 133–4
Cunningham, Chris 116
Cupid (Amor,) 65–6 *see* (Greek) Eros
Curtis, Tony 158
cyborg (cybernetic organism) 28, 115–23, 157–9, 199n. 7, 203n. 5
Cyclops 151
Cyprus 1–3, 11–16, 23–8, 53, 73, 76, 82–3, 89–93, 95, 99–100
Cyrino, Monica S. 26, 184n. 4
Czarniawska, Barbara 180

Daedalus (*Met* Book Eight) 199n. 3
Dali, Salvador 43–4
D'Ambra, Eve 167, 189n. 9 *see* Barolsky
Daniels, Jeff 175–6
Daphne (*Met* Book Two) 65–6, 195n. 1–2
Dark Victory (1939 film dir. Edmund Goulding) 201n. 7
Day, Doris 136, 197n. 25
Day, Robert 200n. 16 *see The Rebel*
Deahl, Alfred 196n. 13
Deahl, Stephen 194n. 27
D'Entre Les Morts (1954 novel by Boileau and Narcejac) 47, 62
de Jarnatt, Steve *see Cherry 2000*
de Palma, Brian 63 *see Obsession*
del Toro, Guillermo 154 *see Splice*
The Devil-Doll (1936 film dir. Todd Browning) 168
Devil Doll (1964 film dir. Lindsay Shonteff) 168
Diana (goddess) 7, 65, 102 *see* (Greek) Artemis

Dick, Philip K. *see Do Androids Dream of Electric Sheep*
Dietrich, Marlene 97
Dionysus 8 *see* (Roman) Bacchus
Do Androids Dream of Electric Sheep (novel by Philip K Dick) 118
Dobkin, Lawrence *see My Living Doll*
Doherty, Lillian E. 184, 203n. 10
Dollhouse (American TV series, 2009–2010) 203n. 6 *see* Joss Whedon
dolls
  in the movies 60, 74, 112, 168–73, 182
  as real life partners, substitutes 115, 126, 162–9
Donen, Stanley 183 *see Funny Face, Singin' in the Rain*
Dorfman, Elena 166–7
Dörrie, Heinrich 205n. 7
Down to Earth (1946 film dir. Alexander Hall) 95–6
Dr Jekyll and Mr Hyde (1932 film dir. Rouben Mamoulian) 193n. 11
Dr Jekyll and Mr Hyde (1941 film dir. Victor Fleming) 193n.11 *see also The Strange Case of Dr Jekyll and Mr Hyde* by Robert Louis Stevenson 200n. 13
Drake, James R. 97 *see Goddess of Love*
Duffy, Stella 204n. 5
Durgnat, Raymond 56

Ebert, Teresa 199n. 5
Echo (*Met* Book Three) 131, 163, 190n. 17, 192n. 10 *see* Narcissus
ecphrasis* 29
Educating Rita
  stage production dir. Willy Russell 85
  1983 film dir. Lewis Gilbert 69, 84–6
elegy (Latin love) 6, 20–1, 190n. 16
Elizondo, Hector 82
Elliot, John 150 *see A for Andromeda*
Elliott, Laura 192n. 6
Elsaesser, Thomas 121
Elsner, Jaś 190n. 12, 191n. 23

Ennius Quintus, (Latin poet and playwright, 239–169BCE) 12, 189n. 4
Enterline, Lynn 32, 194n. 22
Envy 24, 108, 189n. 10 *see* Livor
Epimetheus (brother of Prometheus) 28
Espenson, Jane 4, 148
Euhemerus of Messene (philosopher, mythographer, 3rd century BCE) 189n. 4
Euripides (tragic playwright, 5th century BCE Athens) 6
Alcestis 25
Eurydice (*Met* Book Ten and Virgil, *Georgics* Book Four) 5–6, 119, 147, 190n. 13
Eve (biblical figure) 28, 124, 157
Eve of Destruction (1991 film dir. Duncan Gibbins) 28, 122, 140

Fantham, Elaine 190n. 12
Farr, Shonda 140
Farrow, Mia 69, 175–7
Feeney, Dennis 188n. 5
Feldherr, Andrew 24, 184, 195n. 2
fembots 199n. 6 *see* gynoids
femininity
  cultural constructedness of 4, 28–30, 37, 41, 74, 82–4, 86–90, 92–3, 108, 111–12, 114, 194n. 19 & n. 21
  ideals of 13–14, 30, 37–8, 82, 89–90, 99, 111–14, 127, 144, 178
feminism 67, 113–14, 116
The Fifth Element (1997 film dir. Luc Besson) 205n. 8
film
  eroticism of medium 33
  marketing 35, 37, 91, 192n. 2, 205n. 14
  Pygmalionesque space 33, 36, 57, 183
Fisher, Terence 62–3, 123–6 *see Four Sided Triangle*, *Stolen Face*
Fleming, Rhonda 107
Fleming, Victor 193n. 11 *see Dr Jekyll and Mr Hyde* (1941)
The Fly (1958 film dir. Kurt Neumann) 125

Flynn, Thomas 99
Forbes, Bryan 126–7, 134, 200n. 15
  see The Stepford Wives
Ford, Glenn 195n. 9
Ford, Harrison 94
Four Sided Triangle (1953 film dir. Terence Fisher) 63, 123–5
Frankenstein or A Modern Prometheus (1818 novel by Mary Shelley) 28, 43, 72, 157, 162–3
Fraser, Laura 176
Freud, Sigmund 92
Freund, Karl *see* Orlacs Hände
Funny Face (1957 film dir. Stanley Donen) 196n. 17
The Future Eve (*L'Ève future*, 1886 novel by Auguste Villiers de l'Isle-Adam) 120 *see* android

Gabriel, Yiannis 19
Gardner, Ava 59, 116–17, 159, 198n. 5
Garland, Judy 37–8
Garnett, Tay 107 *see A Connecticut Yankee in King Arthur's Court*
Garrett, Greg 39 *see Hitchcock's actresses*
Gaynor, Janet 192n. 3
Gellar, Sarah Michelle 147, 202n. 14
genetic engineering 152–4, 203n. 6
  see also cloning
Gere, Richard 80–5
Gibbins, Duncan 122 *see Eve of Destruction*
Gibson, John 99 *see* 'Tinted Venus'
Gidley, Pamela 135–6
Gilbert, (Sir) William Schwenk (1836–1911) 80, 186n. 1 *see Pygmalion and Galatea*
Gilda (1946 film dir. Charles Vidor) 114
Gillespie, Craig *see Lars and the Real Girl*
Goddard, Paulette 205n. 9
Goddess of Love (1988 film dir. James R. Drake) 108–13
Gorky, Maxim 199n. 4
Gottlieb, Michael 112 *see Mannequin*

Goulding, Edmund 201n. 7 *see Dark Victory*
Grable, Betty 195n. 1
Graham, Winston 46 *see* novel *Marnie*
Granger, Farley 192n. 6
Grant, Cary 44–5
Grant, Hugh 114
Grant, Mark N. 92, 97
Greenwald, Robert 96 *see Xanadu*
Griffith, Melanie 134–6
Gronberg, Tag 198n. 5
Gross, Kenneth 190n. 13, 191n. 21
A Group of Noble Dames (1891 short story collection by Thomas Hardy) 204n. 2
Grundrisse (1857 political treatise by Karl Marx) 198n. 6
Gunning, Tom 33, 157–8
Gupta, Suman 200n. 11
'Guys n Dolls' (exhibition, Brighton, 2005) 166
gynoid 117, 151 *see* android, automata, cyborg, robot

Hades (god of Underworld, also Underworld) 5, 25, 45, 48, 148
hairdressers (hair stylists) 31, 47, 54, 63, 68, 86–7, 106, 110–12, 118, 120, 151, 170, 188n. 3, 197n. 23, 203n. 11
Hall, Anthony Michael 157
Halliday, Bryant 168
Halliday, Richard 92
Hamilton, Emma 177–9, 205n. 8 & n. 10
That Hamilton Woman (1941 film dir. Alexander Korda) 117–19
Hampshire, Susan 153
Hancock, Tony 200n. 16
Handl, Irene 128, 200n. 16
Haraway, Donna 116–18, 199n. 5, 203n. 5
Hardie, Philip 22, 26, 195n. 2
Hardwick, Lorna P. 188n. 2, 206n. 15
Hardy, Thomas (1840–1928) 204n. 2
  see Barbara of the House of Grebe
Harlow, Jean 192n. 6
Harris, Robert A. 47, 55, 193n. 15

Harrison, Rex 67, 72, 78, 196n. 17
Harryhausen, Ray 199n. 3
Hart, Emma 177 *see* Hamilton, Emma
Havely, Cicely Palser 2
Haymes, Dick 105
Haynes, Michael 150 *see A for Andromeda*
Haynes, Natalie 201n. 2
Hayworth, Rita 96, 114, 198n. 9
Head, Edith 63
Hedren, Tippi 39, 41, 45, 193n. 13
Heliades (*Met* Books Two and Ten) 10
Helmore, Tom 49
Henreid, Paul 62
Hepburn, Audrey 68, 78, 195n. 6, 196n. 17
Hepburn, Katherine 193n. 12
Hephaistus (blacksmith god) 27, 109, 116, 199n. 3 *see* (Roman) Vulcan
Hera (goddess wife of Zeus) 102, 189n. 5 *see* (Roman) Juno
Herakles (Greek hero) 25 *see* (Roman) Hercules
Hermaphroditus (Ovid *Metamorphoses* Book Four) 42, 152, 174–5, 190n. 15, 203n. 5 *see* Salmacis
Hero 100 *see* Leander
Herrmann, Bernard 55, 63, 192n. 8
Hersey, George L. 32, 93, 115–16, 167, 198n. 1
Hesiod (Greek epic poet, writing ca. 700 BCE) 27–8
  Works and Days 27
hieros gamos (sacred wedding, ritual marriage) 25, 191n. 19
High Society (1956 film dir. Charles Walters) 192n. 12
Hiller, Wendy 72
Hitchcock, Alfred 31–81, 95, 152, 161, 192n. 4–10, 193n. 15–21
  see The Birds, North by Northwest, Notorious, Marnie, Spellbound, Strangers on a Train, Vertigo
'Hitchcock et l'art' (exhibition, Montreal and Paris, 2001) 192n. 4
Hitchhiker's Guide to the Galaxy (1979 novel by Douglas Adams) 200n. 8

Hoban, Steve 154 *see Splice*
Hobson, Valerie 58
Hodge, Patricia 182
Holloway, Stanley 130, 132
Holroyd, Mark 70, 78, 196n. 14 & n. 18
Holtsmark, Erling. B. 135
The Holy Machine (2004 novel by Chris Beckett) 118, 200n. 9
Homer (accredited with composition of Greek epics, 8th century BCE) 116–17
 Iliad 116
Homeric Hymn to Aphrodite 27
Hooper, Tom *see The King's Speech*
Horace, Quintus Horatius Flaccus (Latin poet, 65 BCE – 8 BCE) 7
Howard, Leslie 72, 78, 93–4
 see also Pimpernel Smith, Pygmalion
Hoyle, Fred 150 *see A for Andromeda*
Hughes, John 157 *see Weird Science*
Hurran, Nick 176 *see Virtual Sexuality*
Hutton, Betty 197n. 25
Huyssen, Andreas 119

Iliad (epic poem on events in Trojan War) 116
Iliupersis (part of epic cycle on Trojan War) 199n. 2 *see* Arctinus
Indiana Jones (archaeologist hero in adventure movies) 94 *see Pimpernel Smith*
Iscove, Robert 86, 203n. 8 *see She's All That*
ivory, material
 properties of 11, 18–19, 26–7, 31–2, 44, 51, 99, 149, 167, 173–4, 190n.12 n. 12
 symbolic resonances of 4, 14, 18, 29–32, 37, 61, 72, 80, 183, 196n. 15, 202n. 8, 204n. 1
Izod, John 160–5

James, Norman 150 *see A for Andromeda*
James, Paula 11, 189n. 25, 194n. 19 & n. 23, 201n. 2–3

Jason and the Argonauts (1963 film dir. Don Chaffey) 199n. 3
Johnson, Patricia. J. 189n. 3
Jojovich, Milla 200n. 10
Jones, Jennifer 198n. 5
Joshua, Essaka 32, 54, 69–70, 80, 179–80, 195n. 5, 196n. 9
Jowett, Lorna 202n. 13
Jung, Carl 164, 203n. 10
Jupiter (ruler God of Olympus) 12, 65, 99, 106, 109, 111, 198n. 6
 see (Roman) Zeus

katabasis (descent to the Underworld) 135
Katz, James C. 47, 55, 193n. 15
Keaton, Diane 200n. 15
Keel, Howard 136, 197n. 25
Keen, J. M. 1, 14–17, 172, 191n. 20, 204n. 3 *see* Miller, Jane
Kehr, David 51
Kelly, Gene 183 *see Singin' in the Rain*
Kelly, Grace 42–5, 193n. 12
Kelsey, Bill *see My Living Doll*
Kerr, Deborah 58
King, Regina 90
The King's Speech (2010 film dir. Tom Hooper) 195n. 7
Kirchner, Gary 196n. 12
Kitty (1945 film dir. Mitchell Leisen) 205n. 9
Klute (1971 film dir. Alan J. Pakula) 197n. 21
Kneale, Nigel 153 *see The Quatermass Experiment*
Knowles, Bernard 128 *see The Perfect Woman*
Kokoschka, Oscar 168
Koontz, K. Dale 203n. 6
Kord, Suzanne 37, 81–3, 91, 114, 192n. 1, 197n. 22 *see* Krimmer
Korda, Alexander 177–8 *see That Hamilton Woman*
Kracauer, Siegfried 121
Kramer, Clare 144
Krimmer, Elisabeth 37, 81–3, 91, 114, 192n. 1, 197n. 22 *see* Kord

Kris, Ernst see Kurz172
Kristofferson, Kris 192n. 23
Krzyszkowska, Olga 190n. 12
Kubrick, Stanley 201n. 5, 203n. 7
  see *2001: A Space Odyssey*
Kuchar, Gary 194n. 22
Kurz, Otto 172 see Kris

La Belle et La Bête (1946 film dir. Jean Cocteau) 61
La Belle Ferronière (Musée de Louvre, Paris) 49
LaBute, Neil 205n. 6 see *The Shape of Things*
Lacan, Jacques 22, 38, 92
Lactantius (early Christian writer) 167
Lady Hamilton 205n. 11 see *That Hamilton Woman*
Lanchester, Elsa 203n. 4
Lang, Fritz 119–21, 133, 200n. 11 see *Metropolis*
Lars and the Real Girl (2007 film dir. Craig Gillespie) 150, 169–73
Lawrence, Amy 192n. 10
Le Brock, Kelly 158
Leach, Eleanor W. 23, 34, 191n. 22
Leander 100 see Hero
  Tweddle 100–11
Leff, Leonard 34
Leigh, Janet 39
Leigh, Vivien 177–9
Leisen, Mitchell 205n. 9 see *Kitty*
Lerner, Alan Jay 74 see *My Fair Lady*
Leslie, Esther 192n. 2
Lewin, Albert 59 see *Pandora and the Flying Dutchman*
Lewis, Jackie 168
liminality* 18, 23, 47, 87, 118, 145, 147
  see ivory properties of
Lindner, Martin 189n. 4 see Scheer
Liveley, Genevieve 13, 26, 39–40, 116–17, 196n. 15, 199n. 5
The Living and the Dead 47–50, 53, 194n. 26 see *D'Entre Les Morts*
Livor (Envy) 24, 190n. 10, 191n. 18
Llewellyn, Robert 205n. 6 see *The Man on Platform 5*

Loewe, Frederick 74 see *My Fair Lady*
The Lord of the Rings (1954–55 trilogy by J. R. R. Tolkien) 198n. 2
  films dir. Peter Jackson 198n. 2
Lowe, Dunstan 205n. 13
McKinley, Kathryn L. 191n. 22
Mad Love (1935 film dir. Karl Freund) 124
Mahler, Alma 168
Maicanescu, Simona 155
make-over
  of movie stars 37–47, 91
  reversing the Pygmalion myth 18, 56, 67–70, 91, 172
Malleson, Miles 128–30
Maltin, Leonard 135, 160, 164, 168, 176, 198n. 8
Mamoulian, Rouben 193n. 11 see *Dr Jekyll and Mr Hyde*
The Man on Platform 5 (novel by Robert Llewellyn) 204n. 6
Mankiewicz, Joseph L. 189n. 6 see *All about Eve*
Mannequin (1987 film dir. Michael Gottlieb) 108, 112–13
marble 14, 17–18, 50, 63, 72, 80, 86, 95–9, 142, 149, 153, 183–4, 190n. 11
March, Fredric 192n. 5
March, Jennifer R. 198n. 7
Marías, Miguel 193n. 16
Marnie (1964 film dir. Alfred Hitchcock) 40, 45–6, 122, 192n. 8, 193n. 14
Marshall, Garry 67, 80 see *Pretty Woman*, *The Princess Diaries*
Marston, John 32, 53, 194n. 22 see *The Metamorphosis of Pygmalion's Image*
Marsyas (*Met* Book Six) 24
Martin, Al 133 see *My Living Doll*
Martin, Claire 204n. 5
Martin, Mary 92
Martin, Sarah 72–4, 78, 196n. 10 n. 16 & n. 17
Martindale, Charles 188n. 1
Marx, Karl 198n. 6 see *Grundrisse*

masculinity 81, 119
Mason, James 38
Maud, Joan 60
McCarthy, Andrew 112
McDonald, Marianne 206n. 15
Medusa (*Met* Books Four and Five) 153, 191n. 21
Méliès, Georges 87, 197n. 19
Melville, David 189n. 2
Mercury 108, 153, 174 *see* (Greek) Hermes
Mérimée, Prosper 99, 198n. 1 *see La Vénus d'Ille*
'The Metamorphosis of Pigmalion's Image' (1598 poem by John Marston) 32, 53
Metropolis (1927 film dir. Fritz Lang) 28, 35, 118–21, 133, 160, 200n. 10 & n. 11
Metzger, Radley 79 *see The Opening of Misty Beethoven*
Michell, Roger 114 *see Notting Hill*
Mighty Aphrodite (1995 film dir. Woody Allen) 69
Miles, Geoffrey 196n. 2
Miles, Vera 42
Millais, John Everett (1829–1896) 50 *see Ophelia*
Milland, Ray 205n. 9
Miller, Jane 1, 12, 20, 25, 69–71, 75, 78–80, 177, 188n. 1, 191n. 19, 195n. 5 *see* Keen, Jane Michèle
Mills and Boon 204n. 5
mimesis 19
Minerva 24, 109, 189n. 5 *see* (Greek) Athena
mise en scène (composition of cinematic frame) 58, 108, 193n. 16
Miss Congeniality (2000 film dir. Donald Petrie) 69, 88–90
Miss Congeniality 2: Armed and Fabulous (2005 film dir. John Pasquin) 89
Miss Leslie's Dolls (1973 film dir. Joseph G. Prieto) 182
Mitchell-Smith, Ilan 157
Modleski, Tania 39, 45, 48, 194n. 19
The Mona Lisa (Leonardo da Vinci, Musée de Louvre, Paris) 49

The Monkey's Paw (1902 short story by W. W. Jacobs) 202n. 10
Monroe, Marilyn 158, 189n. 6
The Monster and the Woman 125 *see* Four Sided Triangle
Moore, C. L. 118 *see No Woman Born*
Moos, Hermine 168
Morris, Mary 94
Mowbray, Alan 177
Mullen, Barbara 61
Mulvey, Laura 38, 40–1, 98, 122
The Muse (1999 film dir. Albert Brooks) 96
My Fair Lady (1964 film dir. George Cukor) 67, 70–5, 78–9, 196n. 10 & n. 16
My Last Duchess (1842 poem in *Dramatic Lyrics* by Robert Browning) 61
My Living Doll (1960s American TV comedy series) 35, 123, 133
Myer, Valerie. G. 196n. 2
Myrrha (Ovid *Metamorphoses* Book Ten) 3, 29–30, 58, 64–5, 79, 155, 157, 165, 175, 183, 190n. 14, 191n. 18 & n. 22, 195n. 3, 198n. 4, 200n. 12
myths (significance, theories of) 2, 6, 8, 12, 57, 117, 144, 173, 180, 183–5, 194n. 15, 199n. 8

Napoleon 205n. 11
Narcissus (*Met* Book Three) 11–13, 23, 156, 175–6, 190n. 15 & n. 17, 205n. 14 *see* Echo
Nash, Ogden 97
Natali, Vincenzo 154–7 *see Splice*
Newlands, Carole 68
Newman, Kim 200n. 11
Newmar, Julie 133, 201n. 18
Newton-John, Olivia 96
Niccol, Andrew 159–60 *see SIMØNE The Truman Show*
Nixon, Marnie 195n. 6
No Woman Born (1944 short story by C. L. Moore) 118
Nolan, Christopher 123 *see The Prestige*

North by Northwest (1959 film dir. Alfred Hitchcock) 45
Notorious (1946 film dir. Alfred Hitchcock) 41, 44–5, 57
Notting Hill (1999 film dir. Roger Michell) 124
Novak, Kim 41, 45–50, 57, 124
Nugent, Georgia 157

Obsession (1976 film dir. Brian de Palma) 63–4
O'Keefe, Jodi Lyn 86
Olivier, Laurence 172
Olympus 65, 96, 100, 108–11, 116, 151
One Touch of Venus
  1940s stage musical 92
  1948 film dir. William A. Seiter 27, 97–9, 105–11, 159, 183
Onions, John 190n. 11
The Open University 4–5, 200n. 11, 201n. 3, 205n. 8, 206n. 15
  courses
    A103 Introduction to the Humanities 2
    A330 Myth in the Greek and Roman Worlds 4
The Opening of Misty Beethoven (1975 film dir. Radley Metzger) 79–80
Orlacs Hände (1924 film dir. Robert Wiene) 124
Orpheus (Ovid *Metamorphoses* Books Ten and Eleven) 5–7, 12–13, 18, 20, 24–5, 31, 34, 52, 54, 57–8, 87, 105, 107, 119–20, 135–6, 175 *see* Eurydice
Ortloskeit (unspecified, mythical locality) 118
Osiris (major Egyptian god, husband of Isis) 202n. 15
O'Sullivan, Jane 81–5, 98, 118, 191n. 25, 193n. 16, 194n. 19 & n. 21
Ovid, Publius Ovidius Naso (43 BCE – 8 CE) *passim*
  Amores 6
  Ars Amatoria 7, 20
  Epistulae ex Ponto 7
  Fasti 6, 7, 148

Medea 2, 6
Metamorphoses passim
Tristia 7

Paal, Alexander 124 *see Four-Sided Triangle*
Pakula, Alan J. 197n. 21 *see Klute*
Pal Joey
  Rodgers and Hart stage musical 97
  1957 film dir. George Sidney
Paltrow, Gwyneth 205n. 6
Pandora (mythical 'first' woman) 27–8, 41, 119–20, 123, 133, 145, 152, 154–5, 159, 163, 167–8 *see also* Hesiod
Pandora and the Flying Dutchman (1950 film dir. Albert Lewin) 59
Pandora's Box (1929 film dir. G. W. Pabst) 197n. 20
Paphos
  city kingdom of Cyprus 11
  daughter (or possibly son of Pygmalion and the Statue) 1, 11, 165
Pascal, Gabriel 70, 73, 78, 181, 196n. 16 *see* (film) *Pygmalion*
Pasquin, John 2, 89 *see Miss Congeniality*
Pateman, Matthew 202n. 9
patriarchy 4, 12, 67, 126
Patrick, Nigel 130
Paul, Joanna 206n. 15
Payton, Barbara 123–4
Peck, Gregory 43
Peers, Juliette 168
Penry-Jones, Rupert 176
Peregrine Pickle (18th century novel by Tobias Smollett) 71, 205n. 9
The Perfect Woman (1949 film dir. Bernard Knowles) 28, 128–33
Persephone (queen of the Underworld) 47, 152, 194n. 18 *see* (Roman) Proserpina
Perseus (*Met.* Books Three and Four) 2, 153
Persius, Flaccus, Aulus, (Roman satirist 34CE–62CE) 167

Petrie, Donald 88 *see Miss Congeniality*
The Philadelphia Story (1940 film dir. George Cukor) 89, 193n. 12, 197n. 26
Philostephanus, (of Cyrene, wrote *On Cyprus* 3rd century BCE) 191n. 19
Pierson, Frank *see A Star is Born* (1976) 192n. 3
Pimpernel Smith (1941 film dir. Leslie Howard) 93–5
Pixley, Andrew 203n. 1
Plato (Greek philosopher, *ca.*.429–327 BCE)
　Socrates' ideal forms 19
　Symposium 57
Pleshette, Suzanne 39
Plumb, Suzie 168–9
Pluto (Hades, god of the Underworld) 194n. 18
Polley, Sarah 154
Pomeroy, Arthur J. 201n. 4
Poole, Carol 202n. 13
pornography 4, 79
Portman, Eric 59–61
Potter, Amanda 4, 201n. 6, 203n. 15, 205n. 14
Power, Timothy 116
The Prestige (2006 film dir. Christopher Nolan) 123
Pretty Woman (1990 film dir. Garry Marshall) 32, 58, 67–9, 80–5, 87, 176, 197n. 20
Prinze Jr, Freddie 86
Proitides (daughters of Proteus) 189n. 5
Prometheus 27–8, 151, 162–3, 194n. 16
　see Shelley's *Modern Prometheus*
Propertius, Sextus (Latin love elegist writing during reign of Augustus) 20
Propoetides (women of Cyprus) 10, 12–14, 29–33, 41, 44, 53, 72–3, 82, 91, 99, 108, 172, 175, 179, 189n. 5, 191n. 22, 194n. 17
prostitution 12, 17, 23, 84, 189n. 4

puella, (girl, girlfriend, mistress) 20–1, 71
Purple Rose of Cairo (1985 film dir. Woody Allen) 175–6
Pygmalion
　mythological figure *passim*
　Pygmalion 1938 film dir. Anthony Asquith 72–9
　Pygmalion (1914 London stage production) 66–79
Pygmalion and Galatea (1871 play by W. S. Gilbert) 31, 80, 186n. 1
Pyramus (*Met* Book Four) 190n. 15
　see Thisbe

The Quatermass Experiment (1953 British TV series, created by Nigel Kneale) 153

Radio Days (1987 film dir. Woody Allen) 69
Raeburn, David 188n. 5, 189n. 2
Rains, Claude 44
rape 37, 46, 143, 155, 203n. 5
The Real World (MTV reality show 1992– present) 86
Rear Window (1954 film dir. Alfred Hitchcock) 44–5
The Rebel (1960 film dir. Robert Day) 200n. 16
Red Dwarf (1990s British TV series) 205n. 6 *see* Robert Llewellyn
Reverentia (sense of awe, modesty) 20–2, 51, 71, 91
Richardson, Kathleen 117
Ritter, John 146
Rizov, Vadim 203n. 3–5
Roberts, Julia 80–3, 87, 114, 197n. 20
Roberts, Rachel 161
Robertson, Cliff 63–4
Robertson, Jennifer 199n. 6
robot* 4, 28, 35, 115–18, 126, 168–9, 199n. 6 & n. 8, 203n. 6
　see also androids, artificial life, automata, cyborgs, gynoids
Roc, Patricia 128, 131–2

Roisman, Hanna 206n. 15
Romain, Yvonne 168
Roman, Ruth 192n. 6
Romney, Edana 58–62
Romney, George 177–8
Rosati, Gianpero 194n. 18, 204n. 1
Rose, Peter 184
Ross, Katherine 127
Rossum's Universal Robots (1923 play by Karel Čapek) 203n. 6
Rozsa, Miklos 43
Rudd, Paul 176
Rutten, Kris 68–9, 184
Ryder, Winona 163, 205n. 6

Saint, Eve Marie 39, 45
St John, Rogers, Adela 192n. 3 *see What Price Hollywood*
Salmacis (*Met* Book Four) 42, 157, 174–6, 190n. 15, 203n. 5
 see Hermaphroditus
Salzmann-Mitchell, Patricia. B. 27
San Juan, Olga 106
Sanders, George 189n. 6
Der Sandman (1816 short story by E. T. A. Hoffmann) 120
Satisfaction Guaranteed
 1968 short story by Isaac Asimov 204n. 4
 televised by BBC 1960s 204n. 4
Scheer, Tanja S. 189n. 4 *see* Lindner
Scooby-Doo (American TV cartoon series, 1969–1972 films 2002 2004) 202n. 14
Scorsese, Martin 196n. 10 *see My Fair Lady* (restoration)
Scott, Katie 92–3, 198n. 5, 205n. 12
 see Arscott
Scott, Lizabeth 62–3
Scott, Ridley 118, 200n. 10 *see Blade Runner*
Scourfield, David 201n. 3
SF (science fiction) 118, 133, 204n. 6
Seed, David 199n. 7, 203n. 2
Seiter, William A. 97 *see One Touch of Venus*

Selznick, David. O. 192n. 9, 198n. 5
Shadowplay film blog 61
Shahabudin, Kim 205n. 13
The Shape of Things (2003 film dir. Neil LaBute) 176
Sharrock, Alison 18–27, 56, 189n. 10, 190n. 12 & n. 14
Shaw, George Bernard (1856–1950) 2–3, 66–79, 84–6, 89, 91, 94, 107, 133, 162, 177, 188n. 1, 194n. 24, 195n. 4 & n. 5, 196n. 8 n. 16 & n. 18 *see Back to Methuselah Pygmalion*
Shelley, Mary 28, 72, 85, 156, 196n. 14 *see* Frankenstein: or The Modern Prometheus
She's All That (1999 film dir. Robert Iscove) 31, 86–7, 174, 203n. 8
Shirley, Bill 76
Shonteff, Lindsay 168 *see Devil Doll*
Sidney, George 197n. 25 *see Annie Get Your Gun*
Siemann, Catherine 201n. 1
SIMØNE (2002 film dir. Andrew Niccol) 161–5, 169, 171–3
simulacrum 150, 167 *see* Baudrillard
 ghost 52, 179, 190n. 13
 image 20–1, 26, 39, 56, 147, 150, 167, 172, 174, 202n. 13
 likeness (Doppelgänger) 159, 161–3, 202n. 9 & n. 15
 reflection 77, 127, 175
Sinclair, Hugh 60
Singin' in the Rain (1952 film dir. Gene Kelly and Stanley Donen) 183
Slayage (Wilcox and Lavery website archive of Joss Whedon studies) 34, 137
Smith, Amelinda 141
Solaris (1973 film dir. Andrei Tarkovsky) 203n. 9
Some Like it Hot (1959 film dir. Billy Wilder) 158
Sorvino, Mira 69

Spellbound (1945 film dir. Alfred
    Hitchcock) 42–4
Spielberg, Steven 94 *see* Indiana Jones
Splice (2009 film dir. Vincenzo
    Natali) 150, 154–7, 203n. 3–5
Stables, Kate 160, 162–3, 171
Stafford, Roy 205n. 14
A Star is Born
  1937 film dir. William A.
    Wellman 192n. 3
  1954 film dir. George Cukor 37–8
  1976 film dir. Frank Pierson 192n. 3
statues
  (moving) in ancient world 4, 14, 18,
    26, 32–3, 77, 98, 115, 167
  (moving) on screen 18, 27, 33, 91,
    98, 177–8
Steiner, Deborah T. 27
The Stepford Wives
  1972 novel by Ira Levin 126
  1975 film dir. Bryan Forbes 84,
    126–8, 134, 142
Stewart, James 45, 48–55, 84
Stoichita, Victor, I. 19–20, 32, 39, 50,
    55–8, 98, 115, 167, 189n. 8,
    191n. 25, 192n. 7, 193n. 16,
    194n. 23, 195n. 28, 197n. 26
Stolen Face (1952 film dir. Terence
    Fisher) 62–3, 124
Stone, Sharon 96, 164
Storey, John 180
Strangers on a Train (1951 film dir. Alfred
    Hitchcock) 192n. 6 , 198n. 5
Stray, Christopher 206n. 15
Streisand, Barbra 192n. 3
Sueurs Froides 194n. 17 *see* Vertigo
Sutherland, Donald 197n. 21
Sutherland, Kristine 145
Symposium 57 *see* Plato

The Talking Stone (1955 short story by
    Isaac Asimov) 203n. 9
Talus (or Talos, bronze monster) 116,
    199n. 3 *see Argonautica*
Tarkovsky, Andrei 203n. 9 *see Solaris*
Taylor, Doug 156 *see Splice*
Taylor, Elizabeth 86

Taylor, Laurie 188n. 3
The Terminator (1984 film dir. James
    Cameron) 119, 122
Thisbe, (Ovid *Metamorphoses* Book
    Four) 190n. 15 *see* Pyramus
Thomas, Deborah 147, 201n. 7 & n. 17,
    202n. 10
Thomson, David 195n. 1
Tibullus, Albius, (Latin love elegist
    died 19 BCE) 20
'Tinted Venus' (statue by John
    Gibson) 99, 105
The Tinted Venus (a Victorian farcical
    romance by F. Anstey) 97–105
Tiresias (*Met* Book Three) 23, 160
Titans 28
Tolkien, J. R. R. 198n. 2 *see The Lord of
    the Rings*
Tonkin, Boyd 201n. 1
Trachtenberg, Michelle 202n. 12
Tracy, Spencer 193n. 11
La Traviata (opera by Giuseppe
    Verdi) 83
The Truman Show (1998 film dir. Peter
    Weir) 159
Turner, Lana 193n. 11
Twain, Mark 107 *see A Connecticut
    Yankee in King Arthur's Court*
2001: A Space Odyssey (1968 film dir.
    Stanley Kubrick) 203n. 7,
    210n. 5

umbra (reflection, shade, ghost) 62,
    194n. 18

Vas, Steven 124 *see* Four-Sided Triangle
Venus *passim see* (Greek) Aphrodite
La Vénus d'Ille (1837 short story by
    Prosper Mérimée) 198n. 1
Verdoodt, Ive 68–9, 184
Vertigo (1958 film dir. Alfred
    Hitchcock) 32, 36–58, 164, 167,
    173, 184
Viarre, Simone 25, 191n. 18 & n. 22
Vidor, Charles 198n. 9 *see Gilda*
Virgil (Publius Virgilius Maro,
    70–19BCE) 5, 7, 201n. 2

Aeneid 198n. 4, 199n. 2
Georgics 5
Virtual Sexuality (1999 film dir. Nick Hurran) 176-7
von Harbo, Thea 120, 200n. 11
  see Metropolis
Vulcan 27, 109, 116, 198n. 6
  see (Greek) Hephaistus
Waine, Mike 192
Walker, John 198n. 9
Walker, Robert 105-7
Walters, Julie 85-6
wax, properties of 18-19, 60-1
  as Ovidian simile 102
  compared with plasticity of cinema screen 33, 61, 165 *see* Bloom
Weill, Kurt 97 *see One Touch of Venus*
Weir, Peter 160 *see The Truman Show*
Weird Science (1985 film dir. John Hughes) 157-9
Weisz, Rachel 176
Weldon, Fay 182 *see The Cloning of Joanna May*
Welles, Orson 1 *see Citizen Kane*
Wellman, William 192n. 3 *see A Star is Born*
Whale, James 125, 156, 168, 203n. 4
  see Bride of Frankenstein
What Price Hollywood
  1932 novel by Adela St John Rogers 192n. 3
  1932 film dir. George Cukor 192n. 3
Wheatley, Alan 60
Whedon, Joss 34, 147-8, 201n. 1 n. 4 & n. 17, 202n. 10, 203n. 6 *see Buffy the Vampire Slayer, Dollhouse*
Wheeler, Stephen M. 184
White, Vanna 99, 108-10, 142, 159
Williams, Esther 86
Williams, Linda 79
Williamson, Milly 205n. 14
Willis, Bruce 200n. 10
Wilson, Ivy Crane 96
Winkler, Martin, M. 96-7, 135, 180, 184
Wollen, Peter 42
Wood, Evan Rachel 162
Wood, Gaby 32, 167, 190n. 13, 197n. 19
Wright, Peter 203n. 2

Xanadu (1980 film dir. Robert Greenwald) 96

Young, Terence 58 *see Corridor of Mirrors*

Zambaco, Maria 14
Zeus 27, 57, 102, 150 *see* (Roman) Jupiter

www.ingramcontent.com/pod-product-compliance
Lightning Source LLC
Chambersburg PA
CBHW071828300426
44116CB00009B/1479